How to Localize Marxism in (

This book explores frontier issues concerning the localization of Marxism in China by examining historical processes, cultural implications, and contemporary perspectives on this process of indigenization.

Emerging in the 1840s in Germany, Marxism has evolved from a German, European, and Western idea into a Chinese, Asian, and Eastern one. This title seeks to answer the question of how Marxism has been adapted to the Chinese context and how it migrated the regions. The first three chapters chart the history of the dissemination of Marxism to adapt to Chinese conditions across three periods – revolutionary times before 1949, the period of socialist construction after 1949, and the reform and opening-up since 1978. The subsequent two chapters analyze the experience of the development of socialism with Chinese characteristics, featuring synergistic integration with traditional Chinese culture and the combining of the basic principles of Marxism and China's real-life situation. The final chapter advances suggestions on how to further promote the localization of Marxism and how to develop contemporary Chinese Marxism, faced with new historical conditions.

The book will appeal to scholars, students, and general readers interested in contemporary Marxism, Marxism in China, and contemporary Chinese history, politics, and society.

Guo Jianning is a Distinguished Professor at Tsinghua University, China. His main research areas are the adaptation of Marxism in China, contemporary Chinese Marxism, and contemporary Chinese philosophy and culture.

How to Localize Marxism in China

Edited by
Guo Jianning

Routledge
Taylor & Francis Group

LONDON AND NEW YORK

First published in English 2023
by Routledge
4 Park Square, Milton Park, Abingdon, Oxon OX14 4RN

and by Routledge
605 Third Avenue, New York, NY 10158

Routledge is an imprint of the Taylor & Francis Group, an informa business

© 2023 selection and editorial matter, Guo Jianning; individual
chapters, the contributors

English Version by permission of China Renmin University Press

British Library Cataloguing-in-Publication Data
A catalogue record for this book is available from the British Library

Library of Congress Cataloging-in-Publication Data
Names: Guo, Jianning, author.
Title: How to localize marxism in China / Jianning Guo.
Description: New York, NY : Routledge, 2023. | Includes bibliographical
references and index.
Identifiers: LCCN 2022032825 (print) | LCCN 2022032826 (ebook) | ISBN
9781032410265 (hardback) | ISBN 9781032410579 (paperback) | ISBN
9781003356042 (ebook)
Subjects: LCSH: Socialism—China—History. | China—History.
Classification: LCC HX418.5 .G8665 2023 (print) | LCC HX418.5 (ebook) |
DDC 335.43/45—dc23/eng/20220714
LC record available at https://lccn.loc.gov/2022032825
LC ebook record available at https://lccn.loc.gov/2022032826

ISBN: 978-1-032-41026-5 (hbk)
ISBN: 978-1-032-41057-9 (pbk)
ISBN: 978-1-003-35604-2 (ebk)

DOI: 10.4324/9781003356042

Typeset in Times New Roman
by codeMantra

Contents

Contributors

Guo Jianning is a Distinguished Professor at Tsinghua University, China. His main research areas are the adaptation of Marxism in China, contemporary Chinese Marxism, and contemporary Chinese philosophy and culture.

Zhong Tian'e is a lecturer at Beijing University of Chinese Medicine, China. Her main research area is the adaptation of Marxism in China.

Zhao Jianchun is an associate professor at the School of Marxism at North China Electric Power University (Baoding). His main research fields are the sinicization of Marxism, contemporary Chinese Marxism, and contemporary Chinese philosophy and culture.

Bai Yang is a lecturer at the Department of Ideological and Political Theory Teaching at the China Conservatory of Music, China. Her main research areas are university culture and youth issues.

Liu Ying is an associate professor at the School of Marxism at Beihang University, China. Her research interests lie in Marxist Philosophy, culture and value problem, and educational theory.

Introduction

Localization and Marxism in Modern China

Guo Jianning

To develop contemporary Chinese Marxism, we must vigorously promote the localization of Marxism. Emerging in the 1840s in Germany, Marxism evolves from a German, European, and Western idea into a Chinese, Asian, and Eastern one, which involves the adaptation of Marxism. The introduction focuses on the historical process, cultural connotations, and contemporary perspectives of Marxism adaptation.

History of Marxism Localization in China

In the history of the development of Marxism in China, introduction, dissemination, and adaptation are three closely related and distinct concepts. In my view, before the October Revolution, Marxism was introduced in a fragmentary and partial manner. Only excerpts were translated and many ideas were retold. After the October Revolution, Marxism was disseminated widely. Its influence in China was greater, its content more extensive, and its system more complete. The Yan'an Period (1935–1948) saw the localization of Marxism and the formation of Mao Zedong Thought, which marked the first leap in the theoretical achievements of the adaptation of Marxism. The adaptation of Marxism is a process, which means it is important to study it from three levels: introduction, dissemination, and adaptation. If we do not analyze the difference and mix the three, or equate the introduction and dissemination with the adaptation, we are not recognizing the diachronic nature of the adaptation of Marxism and simplifying its process. We are also not realizing the complexity of it and simplifying its form. We are not seeing the full picture of it and simplifying its connotation.

In terms of the introduction of Marxism to China, Marx the name first appeared in China in 1899 when the British missionary Timothy Richard mentioned it in *Globe Magazine*, No. 121. The first Chinese person to introduce Marx was Liang Qichao, who introduced his life in *Xinmin Congbao*, No. 18, October 16, 1902. The first Chinese person to mention the *Communist Manifesto* was Zhu Zhixin, who introduced the book in his *Short Biography of German Social Revolutionaries*, published in November 1905. The influence of Japanese scholarship in Marxism was greater. For example, Kotoku

DOI: 10.4324/9781003356042-1

Shusui's *The Essence of Socialism* and Hajime Kawakami's *The Story of Poverty* and *An Introduction to Das Kapital* were translated into several Chinese versions.

From the point of view of the spread of Marxism and its adaptation, the following five important points should be noted:

First, Chen Duxiu, Li Dazhao, and the initial stage of the spread of Marxism in China, when the introduction of materialist view of history was the key. In his *History of Chinese Thought in the Last Fifty Years*, Guo Zhanbo says that Mr. Li was the first and most steadfast advocate of the materialistic view of history and that he paved the path for the surge of dialectics, materialism, and the materialistic view of history in China today. Not only did Li Dazhao open a column entitled "Marx Studies" and publish a special issue entitled "Marxist Studies" in *The Morning Bell* and *La Jeunesse*, but he also wrote a passage named "My View on Marxism" and books entitled *Lectures on the History of Thought on Historical Studies* and *The Essentials of History*, which opened up a new study of history from the perspective of Marxism in China. Chen Duxiu's "two key points", that are the productive forces and productive relations, the economic base, and the superstructure, exerted a great impact on the spread of the materialist view of history in China.

Second, Qu Qiubai and the full spread of Marxism in China. While Chen Duxiu and Li Dazhao focused on the Marxist materialist view of history, Qu Qiubai was the first to introduce dialectical materialism and historical materialism in a more comprehensive way, publishing three books from 1923 to 1924: *Introduction to Social Philosophy*, *Modern Sociology*, and *Introduction to Social Science*. By promoting and explaining dialectical materialism and historical materialism as a whole, he made the spread of Marxism in China more systematic and laid the foundation for the popularization, systematization, and adaptation of Marxism.

Third, Ai Siqi and the popularization of Marxism. From November 1934 to July 1935, Ai Siqi published 24 philosophical speeches in *Life of Reading*, which were collected and published in January 1936 and renamed *Popular Philosophy* when the fourth edition was released in 1936. In 4 chapters and 24 sections, the book contains more than 100,000 words discussing dialectical materialism in terms of ontology, epistemology, methodology, and dialectics. It tells philosophy in an easy-to-understand way, in the form of everyday conversation, and in a language that is accessible to the general public. It embeds profound philosophy into vivid stories, making it close to life and practice so that philosophy can be easy for the public to understand and grasp. *Popular Philosophy* was so well received that 32 editions were printed before the founding of the People's Republic of China. Incorporating issues of public concern, *Popular Philosophy* is a successful example of explaining Marxism and promoting the popularization of Marxism.

Fourth, Li Da and the systematization of Marxism. Li Da has long been engaged in the study of Marxist theory and has co-translated with Lei Zhongjian the Soviet Union's *A Course in Dialectical Materialism* by Silokov and Eisenberg into Chinese. In May 1937, Li Da's masterpiece, *Outline of Sociology*, was published by the Bigengtang Bookstore, containing more than 400,000 words on Marxist philosophy, which included materialism, dialectics, epistemology, and the materialistic view of history. Mao Zedong paid special attention to Li Da's *Outline of Sociology*. He not only wrote many annotations on the book, which totaled about 3,500 words, but also recommended the book to the students of the Chinese People's Counter-Japanese Military and Political University for study.

Fifth, Mao Zedong and the stage of localization of Marxism. In order for Marxism to take root and blossom in China, it must not only be combined with Chinese practice but must also be integrated into certain Chinese forms. This is what Mao Zedong said,

> Communists who have become part of the great Chinese nation and are linked to it in flesh and blood, and who talk about Marxism out of the Chinese context, are merely talking about the abstract and empty Marxism. Therefore, how to specify Marxism in China, how to give it a Chinese feature in its every expression, that is to say, how to apply it in accordance with Chinese characteristics, has become a problem that the whole Party needs to get aware of and to solve immediately. Pure Western teachings must be abolished, and the empty and abstract words must be stopped, and dogmatism must be replaced by a fresh and lively Chinese style and spirit that is pleasing to the people of China.[1]

It is important to note that the notion "to specify Marxism in China" was a revised version in the *Selected Works of Mao Zedong* published in 1949 after the founding of PRC, and the original notion in Mao Zedong's report to the Sixth Plenary Session of the Sixth Central Committee of CPC in October 1938 was "to adapt Marxism to Chinese conditions". Mao Zedong is the main representative of the localization of Marxism, and Mao Zedong Thought is the expression of the effort.

The contribution of Mao Zedong Thought to the adaptation of Marxism is mainly reflected in three aspects: first, at the level of philosophical theory, i.e., the theoretical discussion in *On Practice* and *On Contradiction*; second, at the level of ideology, i.e., the ideological approach of seeking truth from facts; and third, at the level of practical work, i.e., the elaboration of the military dialectics, the dialectics of the united front, and the dialectics of the methods of leadership and work. Therefore, the significance lies in the fact that these three aspects correspond to the three combinations below: the first is the integration of Marxism and Chinese philosophy at the level of philosophy. As we know, *On Practice* expounds Marxist epistemology, and it has a subtitle: *On the Relation Between Knowledge and Practice, Between Knowing and Doing*. This indicates that the relationship between cognition and practice as taught in Marxist philosophy is also the relationship that between knowing and doing as taught in ancient Chinese philosophical epistemology. The integration of the two in Marxist philosophy is equivalent to the unity of knowing and doing in the Chinese counterpart, and Mao's *On Practice* combines Marxist epistemology and Chinese philosophy. *On Contradiction* is an exposition of the Marxist dialectics, which emphasizes the unity of opposites, the conflict and unity of contradictions, and the universality and particularity of contradictions. By contrast, the ancient Chinese dialectics is characterized by thoughts of "one *yin* and one *yang* is called the Way", "two things complementing each other", "the opposites complementing each other", etc. Mao Zedong's *On Contradiction* embodies a combination of Marxist dialectics and its ancient Chinese counterpart. Second, the combination of Marxism and Chinese culture was achieved at the level of the ideology. In the Eastern Han Dynasty, Ban Gu's *The Book of the Han Dynasty: The Biography of Prince Hejianxian* describes Liu De, the son of Emperor Jing (Liu Qi), as a man who "cultivated his studies of ancient times and sought truth from facts". Mao Zedong gave it a new interpretation in his "Reform Our Study". He pointed out that "facts" means all things that exist objectively, and "truth" refers to the internal connections between objective things, i.e., laws, and "seek" is to "study" or "research". "Seeking truth from facts" is the line of thought of the Party and the essence and soul of Mao Zedong Thought, which embodies the combination of Marxism and traditional Chinese culture. Third, the dialectics at the level of practical work realizes the combination of Marxism and Chinese practice. Marxism was applied to all aspects of practical work, permeating all areas such as the military, the united front, and Party building. The above three combinations show that the Marxism from Germany has been combined with Chinese philosophy, culture, and practice and has begun to merge into a whole. Marxism has taken on Chinese characteristics, style, and spirit. Marxism has been adapted, so it is Marxist and Chinese thinking simultaneously.

In short, Mao Zedong's contribution to Marxist philosophy in 1937 with his *On Practice* and *On Contradiction*, his argument of the "adaptation of Marxism to Chinese conditions" at the Sixth Plenary Session of the Sixth Central Committee of CPC in October 1938, the elaboration on the theory of the New Democratic Revolution in his *On New Democracy* in 1940, the Party's line of thought of "seeking truth from facts", and the establishment of Mao Zedong Thought as the guiding ideology of the Party at the Seventh Congress of CPC in 1945 all marked the realization of the localization of Marxism during the Yan'an period. From the translation and introduction of Marxism at the time of its introduction, to the study and interpretation of Marxism at the time of its dissemination, to the comprehensive practice of Marxism at the time of its adaptation, the process gave birth to a Chinese version of Marxism.

In terms of the "second combination" of Marxism and Chinese reality during the period of socialist construction (1949–1978), Mao Zedong published *On the Ten Major Relations* in April 1956, in which he elaborated on the ten major relations and stressed the importance of learning from the history of the Soviet Union and mobilizing all positive factors.[2] Later, Mao Zedong published *On the Correct Handling of the Contradictions Among the People* in February 1957, in which he discussed the two types of contradictions and emphasized the distinction between the two. The above two discussions were the application and development of Marxism during the period of socialist construction.

In 1978, the Third Plenary Session of the Eleventh Central Committee of the CPC was held, and China entered a new period of reform and opening up. Discussion on what socialism is and how to build it, what kind of Party to build and how to build it, and what kind of development to achieve and how to develop, led to Deng Xiaoping's theory, the important thought of the "Three Represents" and the scientific outlook on development, which formed the theoretical system of socialism with Chinese characteristics. These include the discussion on the essence and fundamental tasks of socialism, the primary stage of socialism, reform and opening up, the socialist market economy, the organic unity of the Party's leadership, the people's position as masters of the country, and the rule of law, the advanced socialist culture, the promotion of scientific development, the construction of a harmonious society, and the founding of the Party for the public and the rule of law for the people. These statements further the localization of Marxism and are the new achievements of the effort.

Socialism with Chinese characteristics has been the theme of all the Party's theories and practices since the reform and opening up of China. The new era calls for focusing on new issues, and new ideas would lead the way to a new journey. Xi Jinping Thought on Socialism with Chinese Characteristics for a New Era, the latest achievement of the localization of Marxism, answers the question of what kind of socialism with Chinese characteristics to uphold and develop in the new era and how to stick to and develop it and deepens the understanding of the laws of governing of the Communist Party, the laws of socialist construction and the laws of development of human society.

First, General Secretary Xi Jinping raised the important concept of Marxism of contemporary China and Marxism of the 21st century. The year 2018 marks the 200th anniversary of Marx's birth. The development of Marxism of contemporary China is a major issue in the study of Marxist theory in China. Xi Jinping Thought on Socialism with Chinese Characteristics for a New Era is the salient embodiment of contemporary Chinese Marxism. From the macro-strategic level, it mainly includes: to unite the powerful force of national rejuvenation by the Chinese Dream; to achieve national prosperity, national revitalization, and people's happiness; based on the theme of adhering to and developing socialism with Chinese characteristics to firmly establish confidence in our path, theory, system, and culture; to promote the four-pronged comprehensive strategy: build a moderately prosperous society, deepen reform, establish the rule of law and manage the Party strictly; to lead the new development with the new development concepts and pursue the visions of innovative, coordinated, green, and open development that is for everyone; to put the people at the center and take the people's aspiration for a better life as the goal of struggle. At the level of application, it includes: taking high-quality development as the key, to promote stable, sustainable and healthy economic development and to advance the construction of socialist economy with Chinese characteristics; to persist in the Party's self-revolution and comprehensive strict self-governance, improve the Party's governing ability and advance the construction of socialist politics with Chinese characteristics; to cultivate and promote socialist core values, strengthen cultural confidence and advance the construction of socialist culture with Chinese characteristics; to ensure and improve people's livelihood, promote social equality and justice, and advance the construction of socialist society with Chinese characteristics; to strengthen the construction of socialist ecological civilization with Chinese characteristics by obeying the principle that green water and mountains are the paramount assets; to strengthen the reform of the army and national defense with the goal of preparing for war and being able to win; and to build a community of shared future for humankind and carry out the Belt and Road initiative so as to achieve interconnection, openness, inclusiveness and win-win cooperation in diplomacy. All these aspects form a rich and interconnected whole, which is a guide for action to achieve the Chinese Dream of the great rejuvenation of the Chinese nation.

Second, General Secretary Xi Jinping has linked the "adaptation of Marxism to Chinese conditions" with "socialism with Chinese characteristics", "Chinese discourse", and "Chinese solutions". As we all know, "adaptation of Marxism to Chinese conditions" and "socialism with Chinese characteristics" are the two central concepts of the Communist Party of China since the 20th century. The former term was proposed by Mao Zedong, while the latter by Deng Xiaoping, and Xi Jinping has made important contributions to both. On the former topic, Xi Jinping emphasized the development of Marxism of contemporary China and Marxism of the 21st century. With regard to the latter, Xi Jinping has put forward a series of new ideas and strategies, which usher in a new era for socialism with Chinese characteristics. In addition, Xi Jinping has made his own original contribution by introducing two more concepts concerning China. The first is "Chinese discourse", i.e., the construction of the disciplinary system, academic system, and discourse system of contemporary Chinese philosophy and social sciences, and the other is "Chinese solutions", i.e., the provision of Chinese solutions for the better development of human society. With not only "adaptation of Marxism to Chinese conditions" and "socialism with Chinese characteristics" but also "Chinese discourse" and "Chinese solutions", a more comprehensive system reflects great wisdom, thinking, and great logic. It should be emphasized that the four China-related concepts mentioned above basically correspond to the "four confidences". The "adaptation of Marxism to Chinese conditions" mainly corresponds to "confidence in theory", "socialism with Chinese characteristics" to "confidence in path", "Chinese discourse" to "confidence in culture", and "Chinese solutions" to "confidence in the system". In this way, the four China-related concepts are combined with the "four confidences". This should be the most important contribution of Xi Jinping Thought on Socialism with Chinese Characteristics or a New Era, which requires our earnest thinking, in-depth understanding, and comprehensive grasp.

Third, Xi Jinping Thought on Socialism with Chinese Characteristics for a New Era highlights the people-centered value orientation. From the idea of "not forgetting our initial pursuit and remembering our mission, to work for the happiness of the Chinese people and the rejuvenation of the Chinese nation" to the idea that no one should be left behind in building a moderately prosperous society and on the road to common prosperity, Xi Jinping's thought is full of considerations for the people, reflecting the idea of people-centered development. The people-centered approach embodies the Marxist materialistic view of history, and for the interest of the people is the fundamental political position of our Party. The foundation of the Party's governance lies in the people, and the source of its strength also lies in the people. At the end of the First Plenary Session of the 19th Party Central Committee of CPC, General Secretary Xi Jinping made a remarkable statement when he met with journalists, saying,

> History is written by the people and all achievements are attributed to them. As long as we are deeply rooted in the people and rely closely on them, we will be able to gain infinite strength and move forward through thick and thin.[3]

As socialism with Chinese characteristics enters a new era, the main conflict in our society has been transformed into the one between the people's growing need for a better life and unbalanced and insufficient development. The change in the main conflict of our society determines that we must make the people's desire for a better life the goal of our struggle, constantly enhance the people's sense of achievement, happiness, and security, and constantly promote the common prosperity of all the people. We will rely on the people to create a great work in history, lead the people to create a better life, and view benefiting the people as the greatest political achievement.

Cultural Connotations of Marxism Localization in China

Since the 18th Congress of CPC, General Secretary Xi Jinping has spoken on many occasions about culture, especially the essence of traditional Chinese culture and virtues, which can be said to be an important feature of Xi Jinping's governance and has attracted extensive attention at home and abroad.

First of all, he attached great importance to the essence of traditional Chinese culture. He pointed out that Chinese culture is the spiritual gene and unique identity of our nation. To abandon tradition and discard the fundamentals is to cut off one's spiritual lifeline. The cultivation and promotion of socialist core values must be based on the essence of traditional Chinese culture, which shall become an important source that nurtures socialist core values. Fine traditional Chinese culture is our greatest strength and cultural soft power, and it is the foundation for us to stand firm in the world's intellectual and cultural turbulence. In 2013, General Secretary Xi Jinping pointed out that the road of socialism with Chinese characteristics has been developed through the great practice of reform and opening up for more than 30 years, through the continuous exploration of the People's Republic of China for more than 60 years, through the in-depth summary of the history of the Chinese nation for more than 170 years since the early modern era, and through the inheritance of 5,000-year-old civilization of the Chinese nation. The insightful meaning of this statement lies in connecting 30 years of reform and opening up with 5,000 years of Chinese history and linking the Chinese path with Chinese civilization, which indicates that the former cannot be separated from the latter and that the Chinese path is rooted in Chinese civilization, so the long history and deep cultural heritage are embedded in our chosen path. One of the basic ideas that runs through Xi Jinping's important remarks on cultural construction, especially on the concept of fine Chinese culture, is that it is necessary to adhere to the stance of Chinese culture, to treat the essence of traditional Chinese culture in an objective, scientific and respectful manner, to modernize Chinese culture, to activate its vitality, and to enhance its influence and appeal.

Second, he comprehensively elaborated on the basic meaning of the essence of traditional Chinese culture. He points out that Chinese culture highlights the following beliefs: "the people are the foundation of the state", "the unity of heaven and man", and "harmony in diversity"; "as nature's movement is ever vigorous, so must a gentleman ceaselessly strive along", and "when the great way prevails, the world is equally shared by all"; "the rise and fall of the world is the responsibility of each man" and the state shall be ruled by virtue and the people be educated by culture; "the mind of the superior man is conversant with righteousness", "the superior man is satisfied and composed" and "the superior man in everything considers righteousness to be essential"; "be sincere in what has been said and to carry out what has been promised" and "how a man without truthfulness is to get on"; "virtue is not left to stand alone. He who practices it will have neighbors", "a benevolent man loves all men", "helping men to practice virtue", "not to do to others as you would not wish done to yourself", "render all friendly offices to one another in their going out and coming in, aid one another in keeping watch and ward", "treat with the reverence due to age the elders in your own family, so that the elders in the families of others shall be similarly treated; treat with the kindness due to youth the young in your own family, so that the young in the families of others shall be similarly treated", "help the poor and the needy", "inequality rather than want is the cause of trouble", and so on.

These ideas and concepts not only boast distinctive national characteristics but also timeless values. He highlighted the need to probe into and expound the contemporary values of the essence of traditional Chinese culture, i.e., benevolence, people-oriented, integrity, justice, harmony, and great unity. He also pointed out that traditional Chinese culture contains important inspirations for solving contemporary problems faced by humankind, such as the ideas that the law of the Tao is its being what it is and the unity of man and heaven, that the world shall be equally shared by all and of great unity, that of self-improvement and virtue supporting things, that of putting the people first and working for the peace, prosperity, and happiness of the people, that of governance by virtue and government as rectification, that of daily renovation, establishing the new by discarding the old, and advancing with the times, that of being down-to-earth and practical, that of applying knowledge to the practice and uniting knowledge and practice, that of pooling wisdom and efforts for public benefits, that of loving people with benevolence and cementing peaceful relations by upholding good faith, that of being upright in politics and diligent in public service, that of adhering to frugality and abstaining from extravagance, that of being neutral and seeking common ground while preserving differences, and that of not forgetting danger, death, and disturbance even in safety.

Third, he remarks on the methodology of treating traditional culture correctly. He pointed out that only by not forgetting the past can we open up the future, and only by being good at inheritance can we better innovate. Traditional culture should be treated with discrimination and inherited with selection. The relationship between inheritance and innovative development should be handled well, with an emphasis on innovative transformation and innovative development. The advocacy of "innovative transformation" and "innovative development" has particular methodological significance. As the "Double Hundred" policy of "letting a hundred flowers blossom, and a hundred schools of thought contend" proposed by Mao Zedong back then, the "Double Innovative" proposal today is the guideline for the correct treatment of traditional culture and the construction of contemporary Chinese culture today and is also the focus and difficulty faced by current cultural construction.

Finally, he highlighted the significance of confidence in culture. Cultural confidence is a nation's awareness, firm identification, persistent pursuit, inheritance, and innovation of its cultural spirit. Xi Jinping emphasizes that cultural confidence is a more fundamental, deeper, and more enduring power and a more profound, broader, and stronger confidence. Cultural confidence is powerful support for the confidence in our path, theory, and system, and is a powerful force for the great rejuvenation of the Chinese nation. Cultural confidence not only reflects the heritage but also the consistency of the Chinese nation. We shall bring cultural confidence into full play during our path toward great rejuvenation and let the light of cultural confidence shine on our way. Cultural confidence is about a unity of the essence of traditional Chinese culture, revolutionary culture, and advanced socialist culture. First, the essence of traditional Chinese culture is the spiritual gene and lifeline. Chinese culture is the genetic and unique identity of our nation. To abandon our traditions and discard our fundamentals is to cut off our spiritual lifeline. We must forge ahead by continuing the cultural lineage of the nation, and realize the innovative transformation and innovative development of traditional culture. Second, revolutionary culture is a valuable spiritual treasure and motivation. When we move forward, we must not forget the road we have traveled. No matter how far we go, no matter how glorious the future will be, we must not forget the past we have journeyed or why we started. From "not forgetting our initial pursuit" to "getting prepared for the new Long March", revolutionary culture is an indispensable and important element and spiritual support. Third, advanced socialist culture leads our way forward. The culture of socialism with Chinese characteristics is an important force that unites and inspires people of all ethnic groups in China. It is rooted in the 5,000-year history of Chinese civilization and in the practice of socialism with Chinese characteristics, featuring distinctive characteristics of the times. It reflects the basic character of China's socialist economy and politics and plays a significant role in economic and political development. The insightful elaboration on "cultural confidence" shows that our understanding of cultural issues has reached a new height. The discussion on the confidence in our path, theory, system, and culture of socialism with Chinese characteristics shows that our knowledge of socialism with Chinese characteristics has been raised to a new level. The remarks on the path, theory, system, and culture of socialism with Chinese characteristics indicate that the path is our route, theory our guide, system our guarantee, and culture our foundation, which are all unified in the great practice of socialism with Chinese characteristics.

Sticking to cultural confidence and achieving the great rejuvenation of the Chinese nation is a process of mutual integration and reinforcement. On the one hand, cultural confidence embodies the strength and morale of the nation, which is an indispensable and vital support for national rejuvenation.

> The Chinese nation has always had a strong sense of cultural pride, but during the Opium War, when China was reduced to a colony and a semi-colony under the powerful attacks of the West, their cultural confidence was seriously damaged.[4]

The Western powers used guns and cannons to blow open the doors of China. Then, Western learning was introduced to the then impoverished and backward China. Despite the Western blows, the Chinese cultural spirit did not decline, which continued to support the nation.

> In the thousands of years of history, the Chinese nation has never had smooth sailing and has encountered numerous difficulties and hardships, but

we survived and came through. One of the important reasons is that generations of Chinese people have cultivated and developed a unique and profound Chinese culture, which has provided strong spiritual support for the Chinese nation to overcome difficulties and live on.[5]

On the other hand, the Chinese Dream of achieving the great rejuvenation of the Chinese nation is a 100-year-old pursuit of the Chinese people, which well represents our cultural confidence. General Secretary Xi Jinping's in-depth remarks on the Chinese Dream have a strong resonance both at home and abroad, and become a spiritual banner that unites and leads Chinese people all over the world. Now, we are closer to the goal of the great rejuvenation of the Chinese nation, and more confident and capable of achieving this goal than in any period of history. As Xi Jinping pointed out,

> Standing on a vast land of 9.6 million square kilometers, absorbing the cultural nutrients accumulated through the long-term efforts of the Chinese nation, and possessing the majestic strength of 1.3 billion Chinese people, we have an incomparably broad stage, an incomparably deep historical heritage, and an incomparably strong determination to move forward. Chinese people should have the confidence to do so. We say that we need to be confident in our path, theory, and system of socialism with Chinese characteristics, but in essence, we need to be committed to cultural confidence.[6]

If Marxism, a German-origin idea and doctrine from Europe, is to take root, sprout, blossom, and bear fruit in the Chinese context, to change from a European form to a Chinese modality, and to take on Chinese characteristics, Chinese style, and Chinese spirit, it must be adapted to the Chinese practices and culture. That is to say, we should adapt Marxism to the Chinese conditions.

As we know, the debate of cultural views during the May Fourth Movement was represented by the radicalism of Chen Duxiu and Li Dazhao, the conservatism of Liang Shuming, and the liberalism of Hu Shih. Later, Chen and Li embraced the materialist view of history and became Marxists. Thus, Marxism, conservatism, and liberalism constituted the basic structure of Chinese thoughts and cultures in the 20th century. If we ask why such a situation occurred and why Marxism could be spread and established in China, the following two points concerning cultural roots are worth noting:

First, Marxism is the product of a dilemma. Culturally speaking, the spread and establishment of Marxism in China was a result of the fact that the Chinese were caught in a dilemma of whether to affirm or deny Western and Chinese cultures after the Opium War. On the one hand, Chinese people wanted to welcome Western culture, which was their master in terms of modernization. However, the master was an aggressor who always bullied the pupil, so Western culture should be rejected in this aspect. On the other, in the face of the invasion of Western culture and China's defeat, traditional Chinese culture, which is not adapted to the times, has to be rejected. Nevertheless, the national identity, national emotion, and national spirit in Chinese culture have to be affirmed. Since the early modern era, the mixed needs to affirm and deny constitute the contradictory and complex backdrop for the Chinese to make sense of culture, and many propositions and paradoxes about cultural understanding since then are related to this background. Wang Guowei summarized the complicated attitude as "loving what one does not believe and believing what one does not love", with the former referring to Chinese culture and the latter to Western culture. Scholar Joseph R. Levenson also noted this dilemma of "sense and sensibility". On the one hand, Chinese culture (mainly Confucianism) is a great heritage, but it also has a lot of outdated teachings. On the other hand, Western culture can be both a teacher of civilization and a symbol of power, hegemony, and aggression. Chinese people decided to learn from the fruits of Western civilization and prevent the evils of Western society, so a possible and appropriate way out is to accept Marxism, an "anti-Western philosophy from the West". In other words, Marxism is "Western", but it is also anti-Western in that it exposes the conflicts, crises, and evils of Western capitalism. Such a philosophy satisfies the mixed needs of the Chinese people to learn from Western civilization while at the same time preventing its evils.

Second, it was the result of two crises. The first was the crisis of Confucianism. The abolition of the imperial examination in 1905 and the 1911 Revolution led to the withdrawal of Confucianism from education and politics. During the New Culture Movement in 1915 and the May Fourth Movement in 1919, Chen Duxiu, Li Dazhao, and Hu Shih made fierce criticisms and attacks on Confucianism, which led to an overall breakdown of Confucianism in terms of its morality, ethics, cultural spirit, and value identity. In 1918, Oswald Spengler's *The Decline of the West* revealed the crisis of Western culture. Later on, Liang Qichao's *Thoughts during My Journey in Europe* also exposed the decline of Western culture and led him to cultural conservatism. What was more severe was that the Paris Peace Conference transferred German privileges in Shandong to Japan in January 1919. The imperialist hegemony angered the Chinese people, especially the intellectuals, and triggered the May Fourth Movement. The triumph of western powers over justice stimulated Chinese nationalism, and the cry for saving the country overwhelmed that for enlightening the people. Meanwhile, it also led to Chinese people's disillusionment with the Western way. In such a situation, it is not difficult to understand why the Chinese turned to Marxism and socialism.

The link of Marxism to Chinese culture plays a crucial role. Only through the integration of Marxism with Chinese culture can the spread and establishment of Marxism in China as well as the localization of Marxism become a reality. There is a certain convergence and similarity between Confucianist *gongxing* (practice what you teach) and the Marxist theory of practice, between the advocacy of "the rise and fall of the world is related to every individual" in Chinese culture and the Marxist emphasis on transforming the world, between "what is opposite to each other is also complementary to each other", "things turn into opposites when they reach extremes" in Chinese philosophy and Marxist dialectics, and between "Society of Great Harmony" in Confucianism and the Marxist social ideal of communism. The materialism and dialectics contained in traditional Chinese culture and philosophical thought are the ideological and cultural basis for the spread and development of Marxism in China and for Chinese people to accept it. This can be further illustrated by the following examples.

For example, "seeking truth from facts". We all say that seeking truth from facts is the fundamental point, starting point, and essence of Mao Zedong's philosophical thought. In fact, seeking truth from facts is borrowed from an ancient Chinese saying. In the Eastern Han Dynasty, Ban Gu's *The Book of the Han Dynasty: The Biography of Prince Hejianxian* describes Liu De, the son of Emperor Jing (Liu Qi), as a man who "cultivated his studies of ancient times and sought truth from facts". Mao Zedong gave it a new interpretation in his "Reform Our Study". He pointed out that the "facts" means all things that exist objectively, and "truth" refers to the internal connections between objective things, i.e., laws, and "seek" is to "study" or "research".[7]

Another example is philosophy. Mao's epistemology is in fact an interpretation and summary of the traditional Chinese philosophical view of knowing and doing. In fact, the subtitle of his "On Practice" is "On the Relation Between Knowledge and Practice, Between Knowing and Doing". Mao's doctrine of contradiction is also linked to the traditional Chinese philosophical concept of *yin* and *yang*. In November 1956, at the Second Plenary Session of the Eighth Central Committee of CPC, Mao said that *yin* and *yang* combined is called the Way, which was exactly the ancient theory that everything has two aspects.

Yet another example is the military. Mao Zedong mentioned Sun Tzu's art of war most frequently, and he particularly appreciated and discussed the phrase "If you know yourself and your enemy, you will never be in danger in a hundred battles". He also often referred to many ancient cases of warfare, such as "make a feint to the east but attack in the west" and "relieve the besieged by besieging the base of the besiegers". In March 1945, when talking about the approach we should take if the Kuomintang attacked the liberated areas, he said,

> The first rule is from the philosophy of Lao Tzu, which is called 'not to be the first in the world'. That is to say, we would not fire the first shot. Secondly, it is the philosophy from *The Commentary of Zuo*, which says 'Retreat and avoid the enemy'. This means that if they are coming, we should give way. The third rule is the 'etiquette of reciprocity' as stated in *The Book of Rites*, which means we will not attack others if we are not attacked, but if we are, we must fight back.[8]

This is not about quoting what Marx and Engels argued for, but about what Lao Tzu, *The Commentary of Zuo*, and *The Book of Rites* said. Traditional culture has become a way of thinking and wisdom of action. In the words of an old saying, it has been "melted in the blood".

Here it is necessary to probe into the question of the content and form of culture. Form and content cannot be separated. National identity exists in the unity of content and form. In other words, national identity is a kind of form, but it is beyond form. It not only reflects in form but also in content. Only when national identity manifests itself in both form and content can it be truly alive. Therefore, it is not enough to treat national identity as merely a form. Accordingly, I believe that the localization of Marxism calls for not only the form but also the content of national identity and entails an inner cultural gene and association. The strong vitality of Chinese culture lies not only in its compatibility and flexibility but also in its openness and modernity. From "seeking truth from facts" and "unity of knowledge and action" to "people-oriented" and "all-round moderate prosperity", all of the proposals are permeated with the essence of traditional Chinese culture, demonstrating the cultural significance of Marxism adapted to Chinese conditions.

The localization of Marxism consists of two dimensions: adapt it to Chinese practice and to Chinese culture. In other words, the adaptation of Marxism includes not only the interpretation of practice but also that of culture. At present, the practical dimension calls for adapting Marxism to socialism with Chinese characteristics, to reform and development. The cultural dimension requires us to establish cultural confidence and promote the essence of traditional Chinese culture. The adaptation of Marxism is the result of combining Marxism with Chinese practice and Chinese culture. With a high degree of awareness of Marxist theory and cultural confidence, we should create a Marxist discourse system with Chinese characteristics, Chinese style, and Chinese spirit on the basis of learning from the achievements of human civilization. At the same time, the study of contemporary Marxism in China should take an open vision, a global perspective, and an international outlook. We shall not shut the door and refuse to communicate with the world. Marxism of China must have a greater say and influence in international exchanges and dialogs so that Marxism is not only adapted to Chinese conditions but also reaches globalization.

Marxism must be integrated not only with Chinese practice but also with Chinese culture. The essential content of Marxism's localization must be developed in these two dimensions so as to reveal its practical and cultural significance. How to stick to the Chinese cultural stance and continue the national cultural lineage is not only a major task for the study of Chinese culture but also a crucial issue for the localization of Marxism. From the above two dimensions, the combination of Marxism with Chinese practice has been largely successful, and we have taken a Chinese path that has attracted worldwide attention. However, the combination of Marxism with Chinese culture is still on the way, and there are many difficulties to be solved. The adaptation of Marxism now depends on the integration and convergence of Marxism and Chinese culture. This is not only more difficult but also more significant, calling for our joint and continuous efforts, which is the mission and responsibility of us, researchers of theories.

Contemporary Perspectives of Marxism Localization in China

Marxism has been in existence for more than 170 years and has been interpreted in different ways by the academic community. In terms of its form, the primary form is the theory of Marx and Engels, and the secondary is the theory of Lenin and Stalin, and the tertiary is Mao Zedong Thought and the theoretical system of socialism with Chinese characteristics. In terms of expression, there are three main types of Marxism: Soviet Marxism, Western Marxism, and Chinese Marxism. There are also various interpretations titled "Marx in his early years", "Marx in his later years", "Marx and Engels", "Marx on the platform", "Marx in the forum", "Marx in the textbook", and "Marx in the text", as well as various references to him such as "Back to Marx", "Rereading Marx", "Reading Marx", "Looking into Marx", "Approaching Marx", "Marx walking with us", and "Marx is contemporary with us". We need to study the text to grasp the true spirit of Marxism. Based on practice, we would promote the development and innovation of contemporary Chinese Marxism.

In recent years, the Central Committee of CPC has launched the research and construction project of Marxist theory, established Marxist theory as a first-level discipline, and set up schools of Marxism, which was of great significance and played a positive role in promoting the construction and academic development of Marxist disciplines. Though the number of books, forums, and research topics on Marxist theory is remarkable, the division of discipline is not very clear, and the problem of poor-quality and repeated research is still serious. In terms of the overall situation of Marxist research and teaching, the achievements are not small, but there also exist many problems and challenges. Three relationships need to be dealt with in research. First, the relationship between politics and academics. Marxist theory is a discipline, which is academic in nature. At the same time, it is also an ideology, which is political in nature. Second, the relationship between theory and practice. Marxism is a theory, but its essence is practical, revolutionary, and critical, so it must be closely integrated with contemporary Chinese practice. Thirdly, the relationship between text and textbook. We must not only read Marx's original classics but also prepare new teaching materials that reflect the new achievements in adapting Marxism to Chinese conditions. For teaching, the following three relationships need to be dealt with. First, the relationship between public and professional courses. At present, the courses of general ideological and political theory in universities are undertaken by the departments of Marxism as public courses, while professional courses, such as Marxist philosophy, are undertaken by other relevant departments. The second is the problem of repetition and overlapping. Repetition refers to the recurrence of similar Marxist courses at the secondary, undergraduate, master, and doctoral levels, while overlapping, a more prominent problem, refers to the intersection of six second-level disciplines under the first-level discipline of Marxist theory. Third, the attendance rate and the number of students raising their heads in the class. Though the attendance rate of courses of ideological and political theory is quite high, only a few students raise up their heads and listen to the lecturers. Many of them are reading books about their majors or looking at their mobile phones. We should face up to and solve these problems and strive to improve the academic standard and quality of teaching in Marxist studies.

In terms of the methodology of Marxist studies, the following are particularly important:

First is the relationship between classics and contemporary reality. The early dissemination of Marxism in China was mainly through translation (e.g., excerpt translation, reporting, introduction). The original Marxist texts, i.e., the original form of Marxism, were not sufficiently studied. The Chinese received Marxism through people of Japan and the Soviet Union. Out of different perspectives, understandings, and translations, some of the expressions may not be accurate, and there may have been non-Marxist additions to them, which made the study and publicity of Marxism in early modern China difficult and induced early Chinese Marxists to treat Marxism in a simplified and mechanical way. This, I am afraid, was one of the reasons for the call for a "return to Marx" in Chinese philosophical studies at the end of the 20th century. It is therefore important to combine the uniqueness of the text with the diversity of interpretation, and the historical background of the text with the modern context of interpretation. We should study the text in order to grasp the true spirit of Marxism and base ourselves on practice to promote the development and innovation of contemporary Marxism in China.

Second is the relationship between politics and academics. Some of the leading figures who propagated Marxism in China, such as Li Dazhao, Chen Duxiu, Qu Qiubai, and Mao Zedong, were not professional philosophers but had dual identities and roles as revolutionists and philosophers, which I think is related to the politicization of contemporary Chinese philosophy. This phenomenon is worth noting when we study the history of the spread of Marxism in China and the localization of Marxism.

Third is the relationship between theory and practice. Due to the urgent needs of China's social development, soon after the introduction of Marxism into China and as the research of it was still in its infancy, the issue of application was already on the agenda. It can be said that the dissemination and application of Marxism in China were almost simultaneous, and theory was quickly transformed into practice. This is also an important feature of the spread of Marxism in China.

Fourth is the relationship between China and the Soviet Union. The Japanese channel had an important influence on the spread of Marxism in China. It can be said that Marxism from Japan played a leading role in its spread in China before 1927. Thereafter, especially after the 1930s, this role was gradually taken over by Marxism from the Soviet Union. The major branch of Marxism imported from the Soviet Union was Marxist philosophy in the form of textbooks. This systematic and authoritative form of Marxist philosophy had replaced Japanese-sourced Marxism and come to dominate Chinese philosophy for half a century. On the whole, neither Li Da's *Outline of Sociology* nor Ai Siqi's *Dialectical Materialism and Historical Materialism* have broken through the influence of Soviet philosophy textbooks. Reform and breakthrough in real sense took place after the mid-1980s.

In 2016, President Xi Jinping pointed out that we should be good at integrating the resources of Marxism, of the essence of traditional Chinese culture, and of philosophy and social sciences from abroad in his speech at the Symposium on Philosophy and Social Sciences. This proposal is very important and relevant. In contemporary China, Marxism, Chinese culture, and Western culture all have their own discourse systems and research paradigms. Although we all attach importance to dialog, there has not yet been much substantive communication and progress. As for the future of Chinese philosophy and social science, Zhang Dainian has proposed a "theory of comprehensive innovation", which means Chinese philosophy of the 21st century should make innovations in combination with modern academics from the West and traditional Chinese culture. The pathway is right, but the question now is how to carry out specific work and make in-depth exploration so as to achieve substantial progress and major breakthroughs.

At present, there are numerous philosophical and social science researches, including Marxist theory researches, in China, but few of them are of high quality. Research topics, projects, and forums are many, and papers, publications, and awards are countless. However, it is common to see repetitive research without much progress. Enhancing academic quality and standards and overcoming low-level repetition are issues that must be resolved in order to build philosophy and social sciences with Chinese characteristics and develop Marxism of contemporary China. The development and innovation of philosophy and social science is a process of continuous exploration and accumulation, which cannot be achieved overnight. We must withstand loneliness and temptation, keep the bottom line, aspire to study with earnestness and sincerity, and strive to be the role models of the people.

The basic experience of the localization of Marxism, and the basic requirement for the development of Marxism of contemporary China is to base the effort on Chinese practice and stand at the forefront of the times with a historical perspective. Under the new historical conditions, the adaptation of Marxism must entail three dimensions, i.e., reality, history, and the times.

The Dimension of Reality

We should consistently uphold and develop socialism with Chinese characteristics. In the 40 years of reform and opening up, we have taken a Chinese path and made the great leap from "keeping up with the times" to "catching up with the times" to "leading the times". Socialism with Chinese characteristics has answered the difficult question of how to build socialism in a country like China, which is economically and culturally backward. Our unique cultural traditions, history, and basic national conditions dictate that we must follow a development path that suits our own needs. China's orderly governance and the West's confusion in politics show that the Western model of development is just "a" model of modernization but not "the" model. As the influence of socialism with Chinese characteristics is expanding, the Communist Party of China and the Chinese people are fully confident that they can provide a Chinese solution to humankind's search for a better social system.

We shall consistently push forward the new great project of Party building. To realize the great dream, we must carry out a great struggle, build a great project, and promote a great cause. The great struggle, project, cause, and dream are closely linked, coherent, and interactive, among which Party building plays a decisive role. We need to analyze the various factors that affect the Party's advanced nature and weaken its purity, fully understand the difficulty and magnitude of the comprehensive strict governance of the Party, carry out self-revolution with a resolution, and promote the great social revolution with the Party's self-revolution. We shall maintain a firm belief, stick to our political stance, take our responsibility, improve our capability and stay away from corruption.

We shall consistently stay alert to risks and challenges. The great achievements of socialism with Chinese characteristics are unprecedented, so are the new problems and challenges we face. General Secretary Xi Jinping proposed in his speech on July 26, 2017 that we should prepare for danger and long-term risks even in times of peace. In the report of the 19th National Congress of CPC, he stressed the importance of staying vigilant. In his speech on January 5, 2018, the Party's confidence and sobriety were again reflected in the statement that we should move forward carefully as if walking on thin ice and be vigilant in times of peace. In the face of the treacherous international situation, the complex and sensitive surrounding environment, and the arduous task of reform, development, and stability maintenance, we must keep a clear mind and strategic determination, prevent economic and social risks, and combat environmental pollution. We should also oppose national separatism and achieve the reunification of China. We shall adopt the holistic approach to national security and resolutely safeguard national sovereignty and security. In a word, we must prevent problems before they occur and take the initiative, pushing forward the great cause of socialism with Chinese characteristics.

The Dimension of History

Firstly, from the perspective of 5,000 years of Chinese culture, Xi Jinping Thought on Socialism with Chinese characteristics for a New Era is good at drawing wisdom and experience from the essence of traditional Chinese culture in respect to governing the country. Only by remembering the past can we embrace a better future. History is a mirror, from which we could learn successes and failures, identify gains and losses, and understand the ups and downs. To govern today's China well, we need to have a deep understanding of our history and traditional culture. The 40 years of reform and opening up are intrinsically connected to the 5,000 years of Chinese civilization, and the Chinese path is interlinked with its civilization too. Chinese civilization is the root of socialism with Chinese characteristics, and socialism with Chinese characteristics is rooted in the fertile soil of Chinese culture. Only when we are good at inheriting can we promote and spread the Chinese culture that transcends time and space, transcends national boundaries, and possesses eternal charm and contemporary value. We should forge ahead by continuing the national cultural lineage and enhancing the morale of the Chinese people so as to create new glories of Chinese culture in the great practice of socialism with Chinese characteristics.

Second, in the light of the 500 years of development of socialism in the world, Xi Jinping Thought on Socialism with Chinese Characteristics for a New Era is the persistence in and development of scientific socialism in China. Socialism has evolved from an empty idea to a science, from theory to practice, from the model of one country to the explorations by many nations, and from possessing Chinese characteristics to entering a new era. This new era means exactly a new era of socialism with Chinese characteristics. Socialism with Chinese characteristics has revitalized ancient China, filled it with vitality and creativity, and demonstrated its strong vitality and influence. In order to accomplish the Party's historical mission in the new era, the fundamental requirement is to hold high the great banner of socialism with Chinese characteristics and to have firm confidence in the path, theory, system, and culture of socialism with Chinese characteristics.

Third, the history of China's revolution, construction, and reform shows that socialism with Chinese characteristics did not come up from nowhere but was the result of the Party and the people's painstaking efforts and great sacrifices. Socialism with Chinese characteristics in the new era is the fruit and also continuation of the great social revolution led by the Party. To write a new chapter of socialism with Chinese characteristics in the new era, we must work hard without slackening and carry out relentless struggle, open up a new situation by seizing every minute, and overcome all difficulties and obstacles with courage and determination. We will create miracles, realize our dreams, and win the future through our efforts.

The Dimension of the Times

In this era, with a complex and volatile international environment and the increasingly fierce competition for comprehensive national power, elements of instability and uncertainty that affect peace and development have increased, so we are facing many foreseeable or unforeseeable risks and challenges. To promote the localization of Marxism, we must stand on the frontier of the times, respond to and follow up its trends, grasp its characteristics, fulfill its requirements, answer its questions, and meet its challenges.

We should take an international perspective. The localization of Marxism entails an open vision and an international outlook. We should attach importance to international exchanges, promote the internationalization of Chinese Marxism as the adaptation of Marxism goes on, voice Chinese Marxism more often in international forums, and enhance the influence and say of Chinese Marxism in international exchanges and dialogs.

We should explain "Chinese characteristics" well. Since the reform and opening up, the Communist Party of China has answered a series of major theoretical and practical questions through theoretical innovation based on practice during the successive explorations of socialism with Chinese characteristics, providing creative theoretical guidance that reflects the traits of the times and grasps the laws of development, which opens up a new realm of Marxism. We should transform our advantages over development into those over discourse, our economic strength into cultural soft power, and the influence of the Chinese path into that of Chinese theory. We should relate the Chinese story vividly and spread the Chinese voice effectively so as to well explain what "Chinese characteristics" are.

We should build a Chinese discourse system. The discourse system is, in essence, about cultural autonomy and theoretical originality. We can neither neglect others' opinions nor accept others' discourse while following our own path. The task to answer Chinese questions with Chinese theories and to interpret Chinese paths with Chinese discourse raises higher requirements for theoretical research. We must continue to liberate our minds, seek truth from facts, keep abreast of the times, and innovate on theories in the great practice of socialism with Chinese characteristics.

We should make our original contributions to Marxism. As socialism with Chinese characteristics enters a new era, the practical form of Chinese Marxism, i.e., the Chinese path, has obtained great achievements. We should continue to develop the theory of localization of Marxism, stick to a problem-oriented approach, focus on the realities, get close to the people, and promote theoretical innovation. "Making China's original contribution to the development of Marxism"[9] is the responsibility and mission of contemporary Chinese Marxists.

Notes

1 Mao Zedong. *Selected Works of Mao Zedong*: vol. 2, 2nd ed. Beijing: People's Publishing House, 1991, p. 534.
2 *Selected Readings of Mao Zedong's Works*: vol. 2. Beijing: People's Publishing House, 1986, p. 720.
3 Address by General Secretary Xi Jinping at the meeting of the Standing Committee of the Political Bureau of the 19th CPC Central Committee with Chinese and foreign journalists, October 25, 2017. http://www.xinhuanet.com//politics/19cpcnc/2017-10/25/c_129726443.htm.
4 Peng Zhenhuai: Xi Jinping's Important Remarks on Traditional Culture, August 15, 2014. http://gx.people.com.cn/n/2014/0815/c365334-22004058.html.
5 Central Literature Research Office of the Communist Party of China. *Selected Important Documents Since the 18th National Congress of CPC*: vol. 2. Beijing: Central Literature Publishing House, 2016, p. 119.
6 Xi Jinping. Speech at the Symposium on Philosophy and Social Sciences. *People's Daily,* May 19, 2016.
7 Mao Zedong. *Selected Works of Mao Zedong*, vol. 3, 2nd edition, Beijing: People's Publishing House, 1991, p. 801.
8 Literature Research Office of the CPC Central Committee. *Collected Works of Mao Zedong*, vol. 3. Beijing: People's Publishing House,1996, p. 326.
9 Get Aware of the Significance and Relevance of Marxism, and Continue to Promote the Localization, Modernization, and Popularization of Marxism. *People's Daily*, September 30, 2017.

1 Localize Marxism With Chinese Revolution

Zhong Tian'e

When the Communist Party of China (CPC) was founded, it adopted Marxism as the guiding philosophy for observing China's destiny and solving the problems of the Chinese revolution. The combination of combining Marxism and the Chinese revolutions is also the process of localizing Marxism. In leading the new democratic and socialist revolutions, the members of the CPC, represented by Mao Zedong, insisted on seeking truth from facts and staying independent. In the struggle against dogmatism, against overemphasis on practical experience, and against other erroneous thoughts, they put forward the important proposal of "localizing Marxism" and created the first major theoretical achievement of Marxism in China, i.e., Mao Zedong Thought, which realized the first historic leap in the localization of Marxism and opened up a new path for the development of Marxism in China.

The Proposal of and Elaboration on Localizing Marxism

The primary requirement of the localization of Marxism is the combination of Marxism with the practice of the Chinese revolutions, which is the basic stance, viewpoint, and method for the correct understanding of Marxism and the practice of the Chinese revolutions that the members of the CPC, represented by Mao Zedong, gradually developed in their course of struggle. Based on the practice of the new democratic revolution, they struggled against the erroneous tendency of dogmatizing Marxism and sanctifying the resolutions of the Communist International and the Soviet experience. In April 1945, in his report to the Seventh National Congress of the CPC, Liu Shaoqi summed up the basic experience of the Chinese revolutionary practice and expounded the localization of Marxism and its theoretical fruit, i.e., Mao Zedong Thought, pointing out that Mao Zedong Thought is "a thought that unifies Marxism, Leninism, and the Chinese revolutions". Mao Zedong Thought is both a Chinese and Marxist idea and is a consistently developing and improving version of Chinese Marxism.

DOI: 10.4324/9781003356042-2

The Proposal of Localizing Marxism

In the early days of the spread of Marxism, Li Dazhao, Chen Duxiu, and other early leaders of the Party elaborated, to varying degrees, on how to treat Marxism and how to apply it, and put forward many valuable ideas and perspectives.

In the debate on the relationship between practical issues and theories early on, Li Dazhao made it very clear that "there should be no empty talk about theories" and that "theories should be combined with realities". He proposed,

> Every theory has both an ideal and a practical aspect [...] Applying the ideal to practical politics means variations of the theory will occur according to the time, the place, and the situation. This is also the case with socialism [...] If we take this and that theory and use it as a tool for practical movement, it will definitely change according to the time, the place and the situation.

He also said, "A socialist, in order to enhance the influence of his idea, must study how he can apply his theory as far as possible to the realities that surround him".[1] In his essay "My View on Marxism", Li Dazhao further elaborated the idea that Marxism should evolve from time to time and place to place. In 1923, in his article "Socialism and Social Movements", Li Dazhao further considered the issue of socialism in the light of the particularities of Chinese society, pointing out that the ideal of socialism

> differs from place to place and from time to time, and it is necessary to find the right version to implement so that a new system that combines commonalities and characteristics will emerge (commonalities are universal qualities, characteristics are things that vary at different time and space). When socialism is realized in China in the future, it will be different from that in Britain, Germany, Russia [...][2]

Li Dazhao's dialectical analysis of Marxism and socialism implies that we shall not treat Marxism as dogmas but apply it on the basis of the reality of Chinese society. These ideas and perspectives provide valuable ideological and theoretical resources for advancing the development of Marxism in China.

After its founding, the CPC actively participated in the struggle of the Chinese revolution and began to use Marxism as a weapon of thought to study and solve the practical problems of the Chinese revolution, which starts the painstaking exploration of the localization of Marxism. During the early years of the Party and the Revolutionary period, the CPC conducted in-depth theoretical thinking on the conditions of China and on a series of fundamental issues of the Chinese Revolution, clarified the nature of the Chinese Revolution, formulated the platform of the democratic revolution, put forward the ideas of establishing a united front, maintaining the independence of the proletariat, upholding the leadership of the proletariat and the peasant allies, etc., and made preliminary theoretical achievements in applying Marxism to solve the practical problems of the Chinese Revolution. However, as the Party was just founded, its ideology and theory were not yet mature and unified. After the defeat of the Revolution, three "Left" deviations emerged in the Party, namely blind activism, adventurism, and dogmatism. The "Left" deviations copied the instructions of the Communist International and the Soviet experience, which were divorced from the realities of the Chinese revolution and caused serious trouble and harm to the localization of Marxism and to Chinese revolutions.

Party members represented by Mao Zedong insisted on combining the basic principles of Marxism to the realities of Chinese revolutions, proposing a series of correct ideas, theories, and opinions on Chinese revolutions. The 1935 Zunyi Conference put an end to the dominance of "Left" dogmatism in the Party and established Mao Zedong as the de facto leader of the Party. Mao Zedong began to lead the Party in its efforts to correct the "Left" errors and to summarize the basic experience, both positive and negative, of the Chinese Revolution, making an important contribution to the development of the adaption of Marxism to Chinese conditions. In October 1938, at the Sixth Plenary Session of the Sixth Central Committee of the Party, Mao Zedong made a political report entitled "On the New Stage", in which he put forward for the first time the proposal of "localizing Marxism". Mao pointed out clearly that the theories of Marx, Engels, Lenin, and Stalin were not dogmas, but guides for action. We must learn from their stances and methods in observing and solving problems.

> Marxism must be realized in specific nations. There is no abstract Marxism, only concrete Marxism. By concrete Marxism, I mean Marxism of the Chinese nation, that is, Marxism applied to the concrete struggles of China's concrete environment, not in an abstract way. Communists who have become part of the great Chinese nation and are linked to it in flesh and blood, and who talk about Marxism out of the Chinese context, are merely talking about the abstract and empty Marxism. Therefore, how to specify Marxism in China, how to give it a Chinese feature in its every expression, that is to say, how to apply it in accordance with Chinese characteristics, has become a problem that the whole Party needs to get aware of and to solve immediately.[3]

He also pointed out, "Pure Western teachings must be abolished, and the empty and abstract words must be stopped, and dogmatism must be replaced by a fresh and lively Chinese style and spirit that is pleasing to the people of China".[4]

Mao Zedong's proposal of "localizing Marxism", reflecting the CPC's insistence on combining the basic principles of Marxism with the practice of the Chinese revolution, was a summary of the practical experience of the CPC in the revolution, and undoubtedly played an important role in liberating minds from the fetters of dogmatism and in urging people to research and solve the problems of Chinese revolutions independently based on the realities.

After this proposal was put forward, it was widely accepted and followed by other leaders in the Party. Zhang Wentian, for example, raised the proposal of "adapting organizational work to Chinese conditions", pointing out that

> we must be familiar with the basic principles of Marxism-Leninism in organizational work. However, the various characteristics of Chinese national, political, cultural, and ideological habits must be strictly evaluated to determine the features of organizational work and to adapt it to Chinese conditions.[5]

In terms of publicity and education, he believed that

> we should propagate Marxism-Leninism and increase people's knowledge of their theories nationwide. In particular, we should educate Party members and revolutionary youth with the revolutionary spirit and methods of Marxism-Leninism. We should also use this chance to study the practical problems of the Chinese revolution and to study all aspects of Chinese history and culture. Marxism-Leninism should be adapted to local conditions and made acceptable to the broadest range of the Chinese people.[6]

Here, Zhang Wentian not only put forward but also tentatively elaborated on the idea of localizing Marxism-Leninism, which means the idea should be combined with the practice of the Chinese revolution and with Chinese history and culture. The proposal of "localizing Marxism" played an important guiding role in further unifying the thinking of the Party, strengthening its unity, and contributing to the victory of the Anti-Japanese War (1931–1945).

The Proposal of and Elaboration on Mao Zedong Thought

Mao Zedong made an important contribution to localizing Marxism. Mao Zedong Thought is the major theoretical form of Chinese Marxism. The process of putting forward and establishing Mao Zedong Thought was also the course of gradually localizing Marxism.

With the growing experience in the Chinese revolutionary struggle, the CPC was increasingly aware of building its own theoretical system, and its ideology and theory began to mature. The concept of "Mao Zedong Thought" began to take shape as the CPC was studying, propagating, and researching Mao Zedong's thinking. In March 1941, Zhang Ruxin, a CPC theoretician, first used the term "Comrade Mao Zedong's Thought" in his essay "On the Bolshevik Educators", saying that "the Party should be faithful to the thought of Lenin and Stalin and to Comrade Mao Zedong's Thought" and that "Mao Zedong's writings are a typical crystal of the combination of Marxist-Leninist theory and the reality of the Chinese revolution".[7] On July 1, 1942, Chen Yi published an article stating that Mao had created a "correct system of thought"[8] and outlined Mao's theories on the Chinese revolution in five aspects. On July 6, 1943, Liu Shaoqi used the similar concept of "Comrade Mao Zedong's ideological system" in his article "Liquidating the Menshevik Thinking in the Party".[9] He called on the Party to "study and learn from Comrade Mao Zedong's ideas about the Chinese revolution and other fields" and to "arm ourselves with Comrade Mao's ideas and use Comrade Mao Zedong's ideological system to liquidate the Menshevik ones in the Party". On July 8, 1943, Wang Jiaxiang used the concept of "Mao Zedong Thought" for the first time in his article "The Communist Party of China and the Road to China's National Liberation", stating

> the correct road for the entire process of national liberation in China—
> past, present and future—is Mao Zedong Thought, the path that Comrade Mao Zedong pointed out in his writings and in practice. Mao Zedong Thought is Chinese Marxism-Leninism, Chinese Bolshevism, Chinese communism.[10]

In August 1943, Zhou Enlai made a speech at a welcome meeting in Yan'an, saying "the 22-year history of our Party proves that throughout the entire period of Party history, the views of Comrade Mao Zedong have been developed into a path of Chinese Marxism-Leninism, or Chinese Communism!"[11] In November 1943, Deng Xiaoping also used the concept of "Mao Zedong Thought" in his speech at the mobilization meeting for the Rectification Movement in the Party School of the Northern Bureau. He suggested that after the Zunyi Conference, the Party's undertaking was completely under the guidance of "Chinese Marxism-Leninism, that is, Mao Zedong Thought".[12]

As a major expression of Chinese Marxism, Mao Zedong Thought is the theoretical fruit of the CPC's combination of the basic principles of Marxism with the practice of the Chinese revolution. The concept obtained wide recognition within the Party. In April 1945, *The Resolution on Certain Historical Issues* adopted by the Sixth Plenary Session of the Seventh Central Committee of the CPC solemnly stated,

> Since its inception in 1921, the Communist Party of China has taken the combination of the universal truths of Marxism-Leninism and the

practice of the Chinese revolution as the guideline for all its work, represented by Comrade Mao Zedong's theories and practices on the Chinese revolution.

Comrade Mao Zedong, on behalf of the Chinese proletariat and the Chinese people, creatively applied the scientific theory of Marxism-Leninism, the highest wisdom of humankind, to a large, semifeudal, semi-colonized country like China, where the peasants are the majority, where the immediate task is to fight against imperialism and feudalism on the vast land with a large population, and where the situation is extremely complex and the struggle extremely difficult.[13]

In May 1945, in his *Report on the Revision of the Party Constitution* made at the Seventh National Congress of CPC, Liu Shaoqi comprehensively and systematically expounded Mao Zedong Thought, pointing out that "Mao Zedong Thought is the unification of Marxism-Leninism with the practice of the Chinese revolution, the Chinese communism, and the Chinese Marxism".

Mao Zedong Thought is the continued development of Marxism in the national democratic revolution of the colonial, semi-colonial, and semi-feudal countries of the present era, and it is an excellent example of adapting Marxism to specific national conditions. It grew and developed out of the long revolutionary struggle of the Chinese nation and the Chinese people in the three great revolutionary wars of China—the Northern Expedition, the Agrarian Revolutionary War, and now the War of Resistance against Japanese Aggression. It is both Chinese and Marxist. It has been created through scientific and meticulous analysis, applying the Marxist view of the universe and society, i.e., dialectical and historical materialism, on the basis of solid Marxist-Leninist theory, the characteristics of the Chinese nation, and the rich experience of the modern revolution and the struggle of the people led by the Communist Party of China.

"From his view on the universe to his style of work, we can see Mao Zedong Thought is a consistently developing and improving version of Chinese Marxism and a complete theory of revolution and nation-building for the Chinese people".[14] The report also elaborated on the Mao Zedong Thought in nine aspects, including the analysis of the modern world situation and China's national conditions, as well as theories and policies on New Democracy, the liberation of the peasants, revolutionary united front, revolutionary war, revolutionary base areas, building the New Democratic Republic, building the Party and culture, etc. The formulation of these theories and policies is the superb expression and theoretical summary of Chinese national wisdom.

The general principles of *Constitution of the Communist Party of China*, adopted at the Seventh Party Congress on June 11, 1945, clearly state that

"Mao Zedong Thought, which is the unity of Marxism-Leninism and the practice of the Chinese revolution, shall be the guideline for all the work of the Party, and we shall oppose any dogmatism and overemphasis on experience".[15] This marked the establishment of the guiding status of Mao Zedong Thought in the Party. The proposal of Mao Zedong Thought was the first major theoretical achievement of localizing Marxism and a historical leap forward in combining Marxism with the practice of the Chinese revolution. The practice has proved that Mao Zedong Thought is the scientific guide for the Chinese revolution to gain victory. The development of the Chinese revolution will continue to promote the further enrichment and development of Mao Zedong Thought.

A Significant Achievement in Localizing Marxism

One important aspect of Mao Zedong's contribution to the localization of Marxism is his creative application and development of Marxist philosophy on the basis of Chinese reality, which brought about important achievements in the adaptation of Marxist philosophy to Chinese realities.

"On Practice" and "On Contradiction": Theoretical Elaboration on Chinese Marxism

"On Practice" and "On Contradiction" are two philosophical works by Mao Zedong that summarize the experience of the Chinese revolution, expose the epistemological origin of dogmatism, and systematically defend the adaption of Marxism to Chinese conditions from a philosophical perspective. These two works, which are closely related to the reality of the Chinese revolution, creatively enriched and developed Marxist epistemology and dialectics, being important achievements in localizing Marxist philosophy.

At the end of the Long March and on the verge of the full-scale War of Resistance against Japanese Aggression, the CPC members, represented by Mao Zedong, seriously studied the philosophical works of Marxism and summarized the experience of Chinese revolutions from a philosophical perspective with a view to liquidating the influence of "Left" dogmatism and to solving the problem of combining the basic principles of Marxism with the practice of the Chinese revolution. From April to early July 1937, Mao Zedong taught philosophy at the Chinese People's Anti-Japanese Military and Political University in Yan'an with his lecture titled "Dialectical Materialism (Outline of Lecture)".

"On Practice" is in Section 11, Chapter 2 of the syllabus, and "On Contradiction" is in Section 1, Chapter 3. While writing "On Practice" and "On Contradiction", Mao referred to some Soviet philosophy textbooks of the 1930s translated by Chinese theoreticians, such as *A Course in Dialectical Materialism* (by Silokov and Eisenberg, translated by Li Da and Lei Zhongjian) and *A New Outline of Philosophy* (by M. B. Mitin, translated by Ai Siqi and Zheng Yili). The two essays draw on some of the ideas of these text-books in presenting the basic ideas of Marxist epistemology and dialectics but with some innovation and development.

"On Practice" focuses on Marxist epistemology. It mainly covers the following aspects:

First, it conducts in-depth discussions on the status and role of practice in cognition. Mao Zedong emphasized the dependence of cognition on practice, believing that practice is the source, the driving force, and the purpose of cognition and is the criterion for testing the veracity of cognition. On this basis, he proposed that

> the epistemology of dialectical materialism puts practice in the first place and holds that human cognition cannot be divorced from practice at all. The theory rejects all false beliefs that deny the importance of practice and separate cognition from practice.[16]

Second, the dialectical process of cognitive development was analyzed in detail. Taking into account the historical experience of the Chinese revolution, Mao Zedong put forward the idea of "two leaps" in the process of cognition. He pointed out that the process of cognition was divided into two stages: perceptual cognition and rational cognition, with the latter depending on the former and the former waiting to evolve into the latter. The first leap in the process of cognition is to rise from perceptual cognition to rational cognition, and the second leap is to move from rational cognition to practice. Only when the second leap is finished can we judge whether the cognition is correct and transform cognition into practice.

Third, he revealed the general law of the movement of cognition. He said,

> Through practice, truth is discovered, and through practice, truth is confirmed and developed. Perceptual cognition is actively developed into rational cognition, which then actively guides revolutionary practice and remolds the subjective and objective worlds. Practice-cognition-practice-cognition… This is the infinite cycle of the two elements, which will upgrade to a higher level as the cycle moves on. This is the epistemology of dialectical materialism, and this is the unity of knowledge and action in dialectical materialism.[17]

This exposition reveals the dialectical relationship between cognition and practice and provides a scientific overview and summary of the general law of the movement of cognition.

Fourth, the concrete historical unity of subjectivity and objectivity, theory and practice is clarified in a scientific manner. Mao pointed out that "opportunism and adventurism are both characterized by the split between subjectivity and objectivity, by the separation of knowledge and practice". "Our conclusion is the concrete historical unity of subjectivity and objectivity, theory and practice, and knowledge and action, and we reject all 'Left' or right erroneous ideas that are divorced from concrete history".[18] The exposition reveals the epistemological origins of erroneous ideas.

"On Contradiction" mainly explains the Marxist dialectics, which includes:

First, the two opposing views of the universe. Mao Zedong believed that in the history of human understanding there existed two opposing views of the universe: the metaphysical one sees things from an isolated, static, and one-sided perspective, and the dialectical one sees things from a connected, developing, and comprehensive perspective. He pointed out that "the dialectical view of the universe mainly teaches people to be good at observing and analyzing the contradictory movements of various objects and to discover ways of resolving them on the basis of these analyses".[19] This remark reveals the methodological significance of the dialectical view of the universe.

Second, the universality and particularity of contradiction and the essence of issues concerning contradiction. According to Mao Zedong, the universality of contradiction is its commonality and absolute nature, which means that contradiction exists in and runs through all processes, while the particularity of contradiction is its individuality and relative nature, which refers to the specialty of the object in a contradiction that distinguishes it from other things. The relationship between the universality and the particularity of contradiction is the relationship between commonality and individuality. "This truth about commonality and individuality, about absolute and relative nature, is the essence of issues concerning contradiction. Failing to understand it is to abandon dialectics".[20] Mao Zedong also attached particular importance to the methodological principle of studying the particularity of contradictions and making concrete analysis of specific things, pointing out that

> the use of different methods to solve different contradictions is a principle that must be strictly observed by Marxists-Leninists. Instead of following this principle, the dogmatists, who do not understand the difference between the various revolutionary situations or the different methods that should be used to solve different contradictions, simply apply a formula that they think is immutable, which will only frustrate the revolution.[21]

Third, primary and secondary contradictions, and the primary and secondary aspects of contradictions. Mao pointed out, "If there are many contradictions in any process, one of them must be the primary one, playing a leading and decisive role, while the others are in a secondary and subordinate position". "Of the two contradictory aspects, one must be primary and the other secondary. The primary aspect is the so-called dominant aspect of the contradiction. The nature of things is primarily determined by the primary aspect of the dominant contradiction".[22] He stressed that the study of the primary contradiction and the primary aspect of the contradiction is one of the important methods by which a revolutionary party can correctly determine its political and military strategic and tactical approach, which all CPC members should pay attention to.[23]

Fourth, the identity and struggle of contradictions. The struggle of contradiction refers to the mutual repulsion and opposition of the two sides of the contradiction, while the identity refers to the interdependence and transformation of the two sides of the contradiction. The latter is conditional, temporary, and relative, while the former is unconditional and absolute. The combination of conditional, relative identity and unconditional, absolute struggle constitutes the contradictory motion of all things. We should combine the two in both cognition and practice. Any approach that separates struggle and identity is wrong.

Based on the struggle and historical experience of the Chinese revolution, "On Practice" and "On Contradiction" creatively enriched and developed Marxist epistemology and dialectics, which liquidate the erroneous influence of subjectivism, especially dogmatism, enhance the theoretical awareness of the Party, unify its ideological understanding, establish a correct world view and methodology for the proletarian party, and advance the localization of Marxism. This laid a solid philosophical foundation for the development of Chinese Marxism.

Anti-subjectivism and Line of Thought of Seeking Truth From Facts

Line of thought refers to the world view and methodology in people's understanding of matters and analysis of problems. As a proletarian party leading the Chinese revolution in guerrilla wars in the countryside with most of its members being peasants, it is particularly important to establish a correct Marxist line of thought in order to overcome the various non-proletarian ideas and wrong ideological tendencies that exist in the party and to ensure the ideological unity of the Party. In the early history of the Party, there were three "Left" deviations, the nature of which was subjectivism that separates the subject from the object, theory from practice, and departs from the world view and methodology of a proletarian party. The CPC members, represented by Mao Zedong, put forward and established the line of thought of seeking truth from facts in the course of their arduous exploration of the path of the Chinese revolution and in the process of criticizing and exposing the errors of subjectivism.

"Oppose Book Worship" and the Proposal of Marxist Line of Thought

As early as the revolutions in Jinggang Mountain, Mao Zedong was deeply aware that "the proletarian leadership in ideology is a very important issue".[24] In a letter to Lin Biao on June 14, 1929, he proposed the concept of "line of thought", saying

> we are materialist-historians, and we must examine everything from both the historical and the environmental aspects to grasp the truth. I have now cited various aspects of the historical problems since the founding of the Fourth Army to prove that the recent problems (the military commission problem, the problem of principle) reflect the inevitability of history and the final struggle on a wrong line of thought in history.[25]

Mao Zedong outlined and summarized the causes of the various contradictions and problems within the Red Army from the perspective of the "line of thought", which is in essence about the world view and methodology of a proletarian party. In order to establish a correct line of thought, we must first oppose subjectivism. In December 1929, Mao Zedong proposed to correct "subjectivism" in the resolution of the Ninth Congress of CPC of the Fourth Army of the Red Army. He pointed out that "subjective analysis of the political situation and subjective guidance of work will inevitably result in either opportunism or blind activism". To correct subjectivism is to "use Marxist-Leninist methods to analyze the political situation and assess class forces, instead of subjectivist analysis and assessment", and to "make Party members pay attention to social and economic surveys and studies, so as to decide on the strategy of struggle and methods of work".[26] By linking subjectivism in line of thought to the correctness of the Party's strategies, guidelines, and other political policies, Mao was deeply aware of the need to unify the ideological starting point within the Party.

In order to oppose the subjectivism that existed in the Party and the Red Army, Mao Zedong wrote an article entitled "Investigation" (later revised as "Oppose Book Worship") in May 1930. He highlighted the importance of doing research and made the famous statement that "without investigation, there is no right to speak" and elaborated on the important principle of linking theory and practice. He pointed out,

> We need Marxism in our struggle ... Marxist books need our study, but they must be combined with the actual situation in our country. We need books, but we must correct the book worship that is divorced from the actual situation.

He further suggested that the victory of the Chinese revolutionary struggle depended on the Chinese comrades' understanding of the Chinese situation. He said, "the correct and unshakable strategy of the struggle of the Communist Party...can only emerge from practical experience", and that

> some comrades who have an unchanging, conservative, formal, and empty optimism would think that the present strategy of struggle is as

good as it can be, and that the guidelines of the Sixth National Congress of the Party guarantee permanent victory, and that if only the established methods are followed, there will definitely be victory. These ideas are totally wrong and are not at all the line of thought for Communists to create a new situation out of struggle, but instead a completely conservative one.[27]

Mao Zedong here put forward the line of thought that "communists create a new situation out of struggle". "Out of struggle" means to start from the reality, while "create a new situation" means to insist on looking at problems from the viewpoint of development and change. Therefore, "create a new situation out of struggle" embodies the organic unity of materialism, epistemology, and dialectics and preliminarily defines the scientific significance of the Party's line of thought, which is correct and reflects the world view and methodology of a proletarian party. This line of thought was put forward by the CPC members represented by Mao Zedong on the basis of their opposition to subjectivism and their insistence on linking theory and practice and laid an important ideological foundation for the formal establishment of a Marxist line of thought within the Party.

The Establishment of Seeking Truth From Facts as A
Line of Thought

In May 1941, Mao Zedong made a report named "Reform Our Study" at a meeting of cadres in Yan'an, clearly stating that "the 20 years of the Communist Party of China witnessed the increasing integration of the universal truths of Marxism-Leninism with the concrete practice of the Chinese revolution".[28] The report sharply criticized the subjectivism of separating theory and practice, called on the whole Party to establish a Marxist style of work that links theory and practice, and equated the Marxist attitude of unifying theory and practice with Party spirit.

Mao pointed out that the scientific attitude is the Marxist-Leninist attitude of unifying theory and practice, is to apply Marxist-Leninist theory and methods in making systematic and thorough investigations and studies of the surrounding environment, is to study Marxist-Leninist theory with a purpose, is to combine Marxist-Leninist theory and the actual movement of the Chinese revolution, is to look for positions, views, and methods from Marxism-Leninism in order to solve the theoretical and strategic problems of the Chinese revolution. "This attitude", he said,

is the attitude of 'shooting the arrow at the target'. The 'target' is the Chinese revolution, and the 'arrow' is Marxism-Leninism. The reason why we CPC members are looking for this 'arrow' is to shoot at the 'target' of Chinese and Eastern revolutions with it. This attitude is the attitude of seeking truth from facts. 'Facts' means all things that exist objectively, and 'truth' refers to the internal connections between objective things, i.e., laws, and 'seek' is to 'study' or 'research'. We have to start from the actual situation at home and abroad, in and out of a province, a county, and a district, and draw out from it its inherent rather than imaginary laws, which means we should find out the internal connection of the surrounding events as a guide for our actions. This attitude is the expression of Party spirit and the Marxist-Leninist style of unifying theory and practice. This is the basic attitude a communist should have.[29]

Mao used the term "seeking truth from facts" borrowed from an ancient Chinese text *The Book of the Han Dynasty: The Biography of Prince Hejianxian* for the first time to express the Marxist attitude of unifying theory and practice, giving "seeking truth from facts" a new scientific meaning.

Seeking truth from facts is the essence and core of the Party's line of thought and the fundamental ideological and working method of the CPC. Seeking truth from facts means maintaining the close link between theory and practice. In February 1942, Mao elaborated on the necessity of linking theory and practice and its scientific significance in his report "Rectifying the Party's Style of Work". He pointed out that "Marxist theory should not be treated as dead dogmas. One should be able to master the Marxist theory and apply it, and the purpose of mastering it is to apply it".

The CPC members will only be able to link theory and practice if they are good at making use of the positions, views, and methods of Marxism-Leninism and the principles of Lenin and Stalin on the Chinese revolution, and if they make theoretical creations in all aspects that meet the needs of China on the basis of careful study of the historical and revolutionary realities.[30]

Thereafter, in order to free the Party members from the bondage of subjectivism and dogmatism, the CPC launched a Party-wide Marxist education campaign, namely the Rectification Movement.

After the Yan'an Rectification Movement and the Seventh Congress of CPC, the Party strengthened its consciousness of combining the basic principles of Marxism with the concrete reality of the Chinese revolution, and the line of thought of seeking truth from facts was established throughout the Party. As a comprehensive application and vivid embodiment of Marxist world view and methodology, the line of thought of seeking truth from facts solves the problem of the starting point of the CPC's ideological understanding in theory. It not only embodies the basic beliefs of Marxist philosophy but also reflects distinctive Chinese characteristics and Chinese style, being an important achievement in realizing the localization of Marxist philosophy.

"On Protracted War": The Application of Marxist
Military Dialectics

Another important aspect of Mao Zedong's contribution to localizing Marxist philosophy is his skill in using Marxist philosophical thought to dialectically analyze and study the practical problems of China's revolutionary warfare. His thought contains a wealth of military philosophical ideas and provides important theoretical guidance for the formulation of correct strategies and tactics. From May 26 to June 3, 1938, Mao Zedong made a speech titled "On Protracted War" on the seminar of the Anti-Japanese War. "On Protracted War" is an example of Mao Zedong's use of Marxist positions, views, and methods to comprehensively analyze and study the problems of China's revolutionary warfare and to expound the Marxist military dialectics, which is an application and embodiment of Marxist epistemology and dialectics in the military field.

The speech contains a wealth of ideas on military dialectics, which are mainly reflected in the following aspects:

i   An objective and comprehensive analysis of the characteristics of the Sino-Japanese War and a convincing conclusion that the war against Japanese aggression is a protracted one and that the final victory will go to China.

Mao Zedong comprehensively analyzed the epistemological origin of "the theory of national subjugation" and "the theory of quick victory" since the war broke out. He pointed out,

> Epistemologically speaking, the source of all erroneous views on war lies in idealist and mechanistic tendencies on the question. People with such tendencies are subjective and one-sided in their approach to problems. They either indulge in groundless and purely subjective talk, or, basing themselves upon a single aspect or a temporary manifestation, magnify it with similar subjectivity into the whole of the problem.

Thus, Mao Zedong argued, "Therefore, only by opposing idealist and mechanistic tendencies and taking an objective and all-sided view in making a study of war can we draw correct conclusions on the question of war".[31]

On this basis, Mao Zedong objectively and comprehensively analyzed the characteristics of the Sino-Japanese War. Japan was a powerful imperialist country and China a weak semi-colonial and semi-feudal one. Japan's war was a war of aggression, which was retrogressive and barbarous, while China's war of resistance against Japan was progressive and just. Japan is a comparatively small country, deficient in manpower and in military, financial, and material resources, and cannot stand a long war, while China is a very big country with vast territory, rich resources, a large population, and plenty of soldiers, and is capable of sustaining a long war. There is broad international support for China stemming from the progressive and just character of the war, which is again exactly the reverse of the meager support for Japan's unjust cause. On the whole, Japan has great military, economic, and political-organizational power, but its war is reactionary and barbarous, its manpower and material resources are inadequate, and it is in an unfavorable position internationally. China, on the contrary, has less military, economic, and political-organizational power, but it is in its era of progress, its war is progressive and just, it is moreover a big country, a factor which enables it to sustain a protracted war, and it will be supported by most countries. The above are the basic, mutually contradictory characteristics of the Sino-Japanese War. They have determined and are determining the protracted character of the war and its outcome, namely, that the final victory will go to China and not to Japan.

ii   Application of the law of quantitative and qualitative change, dialectic analysis of change in enemy's and our relative strength in the course of the war, and scientific prediction of war development.

Mao Zedong analyzed the quantitative and qualitative changes in the war between China and Japan. He pointed out that the changes in relative strength will proceed along the following lines in the three stages. In the first stage, the enemy is superior and we are inferior in strength. Changes of two different kinds will occur in the enemy's and our forces, one for the worse and the other for the better. In the case of China, the former one refers to decreases in territory, population, economic strength, military strength, and cultural institutions, while the latter refers to the experience gained in the war, the progress made by the armed forces, the political progress, the mobilization of the people, the development of culture in a new direction, the emergence of guerrilla warfare, the increase in international support, etc. What is on the downgrade in the first stage is the old quantity and the old quality, the manifestations being mainly quantitative. What is on the upgrade is the new quantity and the new quality, the manifestations being mainly qualitative. It is the second kind of change that provides a basis for our ability to fight a protracted war and win final victory. On the Japanese side, the change for the worse includes hundreds of thousands of casualties, the drain on arms and ammunition, deterioration of troop morale, popular discontent at home, shrinkage of trade, the expenditure of over ten thousand million yen, condemnation by world opinion, etc. This upgrade trend refers to the expansion in territory, population, and resources, but it is transitory and partial. In the second stage, the above changes on both sides will continue to develop. On the whole, Japan will continue on the downgrade and China on the upgrade. This second stage may last quite a long time, during which there will be a great reversal in the balance of forces, with

China gradually rising and Japan gradually declining. China will emerge from its inferior position, and Japan will lose its superior position; first, the two countries will become evenly matched, and then their relative positions will be reversed. Based on the analysis of the changes in the enemy's and our relative strength, Mao argued for the protracted character of the war against Japan and the conclusion that the final victory would go to China, stating,

> China moving from inferiority to parity and then to superiority, Japan moving from superiority to parity and then to inferiority; China moving from the defensive to stalemate and then to the counter-offensive, Japan moving from the offensive to the safeguarding of its gains and then to retreat—such will be the course of the Sino-Japanese war and its inevitable trend.[32]

iii   A systematic elaboration on the theory of conscious dynamic role and emphasis on the importance of conscious agency in winning the final victory in the war.

Mao Zedong stressed that when we say we are opposed to a subjective approach to problems, we mean that we must oppose ideas that are not based upon or do not correspond to objective facts and will lead to failure if acted on, but it does not mean we oppose the human's subjective dynamic role. He systematically expounded the theory of bringing into play the conscious dynamic role of humans. First, whatever is done has to be done by human beings; protracted war and final victory will not come about without human action. Second, for such action to be effective, there must be people who derive ideas, principles, or views from the objective facts, and put forward plans, directives, policies, strategies, and tactics. Third, ideas are subjective, while deeds or actions are the subjective translated into the objective, but both represent the dynamic role peculiar to human beings. We term this kind of dynamic role "human's conscious dynamic role", and it is a characteristic that distinguishes man from all other beings. All ideas based upon and corresponding to objective facts are correct ideas, and all deeds or actions based upon correct ideas are correct actions. We must give full scope to these ideas and actions, to this dynamic role.[33]

Mao particularly emphasized the role of conscious dynamic role in the victory or defeat of war. He argued that victory or defeat in war was certainly decided by the military, political, economic, and geographical conditions on both sides, the nature of the war each side is waging, and the international support each enjoys, but it is not decided by these alone. In themselves, all these provide only the possibility of victory or defeat but do not decide the issue. To decide the issue, subjective effort must be added, namely, the directing and waging of war, human's conscious dynamic role in war. Meanwhile, Mao also elaborated on the relationship between the exercise of human's conscious dynamic role and adherence to objective laws. In seeking victory, those who direct a war cannot overstep the limitations imposed by the objective conditions; within these limitations, however, they can and must play a dynamic role in striving for victory. The stage of action for commanders in a war must be built upon objective possibilities, but on that stage, they can direct the performance of many a drama, full of sound and color, power and grandeur. We do not want any of our commanders in the war to detach themselves from the objective conditions and become a blundering hothead, but we decidedly want every commander to become a general who is both bold and sagacious. Our commanders should have not only the boldness to overwhelm the enemy but also the ability to remain masters of the situation throughout the changes and vicissitudes of the entire war.[34]

iv   Proposal of the famous assertion "The army and the people are the foundation of victory" by applying the basic principles of historical materialism.

It is a basic principle of historical materialism that the masses of the people are the main body of history. Revolutionary war is a war of the masses, and it is only by mobilizing the masses and relying on the masses that war can be waged. This is Mao Zedong's basic view[35]. In "On Protracted War", Mao clearly pointed out that "the army and the people are the foundation of victory" and that "The richest source of power to wage war lies in the masses of the people".[36] He particularly stressed the importance of mobilizing the masses to the greatest extent and the enormous power of the masses to win the final victory in the war against Japan. He said,

> A national revolutionary war as great as ours cannot be won without extensive and thoroughgoing political mobilization...The mobilization of the common people throughout the country will create a vast sea in which to drown the enemy, create the conditions that will make up for our inferiority in arms and other things, and create the prerequisites for overcoming every difficulty in the war. To win victory, we must persevere in the War of Resistance, in the united front, and in the protracted war. But all these are inseparable from the mobilization of the common people.[37]

"Rural Areas to Encircle the Cities", the Theory on Chinese Revolutionary Path

Under the semi-colonial and semi-feudal society of China, the question of what kind of revolutionary path to take in order to ultimately achieve revolutionary victory is a major issue that the CPC must answer and resolve in leading the Chinese revolution. One of the important tasks of the localization of Marxism is to insist on combining the basic principles of Marxism with the national conditions of early modern China and the reality of the Chinese revolution and to explore a revolutionary path that suits the Chinese situation. The CPC members, represented by Mao Zedong, insisted on seeking truth from facts, opposed subjectivism, and creatively opened up a new revolutionary path of using rural areas to encircle the cities and seizing state power with military force during the extremely difficult revolutionary practice, which established the theory of the Chinese revolutionary path and became a shining example of localizing Marxism.

The Failure of the "City-centered Approach"

From the founding of the CPC to the launch of the workers' movement and the collaboration with the Kuomintang in the Northern Expedition, the center of revolutionary work was always in the cities, following a city-centered approach. After the defeat of the Revolution, the CPC issued a manifesto stating that it would continue to support the anti-imperialist and anti-feudal revolutionary struggle. This was followed by the Nanchang Uprising, which inaugurated the Communist Party's independent leadership of the armed struggle.

On August 7, 1927, the Central Committee of the CPC held an emergency meeting in Hankou, Hubei Province (i.e., the August 7th Conference), at which it summed up the lessons learned from the defeat of the Revolution and realized that the Party had made right-deviationist mistakes on three issues that had a bearing on the success or failure of the Revolution. First, in the relationship with the Kuomintang, the Party had adopted a policy of retreat and surrender, giving up the leadership of the proletariat. Second, on the issue of arms, it did not understand the vital importance of the Party's control of arms and failed to arm the workers and peasants and build a strong revolutionary army. Third, it did not actively support and lead the peasant movement and did not dare to meet the peasants' demands for land.[38] For this reason, the August 7th Conference set out the general policy of agrarian revolution and armed resistance against the Kuomintang reactionaries, which brought about a historic change from the defeat of the Revolution to the rise of the Agrarian Revolutionary War. At the conference, Mao Zedong proposed that "we should pay great attention to the military in future. We must know that political power grows out of the barrel of a gun".

The use of revolutionary arms against counter-revolutionary arms was a profound summary by the CPC of the lessons learned from the defeat of the Revolution. From August 1927 to the summer of 1928, the Party organized hundreds of armed uprisings in Hubei, Hunan, Guangdong, Jiangxi, Jiangsu, Anhui, Fujian, Zhejiang, Henan, Shaanxi, and Sichuan. However, the August 7th Conference did not resolve the fundamental question of how to carry out armed struggle and what kind of revolutionary path the Chinese revolution should take. These armed uprisings led by the Party were still aimed at carrying out struggles in the urban areas and capturing the central cities, so the city-centered approach was still followed. Under the brutal reactionary rule of the Kuomintang, and given the disparity in power between the enemy and us, these armed uprisings all ended in failure. It was proved that the city-centered approach was not feasible in a semi-colonial and semi-feudal China.

A New Revolutionary Path for China

The most urgent task facing the CPC was to explore a revolutionary path that could seize state power by armed force and was suitable for China's national conditions. The CPC members represented by Mao Zedong explored the road of the Chinese revolution in a painstaking manner and opened up a new revolutionary path of "rural areas encircling the cities and seizing state power by armed force".

On September 9, 1927, Mao Zedong led the Autumn Harvest Uprising on the Hunan-Jiangxi border. The uprising was aimed at occupying the provincial capital of Changsha, but it was aborted due to the disparity in military strength, the scattered deployment of our military force, and the lack of war experience. On September 14, Mao decided to change his plan to attack Changsha and ordered his troops to gather in Wenjiashi, Liuyang. On September 19, Mao presided over a meeting of the Front Committee in Wenjiashi to discuss the next course of action for the uprising. The meeting accepted Mao's idea of giving up attacking Changsha and transferring the troops to the rural areas in the south, where the enemy's strength was weaker in comparison. After investigation and research, Mao Zedong selected the middle section of the Luoxiao Mountains on the Hunan-Jiangxi border, namely the Jinggang Mountains, as the base for the troops.

The change from attacking major cities to transferring troops to rural areas where enemy's military strength was weaker marked the turn of the Chinese revolutionary path and signified a new beginning of the CPC's leadership in China's revolutionary struggle. In early October 1927, the troops arrived at the old town of Ninggang County, Jiangxi Province, and held an expanded meeting of the Front Committee, which decided to establish a base here and build a peasants' army in the Jinggang Mountains by uniting and reforming them. Mao Zedong led the revolutionary workers and peasants of the Autumn Harvest Uprising on the Hunan-Jiangxi border in carrying out the arduous struggle of land revolution and creating a revolutionary base in the Jinggang Mountains, which gradually opened up a new revolutionary path that suited China's national conditions in practice.

A Theory of China's Revolutionary Path

In the practice of the agrarian revolution, Mao gradually developed the idea of "establishing independent regimes of the workers and the peasants by armed force" and made sufficient theoretical preparations for exploring a new path of the Chinese revolution. Mao summarized the experience of the struggle in the Jinggang Mountain revolutionary base area and elaborated the idea of "establishing independent regimes of the workers and the peasants by armed force" in two writings respectively, namely "Why Is That Red Political Power Can Exist in China?" and "The Struggle in Jinggang Mountains".

He pointed out,

> the long-term survival inside a country of one or more small areas under Red political power completely encircled by a White regime is a phenomenon that has never occurred anywhere else in the world. There are special reasons for this unusual phenomenon. It can exist and develop only under certain conditions.[39]

First, China was an economically backward and semi-colonial country under indirect imperialist rule, which was the fundamental reason why the Red Regime was able to exist and develop. Second, the regions where China's Red political power had first emerged and was able to last for a long time have been those affected by the democratic revolution. Third, the small Red areas would undoubtedly last for a long time and would, moreover, inevitably become one of the many forces for winning nation-wide political power if the nation-wide revolutionary situation continued to develop. Fourth, the existence of a regular Red Army of adequate strength was a necessary condition for the existence of Red political power. It was definitely impossible to create an independent regime, let alone an independent regime that was durable and grows daily, unless there were regular forces of adequate strength. It follows that the idea of "establishing independent regimes of the workers and the peasants by armed force" was an important one which must be fully grasped by the Communist Party and by the masses of workers and peasants in areas under the independent regime.[40] Fifth, the Communist Party organization should be strong and its policy correct.

Mao's systematic exposition of the idea of "establishing independent regimes of the workers and the peasants by armed force" summed up the experience of the revolutionary struggle in founding the revolutionary base in Jinggang Mountains, which provided important theoretical guidance for the land revolution and the establishment of rural revolutionary base areas and laid an important theoretical foundation for the theory of a Chinese revolutionary path.

In January 1930, Mao elaborated on the necessity of establishing independent red regimes of the workers and the peasants by armed force in his letter "A Single Spark Can Start a Prairie Fire". He pointed out clearly that "the theory that we must first win over the masses on a country-wide scale and in all regions and then establish political power does not accord with the actual state of the Chinese revolution", that "China is a semi-colonial country for which many imperialist powers are contending", and that

> in semi-colonial China, the establishment and expansion of the Red Army, the guerrilla forces and the Red areas is the highest form of peasant struggle under the leadership of the proletariat, the inevitable outcome of the growth of the semi-colonial peasant struggle, and undoubtedly the most important factor in accelerating the revolutionary high tide throughout the country.[41]

The idea of viewing "the Red Army, the guerrilla forces and the Red areas" in the rural areas as the most important factor contributing to the national revolutionary upsurge is, in fact, a rural centered approach. The article therefore initially developed the theory of a Chinese revolutionary path, which is to carry out a land revolution, establish and develop a Red regime, and then seize national power when conditions are ripe.

The land revolution, armed struggle, and the construction of revolutionary bases in the countryside are the core ideas of the theory of the Chinese revolutionary path, which are unified and indispensable. The birth of the theory is a shining example of the CPC's insistence on combining the basic principles of Marxism with China's national conditions and the reality of the Chinese revolution. Under the guidance of this theory, the Communist Party mobilized the masses of peasants to carry out armed struggle and agrarian revolution, and created revolutionary base areas in the countryside, so that the spark of revolution eventually became a prairie fire, and eventually the great victory of the New Democratic Revolution was achieved. It has proved to be the only correct theory to guide the Chinese revolution to victory, and is a landmark theoretical achievement in realizing the localization of Marxism.

Notes

1 China Li Dazhao Research Association. *The Complete Works of Li Dazhao*, vol. 3. Beijing: People's Publishing House, 2006, p. 3.
2 China Li Dazhao Research Association. *The Complete Works of Li Dazhao*, vol. 4. Beijing: People's Publishing House, 2006, p. 197.
3 Central Literature Research Office of the Communist Party of China, National Archives Administration of China. *Selected Important Documents Since the Founding of the Party (1921–1949)*, vol. 15. Beijing: Central Literature Publishing House, 2011, p. 651.
4 Central Literature Research Office of the Communist Party of China, National Archives Administration of China. *Selected Important Documents Since the Founding of the Party (1921–1949)*, vol. 15. Beijing: Central Literature Publishing House, 2011, p. 651.
5 Central Literature Research Office of the Communist Party of China, National Archives Administration of China. *Selected Important Documents Since the*

Founding of the Party (1921–1949), vol. 15. Beijing: Central Literature Publishing House, 2011, p. 665.

6 ibid., p. 701.

7 *The Communist*, No. 16, Mar 20, 1941.

8 Party History Research Office of the Central Committee of the Communist Party of China. *History of the Communist Party of China*, vol. 1, part 2, 2nd ed. Beijing: History of the Communist Party of China Publishing House, 2011, pp. 657–658.

9 Central Literature Research Office of the Communist Party of China, National Archives Administration of China. *Selected Important Documents Since the Founding of the Party (1921–1949)*, vol. 20. Beijing: Central Literature Publishing House, 2011, p. 410.

10 Ibid., p. 436.

11 Central Literature Research Office of the Communist Party of China, National Archives Administration of China. *Selected Important Documents Since the Founding of the Party (1921–1949)*, vol. 20. Beijing: Central Literature Publishing House, 2011, p. 512.

12 Deng Xiaoping. *Selected Writings of Deng Xiaoping*, vol. 1, 2nd ed. Beijing: People's Publishing House, 1994, p. 88.

13 Mao Zedong. *Selected Works of Mao Zedong*, vol. 3, 2nd ed. Beijing: People's Publishing House, 1991, p. 952, pp. 952–953.

14 Liu Shaoqi. *Selected Works of Liu Shaoqi*, vol. 1, Beijing: People's Publishing House, 1981, p. 333, pp. 333–334, p. 335.

15 Central Literature Research Office of the Communist Party of China, National Archives Administration of China. *Selected Important Documents Since the Founding of the Party (1921–1949)*, vol. 22. Beijing: Central Literature Publishing House, 2011, p. 389.

16 Mao Zedong. *Selected Works of Mao Zedong*, vol. 1, 2nd ed. Beijing: People's Publishing House, 1991, p. 284.

17 Mao Zedong. *Selected Works of Mao Zedong*, vol. 1, 2nd ed. Beijing: People's Publishing House, 1991, pp. 296–297.

18 ibid., p. 295, p. 296.

19 Mao Zedong. *Selected Works of Mao Zedong*, vol. 1, 2nd ed. Beijing: People's Publishing House, 1991, p. 304.

20 Ibid., p. 320.

21 Ibid., p. 311.

22 Mao Zedong. *Selected Works of Mao Zedong*, vol. 1, 2nd ed. Beijing: People's Publishing House, 1991, p. 322.

23 Ibid., pp. 326–327.

24 Mao Zedong. *Selected Works of Mao Zedong*, vol. 1, 2nd ed. Beijing: People's Publishing House, 1991, p. 77.

25 Central Literature Research Office of the Communist Party of China. *Writings of Mao Zedong*, vol. 1. Beijing: People's Publishing House, 1993, p. 74.

26 Central Literature Research Office of the Communist Party of China. *Writings of Mao Zedong*, vol. 1. Beijing: People's Publishing House, 1993, p. 84, pp. 84–85, p. 85.

27 Mao Zedong. *Selected Works of Mao Zedong*, vol. 1, 2nd ed. Beijing: People's Publishing House, 1991, pp. 111–112, p. 115, pp. 115–116.

28 Mao Zedong. *Selected Works of Mao Zedong*, vol. 3, 2nd ed. Beijing: People's Publishing House, 1991, p. 795.

29 Mao Zedong. *Selected Works of Mao Zedong*, vol. 3, 2nd ed. Beijing: People's Publishing House, 1991, p. 801.

30 Mao Zedong. *Selected Works of Mao Zedong*, vol. 3, 2nd ed. Beijing: People's Publishing House, 1991, p. 815, p. 820.
31 Mao Zedong. *Selected Works of Mao Zedong*, vol. 2, 2nd ed. Beijing: People's Publishing House, 1991, p. 447.
32 Mao Zedong. *Selected Works of Mao Zedong*, vol. 2, 2nd ed. Beijing: People's Publishing House, 1991, pp. 468–469.
33 Mao Zedong. *Selected Works of Mao Zedong*, vol. 2, 2nd ed. Beijing: People's Publishing House, 1991, p. 477.
34 Mao Zedong. *Selected Works of Mao Zedong*, vol. 2, 2nd ed. Beijing: People's Publishing House, 1991, p. 478.
35 Guo Jianning. *A Contemporary Perspective on the Adaptation of Marxist Philosophy to Chinese Conditions.* Beijing: People's Publishing House, 2009, p. 48.
36 Ibid., p. 509, p. 511.
37 Ibid., pp. 480–481.
38 Zhu Qiaosen, et al. *A Study of the Historical Experience of the Communist Party of China.* Beijing: CPC Central Party School Press, 1997, p. 28.
39 Mao Zedong. *Selected Works of Mao Zedong*, vol. 1, 2nd ed. Beijing: People's Publishing House, 1991, pp. 48-–49.
40 Ibid., p. 50.
41 Mao Zedong. *Selected Works of Mao Zedong.* , vol. 1, 2nd ed. Beijing: People's Publishing House, 1991, pp. 97-–98, p. 98, p. 98.

2   Localize Marxism With Socialist Construction

Zhong Tian'e

After the establishment of socialism, China entered a new period of comprehensive socialist construction. In a country like China, which had evolved into a socialist society from a semi-colonial and semi-feudal one through a new democratic one, the path to building socialism emerged as another major issue that the Communist Party of China had to solve under the new historical conditions. The CPC members represented by Mao Zedong continued to adhere to the correct direction of localizing Marxism and made painstaking efforts to explore the path of socialist construction suited to Chinese characteristics. Their original theoretical achievements laid the foundation for the path of socialism with Chinese characteristics in the future. However, as socialist construction was a brand-new undertaking, the Party was not well prepared in terms of thinking and theory for the enormity and complexity of the construction. Facing the complex domestic and international environment, the Party has made major mistakes in exploring its own path of socialist construction. The facts fully prove that only by adhering to the correct direction of localizing Marxism, seeking truth from facts, and combining Marxism with China's construction can we ensure the smooth progression of socialist construction.

A Second-Time Combination of Marxism and Chinese Reality

As the first socialist country in the world, the Soviet Union made outstanding achievements in the cause of socialist construction and provided experience for other socialist countries to draw on. The practice and experience of socialist construction in the Soviet Union have become an important source for other socialist countries to understand socialism. Since socialist construction was a brand-new undertaking, the CPC lacked experience and made insufficient preparations in knowledge. At the very beginning, the Party called for the nation to learn from the Soviet Union. In February 1953, Mao Zedong proposed to learn from the Soviet Union in his speech at the closing session of the Fourth Session of the First National Committee of the Chinese People's Political Consultative Conference. He pointed out that "we must carry out the great task of construction in our country. The

DOI: 10.4324/9781003356042-3

work facing us is difficult and our experience is insufficient; therefore, we must earnestly study the advanced experience of the Soviet Union," and that

> "all must wholeheartedly learn from the strengths of the Soviet Union. We should not only learn from the theories of Marx and Lenin, but must also learn from the Soviet Union's advanced science and technology. We should learn humbly all that we need", and "we must whip up a high tide of learning from the Soviet Union throughout the whole country in order to build our country."[1]

In this way, China's socialist construction inevitably took the path of emulating the Soviet model.

The profound changes in the situation at home and abroad since 1956 prompted the CPC to reconsider the approach of learning from the Soviet Union. On the 20th Congress of the Communist Party of the Soviet Union held in February 1956, Khrushchev sharply exposed and criticized some of the major mistakes made by Stalin in leading their socialist construction, which shocked the socialist camp greatly. The revelation and criticism of Stalin's errors were conducive to the liberation of thinking of the communist parties worldwide, and they began to look for the path of socialist construction suited to their own conditions independently. However, the changes also brought serious confusion to their minds. At home, after over three years construction under the First Five-Year Plan, the shortcomings of the Soviet model were gradually exposed. The CPC increasingly realized that the Soviet experience was not always successful, and that even the successful Soviet experience was not always suitable for China's situation. Learning from the Soviet Union did not mean we stopped our own exploration of a path of socialist construction suitable for China.

In the process of reflecting on the pros and cons of learning from the Soviet experience and studying the 20th Congress of the Communist Party of the Soviet Union and its influence, the CPC members represented by Mao Zedong proposed the historical task of learning from the Soviet Union and carrying out a "second-time combination" of Marxism and Chinese reality.

On March 23, 1956, Mao presided over an expanded meeting of the Secretariat of the Central Committee of the Communist Party of China to discuss the report of the 20th Congress of the Communist Party of the Soviet Union. In response to Khrushchev's criticism of Stalin, Mao believed that though Khrushchev revealed troubles of the past, he stirred up further trouble at the same time. Khrushchev dispelled the myth that everything was right in the Soviet Union, the Communist Party of the Soviet Union, and Stalin, and was in favor of opposing dogmatism. Mao argued that it was time to stop copying everything from the Soviet Union and to think with our own minds. It was time to combine the basic principles of Marxism-Leninism with the reality of China's socialist revolution and construction and to explore the way to build socialism in our country.[2]

On April 4, 1956, Mao Zedong chaired a meeting of the Secretariat of the CPC Central Committee to discuss again the issue of the 20th Congress of the Communist Party of the Soviet Union, and he made it even clearer,

> the question is what we ourselves have learned from it. The most important thing is to think independently and to combine the basic principles of Marxism-Leninism with the reality of the Chinese revolution and construction. It was only after we had suffered great losses during the democratic revolution that we succeeded in achieving such a combination and the victory of the new democratic revolution. Now it is the period of socialist revolution and construction, and we have to make a second-time combination to find out how to build socialism in China

and

> we should consider from all sides how to act in accordance with the Chinese situation and not be superstitious as we were in the past. In fact, we were not completely superstitious in the past, we had our own originality. Now it is all the more important to try to find a concrete path for building socialism in China.[3]

In this discussion, Mao Zedong for the first time put forward the task of a "second-time combination" of Marxism with Chinese reality.

The "second-time combination" of Marxism with Chinese reality is to solve the fundamental problem of China's own path to socialist construction. The introduction of this idea meant the CPC adopted a scientific attitude toward the Soviet model, and the correct direction for the Party to adhere to was signaled, namely to localize Marxism and to keep exploring China's own path to socialist construction.

"On the Ten Major Relationships": The Beginning of Exploration Into a Path Toward China's Socialist Construction

The CPC members represented by Mao Zedong conducted extensive research and in-depth theoretical thinking on how to learn from the Soviet Union and explore a socialist construction path suitable for the Chinese situation. From February to April 1956, Mao Zedong spent 43 days listening to the reports of 34 ministries and commissions on industrial production and economic work, which covered all aspects of socialist construction, on the basis of which he formulated his speech "On the Ten Major Relationships." On April 25, 1956, at an enlarged meeting of the Political Bureau of the Central Committee, Mao Zedong delivered the speech, which set forth a series of important ideas of long-term significance for the construction of socialism in China and was "an opening work of the Communist Party of China in exploring the road of building socialism that suits China's conditions."[4]

Taking the Soviet Union as a reference and following a socialist path suitable for China's situation is the basic idea that runs through his speech. It was in the comparison with the Soviet Union that Mao thought about how to build socialism in China. In particular, the 20th Congress of the Communist Party of the Soviet Union revealed the problems and mistakes in the construction of socialism in the Soviet Union, which aroused Mao's great concern. He said,

> Particularly worthy of attention is the fact that in the Soviet Union certain defects and errors that occurred in the course of their building socialism have lately come to light. Do you want to follow the detours they have made? It was by drawing lessons from their experience that we were able to avoid certain detours in the past, and there is all the more reason for us to do so now.[5]

Meanwhile, he stressed,

> In the social sciences and in Marxism-Leninism, we must continue to study Stalin diligently wherever he is right. What we must study is all that is universally true and we must make sure that this study is linked with Chinese reality.[6]

These statements further clarify the basic idea that the construction of socialism must follow its own path in accordance with national conditions.

Taking the Soviet experience as a reference, "On the Ten Major Relationships" summarizes the lessons learned from the Chinese socialist revolution and construction and focuses on ten major issues in China's socialist construction, also known as the Ten Major Relationships. They include the relationship between heavy industry and light industry and agriculture, the relationship between industry in the coastal region and industry in the interior, the relationship between economic construction and defense construction, the relationship between the state, the units of production and the producers, the relationship between the central and the local authorities, the relationship between Han ethnic group and ethnic minorities, the relationship between Party and non-Party, the relationship between revolution and counter-revolution, the relationship between right and wrong, and the relationship between China and other countries. The discussion of the relationship between heavy industry, light industry, and agriculture, the relationship between industry in the coastal region and industry in the interior, and the relationship between economic construction and defense construction, in fact, is about figuring out a different path of China's industrialization from that of the Soviet Union. In view of the lessons learned from the Soviet Union's unilateral emphasis on the development of heavy industry at the expense of light industry and agriculture, which resulted in a serious imbalance of the three industries and caused serious damage to the daily lives of the people, it was proposed that the ratio of investment in heavy industry to that in agriculture and light industry should be appropriately adjusted, with more input in agriculture and light industry. In the relationship between industry in the coastal region and industry in the interior, coastal industry, especially light industry, shall be made full use of to develop and support industries in the interior and to gradually balance the layout of industrial development. The relationship between economic construction and defense construction should be correctly handled. The military and political costs should be reduced to an appropriate proportion, while the economic construction costs should be increased. Only when economic construction develops rapidly can defense construction make greater progress. The discussion of the relationship between the state, the units of production and the producers, and the relationship between the central and local authorities is in fact a reflection on the shortcomings of a highly centralized planned economic system. In view of the experience of the Soviet Union and our own, it was proposed that a balance must be struck between the state, the collective, and the individual, rather than merely one end of the spectrum. As the national economy develops, wages must be adjusted appropriately. Factories must be given a certain degree of independence and rights, and more attention must be paid to the relationship between the state and the peasants. On the premise of consolidating the unified leadership of the central government, the powers of the local authorities should be expanded to give them more independence, so as to give full play to both central and local initiatives. In addition, in the relations between the Han and the ethnic minorities, we should focus on opposing Han chauvinism as well as local ethnic minorities' chauvinism. We must sincerely and actively help the ethnic minorities in their economic and cultural development and consolidate the unity of all ethnic groups. In the relationship between the Party and the non-Party, we should insist on long-term coexistence and mutual supervision. On the relationship between revolution and counter-revolution, certainly, there were still counter-revolutionaries, but it was stressed that the number of counter-revolutionaries had been greatly reduced and that fewer arrests and killings should be carried out in social crackdowns. In terms of the relationship between right and wrong, it was stressed that a clear distinction between the two should be made for people both within and outside the Party, and that the policy of "learning from past mistakes to avoid future ones and curing the sickness to save the patient" should be adopted for comrades who had made mistakes. On the relationship between China and other countries, it was proposed that we should learn from the strengths of all nationalities and countries, but we must learn them analytically and critically instead of blindly copying them. We must learn from the advanced science and technology of capitalist countries and the scientific aspects of business management methods.

On the basis of the systematic elaboration of the Ten Major Relationships, Mao Zedong put forward the general policy of socialist construction by mobilizing all positive factors to serve socialist construction. He pointed out,

> These ten relationships are all contradictions. [...] Our task is to handle these contradictions correctly. As to whether or not they can be resolved entirely to our satisfaction in practice, we must be prepared for either possibility; furthermore, in the course of resolving these contradictions we are bound to come up against new ones, new problems. [...] We must do our best to mobilize all positive factors, both inside and outside the Party, both at home and abroad, both direct and indirect, and make China a powerful socialist country.[7]

"On the Ten Major Relationships" is a continuation of the CPC's adherence to and development of Chinese Marxism based on the practice of Chinese socialist construction and reflects the theoretical thinking of the CPC members represented by Mao Zedong on a series of major issues of Chinese socialist construction. Mao Zedong later recalled this period and said,

> The first eight years were spent copying foreign experience. But from 1956, when 'On the Ten Major Relationships' was proposed, we began to find a path of our own that was suitable for China [...] and reflect the objective economic laws of China.[8]

Many of the ideas put forward in "On the Ten Major Relationships" are still of great theoretical value and guidance to the development of socialism with Chinese characteristics after the Third Plenary Session of the 11th Central Committee of the Party.

Proactive Exploration Into Socialist Construction in the Eighth Party Congress

On 15 September 1956, the Eighth National Congress of the Communist Party of China was held, the first national congress after the Party had come to power. Guided by the basic spirit of "On the Ten Major Relationships," the Eighth National Congress of the Party explored various aspects of the cause of socialist construction in China and became another milestone in the CPC's exploration of China's own path of socialist construction after the publication of "On the Ten Major Relationships."

In his opening address to the Eighth Congress of the CPC, Mao Zedong once again stressed that "it has always been the ideological principle of our Party to link Marxist-Leninist theory closely with the practice of the Chinese revolution."[9] It was on the basis of this ideological principle that the Eighth Congress correctly analyzed the changes in the domestic situation and the principal contradictions after the completion of the socialist transformation and made a correct judgment on the major problems in Chinese society. The resolution of the Eighth Congress clearly states that the CPC led the Chinese people in completing the bourgeois-democratic revolution and winning the socialist revolution. This resulted in a completely new social outlook of China. The major problem in the old Chinese society, that was, the contradiction between the Chinese people and the rule of imperialism, feudalism and bureaucratic capitalism, had been resolved by the victory of the bourgeois-democratic revolution. Now that this socialist transformation had been achieved, it was clear that the contradiction between the proletariat and the bourgeoisie in China was basically resolved, that the 1,000-year-old history of class exploitation basically came to an end and that the socialist social system was basically established in China. The principal problem in our country is already the contradiction between the people's demand for the establishment of an advanced industrial country and the reality of a backward agricultural country, between the people's need for rapid economic and cultural development and the current situation in which the economy and culture cannot meet the needs of the people. The essence of this contradiction, in the context of the establishment of our socialist system, is the contradiction between the advanced socialist system and the backward social productive forces.[10]

The Party's Eighth Congress was not entirely accurate in its understanding of the principal social problems and failed to see that the socialist relations of production had been established, and that there were still some aspects incompatible with the development of the productive forces, which should be resolved by further liberating the productive forces. Despite what has been mentioned above, the Party's Eighth Congress was correct in its judgment of the principal social problems. It was on the basis of a correct judgment of the main problems that the Eighth Congress proposed that the major task of the Party and the country at present was to concentrate on solving this contradiction, to transform China from a backward agricultural country into an advanced industrial country as soon as possible, and to protect and develop the social productive forces under the new production relations. Shifting the focus to pooling resources on developing productive forces after the socialist transformation "was the most important theoretical contribution of the Eighth Congress and became the consensus of the whole Party at that time. This focus has proved to be correct by history."[11]

On the basis of a correct understanding of the major problems and tasks, the Eighth Congress proactively explored many key theoretical and practical issues in the construction of Chinese socialism and put forward many important guidelines and policies. On the economic front, it formulated a policy of economic construction that was both anti-conservative and anti-adventurous and that was to make steady progress in a comprehensive and balanced manner. The Eighth Congress pointed out that

the pace of development must be proactive so as not to miss the opportunity and fall into the error of conservatism, but it must also be sound and reliable so as not to go awry from the correct proportions of economic development and overburden the people, or to disconnect different sectors from each other so that plans cannot be completed and waste is created, which would be an error of adventurism.[12]

The pace of development of the national economy should be reasonably set according to needs and possibilities, and the plan should be placed on a basis that is proactive, steady and reliable, so as to ensure a more balanced development of the national economy.[13]

"The task of the Party is to pay attention at all times to preventing and correcting right-leaning conservatism or 'Left' adventurism, and to promote the development of the national economy in a proactive, steady and reliable manner."[14] The pace of economic development is a major issue in socialist construction. The idea of developing the national economy in a "proactive and steady" and "comprehensive and balanced" manner, as expounded at the Eighth Congress, is a penetrating summary of the lessons learned from socialist economic construction, showing that the Party had a sober understanding of the speed of socialist construction. Politically, the Congress proposed the expansion of people's democracy and the establishment of a sound socialist legal system. In terms of ideology and culture, the principle of "a hundred flowers blooming and a hundred schools of thought contending" was confirmed as the guideline for the prosperity and development of science, culture, and art, and the vigorous development of culture and education was proposed. In dealing with the relationship between the Communist Party and the democratic parties, the policy of "long-term coexistence and mutual supervision" was adhered to.

In addition, the Eighth Congress also made preliminary explorations into the reform of the economic management system and the state administration system. With regard to the reform of the economic system, it is particularly important to highlight the idea of "three main bodies and three supplements" put forward by Chen Yun at the Congress. He believed that the new economic system would be one in which (1) state and collective management would be the main body of industry and commerce, and a certain number of individual businesses would supplement the main body; (2) planned production would be the main body of industrial and agricultural production, and free production within the scope of state planning in accordance with market changes would supplement planned production; (3) the state market would be the main body, and state-led free markets within a certain scope would supplement the state market.[15] In his report, Zhou Enlai also proposed issues concerning "free market," "free production," and "decentralized management," With regard to the improvement of the state administration system, Liu Shaoqi proposed to "appropriately adjust the administrative powers and responsibilities of the central and local governments" and to "assign part of the administrative powers and responsibilities to the local governments" so as to "give full play to the enthusiasm of the central and local authorities with both enjoying necessary flexibility and exercising mutual supervision."[16] The resolution adopted at the Eighth Congress also clearly stipulates that

> in accordance with the principles of unified leadership, hierarchical management, and catering to specific local conditions and circumstances, the administrative system of the State shall be improved, and the scope of management of enterprises, institutions, planning and finance authorities shall be better divided, and the management authority of provinces, autonomous regions and municipalities directly under the central government shall be appropriately expanded.[17]
>
> The higher state organs often have too much and too rigid control over enterprises, which hinders their initiative and mobility. We should ensure that enterprises have appropriate autonomy in their own management of planning, finance, cadres, staff, welfare, etc., under the unified leadership and plan of the state.[18]

These ideas were important attempts to change the unitary system of public ownership and the highly centralized economic and administrative management system and provided valuable experience for exploring the reform of the socialist economic and administrative systems.

Elaboration on the Theory of Contradictions in Socialist Society

How to understand the contradictions of socialist society is an important theoretical and practical problem facing the practice of socialism. The Soviet Union was the first country to put into practice the theory of scientific socialism, but during their practice, from Lenin to Stalin and the subsequent leaders of the Communist Party of the Soviet Union, there was no systematic elaboration of the contradictions in socialist society.

In his commentary on Nikolai Bukharin's *Economics of the Transition Period*, Lenin pointed out that confrontation and contradiction were two different categories and that "under socialism, confrontation would disappear, while contradiction would still exist,"[19] thus affirming the existence of contradictions in socialist society. However, as Lenin was living in a period of transition from capitalism to socialism in the Soviet Union, he did not probe into the problem of contradictions in socialist society due to the constraints of historical conditions.

After the establishment of the socialist system in the Soviet Union, Stalin denied that there were contradictions in socialist society in the course of his leadership of the socialist construction in the Soviet Union for a long time. In his *On Dialectical Materialism and Historical Materialism* published in 1938, he argued that the social nature of the production process was consolidated by the public ownership of the means of production, hence the productive relations were in perfect accordance with the productive forces.[20] This view had a significant impact on the Soviet Union for a considerable period of time. As the contradictions within Soviet society grew increasingly pronounced, Stalin began to rethink the problem of contradictions in socialist society. In 1952, in his *Problems of the Soviet Socialist Economy*, Stalin acknowledged that there were still contradictions in socialist society. He said,

> The expression 'in perfect accordance' cannot be understood in an absolute sense [...] which should be understood as there is usually no conflict between the production relations and the productive forces in socialist society, and that it is possible for the socialist society to adapt the backward production relations to the productive forces in time [...] Even in a socialist system, there are backward inert forces which do not understand the need to change the production relations, but such forces, of course, are not difficult to overcome and do not bring things into conflict.[21]

He criticized the erroneous view that there was no contradiction between the productive forces and production relations under the socialist system and pointed out that if the policies were not right or not well regulated, there would be contradictions. However, Stalin still lacked a comprehensive and profound understanding of the contradictions in socialist society and held many theoretical biases, which led him to confuse the contradictions between ourselves and the enemy with those among the people in practice, which greatly harmed the construction of socialism in the Soviet Union.

In the history of the world socialist movement, it was Mao Zedong who, for the first time, systematically expounded the problem of contradictions in socialist society and founded the theory of contradictions in socialist society.

After the 20th Congress of the Communist Party of the Soviet Union and the Polish-Hungarian Incident in 1956, the contradictions and problems of socialist society were further revealed. At home, workers' and students' strikes and marches in China's cities increased in the autumn and winter of 1956. Meanwhile, there was also a wave of withdrawals by communal members in the countryside. Some intellectuals sharply criticized the work of the Party and the government after the "Double Hundred Guideline" was put forward. Faced with the complex situation at home and abroad, how to correctly understand the new situation and problems that had arisen, and how to correctly distinguish and deal with the contradictions between ourselves and the enemy and those among the people, grew to be an important issue for the CPC in the practice of socialist construction. On January 27, 1957, Mao Zedong pointed out clearly in his speech at a meeting of party secretaries of provincial, municipal, and autonomous regions that the way to deal with the contradictions between ourselves and the enemy and those among the people in a socialist society was a science that deserved to be studied. In this way, the contradictions in socialist society were distinguished into two categories: the contradictions between the enemy and ourselves and the contradictions among the people. The issue of contradictions among the people was thus brought out.

On February 27, 1957, at the 11th session of the Supreme State Conference, Mao Zedong delivered a speech entitled "How to Deal with Contradictions Among the People," in which he systematically distinguished between the contradictions between the enemy and ourselves and those among the people in a socialist society and the correct handling of the latter. This speech was later collated, revised, and supplemented, which was finally published in *People's Daily* on 19 June of the same year under the title "On the Correct Handling of Contradictions Among the People." The passage formed a relatively systematic theory of contradictions in socialist society, which mainly covers the following aspects:

First, the basic contradictions of socialist society. According to Mao Zedong, socialist society is full of contradictions, and it is these contradictions that drive socialist society forward. In a socialist society, the basic contradiction is still the ones between the productive forces and the relations of production, between the economic base and the superstructure. However, the basic contradictions of socialist society are fundamentally different from those of the old, for the former are not antagonistic and can be constantly resolved through the socialist system itself. The basic contradictions of socialist society are both compatible and contradictory. The socialist relations of production have been established, which are compatible with the development of the productive forces. However, they are still imperfect, and these imperfections are in contradiction with the development of the productive forces. Akin to this compatibility and contradiction between the relations of production and the development of the productive forces, similar situations also occur between the superstructure and the economic base. Therefore, contradictions must be resolved in ways based on specific cases. "The ceaseless emergence and ceaseless resolution of contradictions constitute the dialectical law of the development of things."[22]

Second, two types of contradictions in socialist society. Mao Zedong pointed out, "We are confronted with two types of social contradictions—those between ourselves and the enemy and those among the people. The two are totally different in nature."[23] At the present stage, the period of building socialism, the classes, strata, and social groups which favor, support, and work for the cause of socialist construction all come within the category of the people, while the social forces and groups which resist the socialist revolution and are hostile to or sabotage socialist construction are all enemies of the people. The fundamental identity of the people's interests underlies the contradictions among the people, which are not antagonistic in nature. Mao made a complete explanation of contradictions among the people, arguing that in the conditions prevailing in China today, the contradictions among the people comprise the contradictions within the working class, the contradictions within the peasantry, the contradictions within the intelligentsia, the contradictions between the working class and the peasantry, the contradictions between the workers and peasants on the one hand and the intellectuals on the other, the contradictions between the working class and other sections of the working people on the one hand and the national bourgeoisie on the other, the contradictions within the national bourgeoisie, and so on. There are certain contradictions between this government and the people. These include the contradictions between the interests of the state and the interests of the collective on the one hand and the interests of the individual on the other, between democracy and centralism, between the leadership and the led, and the contradictions arising from the bureaucratic style of work of some of the state personnel in their relations with the masses. All these are also contradictions among the people.

Third, the basic methods to resolve two types of contradictions. Mao Zedong pointed out,

> Since they are different in nature, the contradictions between ourselves and the enemy and the contradictions among the people must be resolved by different methods. To put it briefly, the former entail drawing a clear distinction between ourselves and the enemy, and the latter entail drawing a clear distinction between right and wrong. It is of course true that the distinction between ourselves and the enemy is also one of right and wrong [...] but it is in a different category from questions of right and wrong among the people.[24]

"Under the people's democratic dictatorship two different methods, one dictatorial and the other democratic, should be used to resolve the two types of contradictions which differ in nature—those between ourselves and the enemy and those among the people."[25] He stressed, "The only way to settle questions of an ideological nature or controversial issues among the people is by the democratic method, the method of discussion, criticism, persuasion and education, and not by the method of coercion or repression."[26] The democratic method of resolving contradictions among the people was epitomized as "unity-criticism-unity." To elaborate, that means starting from the desire for unity, resolving contradictions through criticism or struggle, and arriving at a new unity on a new basis.

Fourth, the correct handling of contradictions among the people is the subject of national politics. In a socialist society, there are far more contradictions among the people than another type of contradictions. Mao Zedong highlighted contradictions among the people in his speech, pointing out that "our general subject is the correct handling of contradictions among the people."[27] He particularly stressed that correct policies and methods shall be adopted to handle contradictions among the people appropriately in case such contradictions would be transformed into the ones between the enemy and ourselves. He pointed out,

> The large-scale, turbulent class struggles of the masses characteristic of times of revolution have in the main come to an end, but class struggle is by no means entirely over [...] It is therefore imperative for us at this juncture to raise the question of distinguishing contradictions among the people from those between ourselves and the enemy, as well as the question of the correct handling of contradictions among the people, in order to unite the people of all ethnic groups in our country for the new battle, the battle against nature, develop our economy and culture [...] consolidate our new system and build up our new state.[28]

Mao Zedong's systematic elaboration of contradictions in socialist society is an important theoretical achievement made during the period of socialist construction by adhering to the localization of Marxism, which not only embodied the basic ideas of "On the Ten Major Relationships" but also continued and developed the policies of the Eighth Congress of the CPC. This theoretical achievement is an original development of the Marxist scientific socialism and is of great theoretical and practical significance. However, before the speech was published, the anti-rightist campaign had already begun. Due to an overestimation of the situation, Mao Zedong added to the published speech remarks that were incongruous with the spirit of the original one, stressing that the class struggle was fierce and that the battle for victory between socialism and capitalism had not yet ended. Thus, there exist logical contradictions in the speech "On the Correct Handling of Contradictions Among the People," as well as inaccuracies and imperfections in some of the specific discussions on the two types of contradictions, yet these shortcomings and flaws provide historical lessons to be learned for further refining the theory of contradictions in socialist society in the new era.

The Party's Further Exploration Into the Path of Socialist Construction

Since the summer of 1957, as the anti-rightist campaign intensified, the Party's judgment of the situation gradually turned toward the "Left," overestimating the class struggle under socialist conditions and leading to its enlargement in politics, which was a serious mistake. At the same time, the "Left" errors in the economic field grew again. The "Great Leap Forward" and the "People's Commune" campaigns, which were "impetuous and adventurous, eager for success and transition into communism," were launched. The Party made a major mistake in exploring China's own path of socialist construction. In response to the outstanding problems revealed by the Great Leap Forward and the People's Commune, and taking the

Zhengzhou Conference in November 1958 as a turning point, Mao Zedong and other leaders of the Party began to take measures to correct the "Left" mistakes that went awry from the reality. In the process of correction, the CPC members represented by Mao Zedong carried out in-depth theoretical thinking on many major theoretical and practical issues in the practice of socialist construction and put forward a series of correct ideological and theoretical views.

Thinking and Practice: Emphasis on Surveys and Investigations

Investigation is the concrete application and embodiment of the Marxist worldview and methodology in practical work. In the practice of the New Democratic Revolution, the CPC developed a style of work that attached importance to investigation. In order to find and correct the problems and mistakes that had arisen in the practice of socialist construction, Mao Zedong once again proposed to attach importance to investigation on socialist construction, and hence to find out the guidelines, policies, and solutions to problems. To this end, Mao Zedong set an example by personally taking part in a large number of investigations, which had a positive impact on practice.

From mid-October to early November 1958, Mao Zedong visited Hebei and Henan provinces to investigate the actual situation in the people's communes. It was through this investigation that Mao discovered serious boastfulness and extreme equalitarianism in the people's commune campaigns and began his efforts to correct the "Left" mistakes. The First Zhengzhou Conference was an important one in correcting the "Left" errors based on this investigation. At the conference, Mao Zedong criticized the proposal to abolish currency and commodities and the tendency to hasten the transition from collective ownership to public ownership and from socialism to communism, taking the first step to correct the "Left" errors. After the conference, he raised the issues of collective and public ownership, the line between socialism and communism, and the question of whether or not to preserve commodities at the present stage, arguing that "it is impossible to correct the mistakes in our work without solving these two major theoretical and practical problems."[29] The two questions are key in socialist construction. One is the stage of development of socialist society, and the other is the relationship between socialism, commodity production, and the commodity economy. Since the reform and opening up, the path of socialism with Chinese characteristics has been premised on the correct understanding of these two issues. Mao Zedong's ability to get to the root of the problem at that time was the result of his attention to investigations.

Afterwards, Mao continued his investigation to understand the real situation in the countryside more broadly. In response to the over high targets and boastfulness in industrial and agricultural production, he proposed to adjust the excessive targets, oppose falsification, protect science, and pay attention to the livelihood of the masses. In late February 1959, Mao Zedong went south again to inspect Hebei, Shandong, and Henan provinces to learn more about the specific situation in the countryside, which included the extreme equalitarianism and unpaid-for appropriation of peasants' resources. From this, he discovered some important problems with the collective ownership system of the people's communes and proposed that these problems must be solved, especially those about the gradation of collective ownership within the communes. In this way, Mao began to perceive and delve into the problems from the perspective of collective ownership within people's communes. From February 27 to March 5, 1959, the Central Committee of the Communist Party of China held an enlarged meeting of the Political Bureau in Zhengzhou (i.e., the Second Zhengzhou Conference), at which Mao Zedong pointed out that "within the commune, a transition period is needed to transfer from the small team-level collective ownership to the large commune-level one," and that

> the distinction between the rich and poor have been eliminated by extreme equalitarian distribution, and certain property of the production team has been appropriated without pay, and the banks have called in many loans of the countryside. Equalitarian distribution, unpaid-for appropriation and loans being called in panicked the peasants very much, and these are the key problems in our relationship with the peasants.[30]

Based on Mao's ideas, the Second Zhengzhou Conference established a series of basic policies to rectify the people's communes and curb the extreme equalitarianism, which were important preliminary achievements in correcting the "Left" errors. In March 1959, the enlarged meeting of the Political Bureau in Shanghai formulated "The Eighteen Questions Concerning the People's Commune," which recognized the partial ownership and certain management authority of the production units under the production teams, thus bringing the people's communes, which were "large in size and collective in nature," back to the size and scope of ownership of the original senior and junior communes. All these achievements were the result of the importance attached to investigation and practice during this period.

In January 1961, Mao Zedong made a speech at the Central Working Conference on promoting surveys and investigations, asking the Party to restore the fine tradition of seeking truth from facts and conducting investigations. On March 23, 1961, the Central Committee issued a letter of instruction on carrying out earnest investigation work attached with an article entitled "Investigation" written by Mao Zedong in 1930 (when it was published, its title was changed to "Oppose Book Worship"). The letter pointed out that the shortcomings and mistakes in the work of recent years are basically due to the fact that many officials had slackened their efforts to conduct investigation and research, which was very effective during the years of war and had only read reports on paper and listened to oral presentations. When they went to the people, they only gave a hurried and cursory glance. For a period of time, they had made judgments and decisions on the basis of unrealistic or one-sided materials, indulging in empty talk. This is an important lesson. The letter stressed that investigation was the first and foremost task of leadership. The principle of "starting from reality" and "without investigation, there is no right to speak" must become the first rule of thought and action for all Party cadres.[31] Thereafter, Mao Zedong, Liu Shaoqi, Zhou Enlai, Zhu De, Chen Yun, and other Party leaders organized investigation groups and went to the countryside to conduct investigations and studies. During these investigations, the Party and State leaders formed a new understanding of issues such as the size of the communes and teams, public canteens, the supply system, household plots, and market trade, which gave a strong impetus to the adjustment of policies in agriculture, industry, science and technology, and education and culture.

Mao Zedong's thought and practice of attaching importance to survey and investigation played an important role in correcting the "Left" error that went awry from the reality, restoring the Party's line of thought of seeking truth from facts, promoting the adjustment of the Party's guidelines and policies, and transforming the Party's style of work, which are still of great theoretical and practical value.

Thought on Exploring the Laws of Socialist Construction

In the process of conducting investigations and correcting the "Left" errors, Mao also put forward the idea of exploring the laws of socialist construction. In June 1960, Mao pointed out in his "The Initiative Comes from Seeking Truth from Facts,"

> Truth cannot not be reached at once, but gradually [...] Freedom is from our knowledge of necessity and transformation of the world. The leap from the Realm of Necessity to the Realm of Freedom is accomplished in a long, gradual process of cognition [...] But there is still a great blindness, a great unacknowledged Realm of Necessity, which we do not yet know deeply enough about the socialist revolution and construction. We have to take the second decade to investigate it, to study it, to find out from it its inherent laws, so that we can use these laws for the revolution and construction of socialism.[32]

From January 11 to February 7, 1962, the Central Committee convened an enlarged Central Working Conference in Beijing (i.e., the 7,000 People's Congress), to summarize systematically the lessons learned since the Great Leap Forward Campaign. Mao Zedong once again expounded on the protracted nature and difficulty of exploring the laws of socialist construction. He pointed out,

> There must be a process of understanding the laws of building socialism. Starting from practice, we will grow from lack of inexperience to having experience, from having less experience to having more experience, from the unrecognized Realm of Necessity, which is building socialism, to gradually overcoming blindness, recognizing objective laws, and thus gaining liberty, which is a leap in knowledge to the Realm of Freedom.
>
> We must combine the universal truths of Marxism-Leninism with the concrete reality of socialist construction in China and of the world revolution in the future as closely as possible. We should understand the objective laws of struggle step by step from practice. Be prepared to suffer many defeats and setbacks due to blindness, so as to gain experience and win the final victory.[33]

He also stressed that we still had a great deal of blindness in the construction of socialism. There still existed a large Realm of Necessity in socialist economy which was not yet known to us. We should accumulate experience and study hard in the coming period, and we must work hard to investigate it, study it, and gradually deepen our understanding of it in practice to clarify its laws.[34]

Mao Zedong's ideas on exploring the laws of socialist construction are undoubtedly of great significance for understanding the protracted nature and difficulty of the socialist construction project, overcoming the subjectivist errors of impetuous and adventurous, eager for success and transition into communism, and grasping the objective laws of socialist construction.

Thought on the Development of Commodity Production, Commodity Exchange and Using the Law of Value

In the process of correcting the problem of people's communes, Mao Zedong and other Party leaders considered the theoretical problem of whether or not to develop a commodity economy in a socialist society and put forward the idea that commodity production and commodity exchange should also be developed under socialist conditions.

Mao Zedong proposed that "our country is a very underdeveloped one in terms of commodity production" and that "we must affirm the positive role of socialist commodity production and commodity exchange."[35] He argued that commodity production belonged to a historical category that "has been in existence since ancient times" and that "commodity production should not be confused with capitalism," but "depends on what economic system it is linked to. If linked to the capitalist system, it is capitalist. If linked to the socialist system, it is socialist." He also encouraged, "Don't be afraid, it won't lead to capitalism, for which there is no longer an economic basis."[36] He stressed that we "must use commodity production, commodity exchange and the law of value as useful tools in the service of socialism," "must understand the importance of the role of commodity production under socialist conditions," and that in the period of socialist construction, "socialist commodity production should be greatly developed in a well-planned way." It is therefore clear that Mao's emphasis is on socialist commodity production, which is premised on the socialist economic base and is in the service of socialism.[37] In December 1958, *The Resolution on Certain Problems of the People's Communes*, which was revised and adopted by the Sixth Plenary Session of the Eighth Central Committee of the Party in accordance with Mao Zedong's views, affirmed this idea for the first time in the form of a plenum resolution, stating that there must be a great development of commodity production in the people's communes, as well as commodity exchange between the state and the communes and between the communes. This commodity production and commodity exchange are planned on the basis of socialist public ownership and are therefore not capitalist.[38]

In addition, Mao Zedong further analyzed the erroneous tendency of egalitarianism and over-centralization in the people's commune system as it ignored the law of value. He said that the tendency of egalitarianism denied that the income of each production team and each individual should be different, which denied the socialist principle of distribution according to labor and more pay for more work. The tendency of over-centralization denied the ownership and rights of the production teams and transferred the property of production teams up to the communes. Both tendencies included the denial of the law of value and the exchange of equivalents, which was certainly wrong.[39] Mao Zedong emphasized the need for the exchange of equivalents and prohibited free appropriation. The law of value and exchange of equivalents, which are objective laws, should be observed. In March 1959, in his speech at the Shanghai Conference, Mao further stated that the objective law of value "is a great school, and only by using it can we teach our tens of millions of cadres and tens of thousands of people, and make it possible to build our socialism and communism. Otherwise, nothing is possible."[40] To a certain extent, these ideas had a positive impact on correcting the wrong tendencies of egalitarianism and over-centralization.

Thought on the Development Stages of Socialist Society

In its efforts to correct the mistakes of the "Great Leap Forward" and the People's Commune Campaign, which were out of touch with reality and eager for transition into communism, the Party also developed more theoretical thinking on the question of the development stages of socialist society. In November 1958, Mao Zedong raised the distinction between socialism and communism in his address when he was reading *Problems of the Soviet Socialist Economy* by Stalin. Thereafter, Mao began to think about the timing of China's entry into communism, stating, "We are now poor and blank [...] We are now boasting too much, which I think is untrue and does not reflect objective reality."[41] On the basis of the lessons learned from the "Great Leap Forward" and the People's Commune Campaign, the Sixth Plenary Session of the Eighth Party Congress elaborated more profoundly on distinguishing between socialism and communism, emphasizing that

> it must be soberly recognized that the transition from socialism to communism is a rather long and complex development process. During this entire process, the nature of society remains socialist. Socialist and communist societies are two stages with different degrees of economic development.

"The transition from socialism to communism must be based on a certain degree of development of the productive forces" and "to attempt to force an entry into communism when conditions are not ripe is undoubtedly an illusion that cannot come true."[42]

In his reading of *A Textbook of Political Economy* of the Soviet Union at the end of 1959, Mao Zedong conducted a more in-depth theoretical reflection on the stages of socialist development. He clearly pointed out that "the development of socialism may be divided into two stages, the first being underdeveloped and the second being more developed. The latter stage may take longer time to realize than the former" and "in a country like ours, completing the construction of socialism is an arduous task, and it is wrong to talk about the completion of socialism too soon."[43] Zhou Enlai agreed that the transition from capitalism to communism was a relatively long period, saying "we are now in the first stage, which can be subdivided into many smaller stages."[44] In January 1962, Mao proposed on the enlarged Central Working Conference that "I do think it will take over a hundred years for China to develop its productive power to a great extent and catch up with or even surpass the most advanced capitalist countries in the world."[45] These ideas show that the Party had begun to have a clear understanding of the stage of development of our society and was prepared for the protracted nature and difficulty of socialist construction, which undoubtedly had important theoretical and practical significance.

A New Understanding of the Strategic Objectives of Socialist Modernization

In the course of its efforts to restructure and revive the national economy, the CPC gradually specified its development strategy for socialist modernization. As early as the eve of the founding of the PRC, Mao Zedong proposed the goal of "steadily transforming China from an agricultural nation to an industrial one after the victory of the revolution [...] and building China into a great socialist country"[46] at the Second Plenary Session of the Seventh Central Committee of the Party. After the founding of the PRC, the Communist Party of China gradually deepened its understanding of the country's strategic objectives in the practice of socialist revolution and construction. The Party's general line during the transition period treated socialist industrialization of the country as the main and central task and clearly defined the objectives and tasks of socialist industrialization.

On September 15, 1954, Zhou Enlai proposed "four modernizations" for the first time in his report on the work of the government at the first session of the National People's Congress, which means "building up a strong and modernized industry, a modernized agriculture, a modernized transportation and a modernized national defense." The Eighth Party Congress in 1956 reaffirmed this goal, stating

> the task of the CPC is to develop the national economy in a planned manner, to industrialize the country as rapidly as possible, to carry out the technical transformation of the national economy in a systematic and orderly manner, and to equip China with strong and modernized industry, modernized agriculture, modernized transportation and modernized national defense.[47]

In 1957, Mao Zedong mentioned twice in "On the Correct Handling of the Internal Contradictions Among the People" and "Speech at the National Conference of the Communist Party of China on Publicity" that he wanted to build China into "a socialist country with modern industry, modern agriculture and modern science and culture,"[48] which begins to incorporate "modern science and culture" into the overall vision of modernization.

In August 1957, when presiding over an executive meeting of the State Council, Zhou Enlai stated that industrial modernization "included transportation," and thus "modernization of transportation" was no longer singled out.[49] From December 1959 to February 1960, Mao Zedong further stated in his address on the reading of *A Textbook of Political Economy* of the Soviet Union that "the construction of socialism originally required industrial modernization, agricultural modernization, scientific and cultural modernization, but now we must add national defense modernization."[50] In February 1960, Zhou Enlai changed the term "modernization of science and culture" to "modernization of science and technology"[51] in his speech on the reading of *A Textbook of Political Economy*. In this way, the basic content and objectives of the four modernizations were made clear. In December 1964, Zhou Enlai formally proposed in his report on the work of government at the first session of the Third National People's Congress to "build China into a strong socialist country with modernized agriculture, modernized industry, modernized national defense and modernized science and technology within a not too long historical period," which were the strategic objectives of "four modernizations." At the same time, it was also proposed that four modernizations should be realized in two steps.

> Starting from the Third Five-Year Plan, the development of China's national economy can be planned in two steps: the first is to establish an independent and relatively complete industrial system and national economic system. The second is to fully realize the modernization of agriculture, industry, national defense and science and technology, so that our economy will be at the forefront of the world.[52]

The strategic objectives and steps of realizing the "Four Modernizations" represent an important exploration of the path of socialist construction by the CPC, which has pointed out the fundamental direction for the development of the socialist cause and become a powerful spiritual force that unites people of all ethnic groups in their struggle. The thought of realizing the goals in steps and stages is integral to the methodology of socialist construction.

Thought on Establishing a System of Responsibility in Agricultural Production

In the course of investigation and research, correction of mistakes and adjustment of policies, in order to revive agricultural production, overcome rural difficulties and mobilize peasants' enthusiasm for production, the Party and State leaders also proactively explored production management methods suitable for China's level of productive forces in rural areas, putting forward the idea of establishing a system of responsibility in agricultural production.

The new forms of developing agricultural production, such as "fix farm output quotas for each household" and the "responsibility fields," were first developed by peasants in some places on their own initiative to cope with the difficult situation. Faced with this fact, how to evaluate such forms became an important issue for the Party in the process of resuming agricultural production. The peasants' spontaneous invention of the fixed farm output quotas system prompted Party leaders to consider the management system of agricultural production more deeply. Deng Zihui, Director of the Rural Work Department of the Central Committee of the Communist Party of China, put forward the idea of establishing a system of responsibility in agricultural production on the basis of extensive research and studies in the countryside. He pointed out that

> at the present stage when agricultural production forces are still characterized by human and animal power, leaving some freedom and offering certain private ownership are the most effective ways in mobilizing the peasants' enthusiasm and sense of responsibility for their work.[53]

In response to the management of rural production teams, he proposed to "focus on the establishment of a system of responsibility in production and a clear division of labor," "which is the key for the improvement of collective production and the consolidation of collective ownership in future."[54] In July 1962, in his report on agriculture made at the Central Party School, he elaborated more systematically on establishing a system of responsibility in agricultural production. He made it clear that "in order to mobilize the enthusiasm of the commune members, there must be a strict system of responsibility and a division of labor," that "in agriculture there must also be a system of responsibility, and first of all work should be allotted to individual laborers," that "the system of responsibility in agricultural production is very difficult to implement without combining it with output," and that "we cannot consider the system of responsibility in field management as labor under individual economy. Though people do not work together, the land and means of production are collectively owned, so it is never individual economy."[55] Liu Shaoqi also consistently advocated that a system of responsibility in production must be implemented in the management of agricultural production. When talking about how to consolidate the collective economy, he argued that a system of responsibility must be established. He said, "it is possible for a household to be assigned a piece of land, or for a production group to be assigned a piece of land. The problem is how to link the system of responsibility to output."[56] When Chen Yun was thinking about how to revive agricultural production, he also suggested fixed farm output quotas to households, which was "a unique solution for a unique period" and that "fixed output quotas to households was not complete, and it would be better to allot land to households."[57] He thought this would stimulate the peasants' enthusiasm for production so as to restore agricultural output and solve agricultural difficulties. Deng Xiaoping also proposed,

> I think that the best way of determining production relations is to adopt an attitude that whichever form is easier and faster for the revival and development of agricultural production, whichever form should be taken; whichever form the masses are willing to take, whichever form should be taken, and make it legal if it is not legal.[58]

This is in fact a question of the specific form of realizing public ownership. However, with the re-escalation of the "Left" erroneous tendency, these positive explorations were interrupted.

The positive results achieved by the CPC members represented by Mao Zedong in exploring China's own path of socialist construction are the product of the Party's continued insistence on combining the basic principles of Marxism with the practice of socialist construction in China. The issues it addresses, such as the stage of development of socialist society, the relationship between socialism and the commodity economy, and public ownership and the form of realizing it, are all key theoretical and practical problems facing the construction of socialism. Although some of these ideas were not implemented or were interrupted in the process of implementation, they have accumulated valuable experience for the continued exploration of the path of socialist construction and have provided important ideological and theoretical preparations for clarifying the fundamental questions of "what is socialism and how to build socialism" in the new era. It also laid a solid theoretical foundation for the formation and creation of the theoretical system of socialism with Chinese characteristics.

Notes

1 Central Literature Research Office of the Communist Party of China. *Writings of Mao Zedong*, vol. 6. Beijing: People's Publishing House, 1993, p. 263, p. 264, p. 264.
2 Central Literature Research Office of the Communist Party of China. *Chronology of Mao Zedong (1949–1976)*. Beijing: Central Documents Publishing House, 2013, p. 550.
3 Ibid., p. 557.
4 Central Literature Research Office of the Communist Party of China. *Biography of Mao Zedong*, vol. 4, 2nd ed. Beijing: Central Documents Publishing House, 2011, p. 1433.
5 Central Literature Research Office of the Communist Party of China. *Writings of Mao Zedong*, vol. 7. Beijing: People's Publishing House, 1999, p. 23.
6 Ibid., p. 42.
7 Central Literature Research Office of the Communist Party of China. *Writings of Mao Zedong*, vol. 7. Beijing: People's Publishing House, 1999, p. 44.
8 Central Literature Research Office of the Communist Party of China. *Chronology of Mao Zedong (1949--1976)*, vol. 4. Beijing: Central Documents Publishing House, 2013, pp. 418--419.
9 Central Literature Research Office of the Communist Party of China. *Writings of Mao Zedong*, vol. 7. Beijing: People's Publishing House, 1999, p. 116.
10 National Archives Administration of China, Central Literature Research Office of the Communist Party of China. *Selected Documents of the Central Committee of CPC*, vol. 24. Beijing: People's Publishing House, 2013, p. 248.
11 Party History Research Office of the Central Committee of the Communist Party of China. *History of the Communist Party of China*, vol. 2, part 1, 2nd ed. Beijing: History of the Communist Party of China Publishing House, 2011, p. 396.
12 National Archives Administration of China, Central Literature Research Office of the Communist Party of China. *Selected Documents of the Central Committee of CPC*, vol. 24. Beijing: People's Publishing House, 2013, pp. 78–79.
13 Ibid., p. 180.
14 Ibid., p. 254.
15 Chen Yun. *Selected Works of Chen Yun*, vol. 3, 2nd ed. Beijing: People's Publishing House, 1995, p. 13.
16 National Archives Administration of China, Central Literature Research Office of the Communist Party of China. *Selected Documents of the Central Committee of CPC*, vol. 24. Beijing: People's Publishing House, 2013, pp. 101–102.
17 National Archives Administration of China, Central Literature Research Office of the Communist Party of China. *Selected Documents of the Central Committee of CPC*, vol. 24. Beijing: People's Publishing House, 2013, p. 277.

18 Ibid., p. 85.
19 Central Compilation and Translation Bureau for the Works of Marx, Engels, Lenin and Stalin. *The Complete Works of Lenin*, vol. 60, 2nd ed. Beijing: People's Publishing House, 1990, p. 282.
20 Central Compilation and Translation Bureau for the Works of Marx, Engels, Lenin and Stalin. *Selected Works of Stalin*, part 2. Beijing: People's Publishing House, 1979, p. 449.
21 Ibid., p. 577.
22 Central Literature Research Office of the Communist Party of China. *Writings of Mao Zedong*, vol. 7. Beijing: People's Publishing House, 1999, p. 216.
23 Central Literature Research Office of the Communist Party of China. *Writings of Mao Zedong*, vol. 7. Beijing: People's Publishing House, 1999, pp. 204–205.
24 Ibid. p. 206.
25 Central Literature Research Office of the Communist Party of China. *Writings of Mao Zedong*, vol. 7. Beijing: People's Publishing House, 1999, pp. 211–212.
26 Ibid., p. 209.
27 Ibid., p. 204.
28 Ibid., p. 216.
29 Central Literature Research Office of the Communist Party of China. *Biography of Mao Zedong*, vol. 5, 2nd ed. Beijing: Central Documents Publishing House, 2011, p. 1866.
30 Central Literature Research Office of the Communist Party of China. *Writings of Mao Zedong*, vol. 8. Beijing: People's Publishing House, 1999, p. 10.
31 National Archives Administration of China, Central Literature Research Office of the Communist Party of China. *Selected Documents of the Central Committee of CPC*, vol. 36. Beijing: People's Publishing House, 2013, pp. 381–382.
32 Central Literature Research Office of the Communist Party of China. *Writings of Mao Zedong*, vol. 8. Beijing: People's Publishing House, 1999, p. 198.
33 Ibid., p. 300, p. 302.
34 Ibid., pp. 302–303.
35 Central Literature Research Office of the Communist Party of China. *Writings of Mao Zedong*, vol. 7. Beijing: People's Publishing House, 1999, p. 435, p. 436.
36 Ibid., p. 439, p. 440.
37 Ibid., p. 435, p. 437.
38 Central Literature Research Office of the Communist Party of China. *Selected Important Documents Since the Founding of the People's Republic of China*, vol. 11. Beijing: Central Literature Publishing House, 1995, p. 611.
39 Central Literature Research Office of the Communist Party of China. *Writings of Mao Zedong*, vol. 8. Beijing: People's Publishing House, 1999, p. 11.
40 Ibid., p. 34.
41 Central Literature Research Office of the Communist Party of China. *Biography of Mao Zedong*, vol. 5. Beijing: Central Documents Publishing House, 2011, p. 1867.
42 National Archives Administration of China, Central Literature Research Office of the Communist Party of China. *Selected Documents of the Central Committee of CPC*, vol. 29. Beijing: People's Publishing House, 2013, pp. 303–304.
43 Central Literature Research Office of the Communist Party of China. *Writings of Mao Zedong*, vol. 8. Beijing: People's Publishing House, 1999, p. 116.
44 Central Literature Research Office of the Communist Party of China. *Chronicle of Zhou Enlai (1949–1976)*, vol. 2. Beijing: Central Literature Publishing House, 1997, p. 288.
45 Ibid., p. 302.

46 Mao Zedong. *Selected Writings of Mao Zedong*, vol. 4. 2nd ed. Beijing: People's Publishing House, 1991, p. 1437.
47 National Archives Administration of China, Central Literature Research Office of the Communist Party of China. *Selected Documents of the Central Committee of CPC*, vol. 24. Beijing: People's Publishing House, 2013, p. 224.
48 Central Literature Research Office of the Communist Party of China. *Writings of Mao Zedong*, vol. 7. Beijing: People's Publishing House, 1999, p. 268.
49 Party History Research Office of the Central Committee of the Communist Party of China. *History of the Communist Party of China*, vol. 2, part 2, 2nd ed. Beijing: History of the Communist Party of China Publishing House, 2011, p. 675.
50 Central Literature Research Office of the Communist Party of China. *Writings of Mao Zedong*, vol. 8. Beijing: People's Publishing House, 1999, p. 116.
51 Party History Research Office of the Central Committee of the Communist Party of China. *History of the Communist Party of China*, vol. 2, part 2, 2nd ed. Beijing: History of the Communist Party of China Publishing House, 2011, p. 675.
52 Zhou Enlai. *Selected Writings of Zhou Enlai*, vol. 2. Beijing: People's Publishing House, 1984, p. 439.
53 Deng Zihui. *Writings of Deng Zihui*. Beijing: People's Publishing House, 1996, p. 594.
54 Ibid., pp. 598–599.
55 Deng Zihui. *Writings of Deng Zihui*. Beijing: People's Publishing House, 1996, p. 605, p. 608.
56 Central Literature Research Office of the Communist Party of China. *Biography of Liu Shaoqi*, vol. 2, 2nd ed. Beijing: Central Literature Publishing House, 2008, p. 834.
57 Central Literature Research Office of the Communist Party of China. *Biography of Chen Yun*, vol. 2. Beijing: Central Literature Publishing House, 2005, p. 1321.
58 Deng Xiaoping. *Selected Writings of Deng Xiaoping*, vol. 1, 2nd ed. Beijing: People's Publishing House, 1994, p. 323.

3 Localize Marxism With Reform and Opening Up

Zhao Jianchun

Over the past 40 years of reform and opening up, the development of Marxism in China has been focused on building socialism with Chinese characteristics. Accompanied by the vivid practice of reform and opening up, Marxism has been constantly enriched and developed in order to keep pace with the times. The theoretical achievements made during this period of history are mainly reflected in the theoretical system of socialism with Chinese characteristics.

The Establishment of Socialism With Chinese Characteristics as a Theoretical System

The Theoretical System of Socialism With Chinese Characteristics: A New Chapter of Localizing Marxism

The Communist Party of China has always insisted on combining the basic principles of Marxism with Chinese reality, constantly promoting the localization of Marxism, constantly opening up new frontiers in the development of Marxism in China, and guiding the cause of socialism in China toward victory. In the long-term practice, the Party has made two historic leaps in the localization of Marxism, which gave birth to two major theoretical achievements. The first leap took place during the period of the New Democratic Revolution and gave birth to Mao Zedong Thought, the correct theoretical principles and summaries of experience on the Chinese revolution and construction that have been verified in practice. The second leap took place after the Third Plenary Session of the 11th Central Committee of the Party, which formulated the practically verified theoretical principles and summaries of experience on the construction, consolidation, and development of socialism in China, i.e., the theoretical system of socialism with Chinese characteristics. This is the latest achievement of localization of Marxism.

The Third Plenary Session of the 11th Central Committee of the CPC opened up a new period in the history of reform and opening up. For more than 40 years, all the theoretical and practical explorations of the Party have

DOI: 10.4324/9781003356042-4

centered on the theme of building socialism with Chinese characteristics. In the great practice of promoting reform and opening up and socialist modernization, the Party has persistently conducted theoretical review and innovation and continuously promoted the localization of Marxism under new historical conditions, which has led to the formation and development of the theoretical system of socialism with Chinese characteristics.

Since the reform and opening up of China, the CPC members represented by Deng Xiaoping have re-established the ideological line of seeking truth from facts, rectified the guiding ideology, shifted the work focus of the Party onto economic construction, and started a new exploration of building socialism. At the opening ceremony of the 12th Party Congress, Deng Xiaoping made it clear that we should combine the universal truths of Marxism with the specific reality of China, follow our own path, and build socialism with Chinese characteristics. After the 12th Party Congress, Deng Xiaoping put forward a series of innovative ideas that deepened the Party's understanding of scientific socialism. In 1992, during the Southern Talks, he gave a detailed theoretical overview and elaboration on a series of key problems in the development of socialism with Chinese characteristics, which fundamentally lifted the ideological barriers that were binding people, and strongly promoted the development of the cause of socialism with Chinese characteristics. The 14th Party Congress summarized a series of important ideas of Comrade Deng Xiaoping and named them "Comrade Deng Xiaoping's Theory of Building Socialism with Chinese Characteristics".

In 1997, the 15th Party Congress outlined and discussed this theory of Comrade Deng Xiaoping, renaming it "Deng Xiaoping Theory", and wrote it into the Party Constitution as the guiding ideology.

After the Fourth Plenary Session of the 13th Party Congress, the CPC members represented by Comrade Jiang Zemin continued to promote the cause of socialism with Chinese characteristics and put forward a series of new ideas and arguments, which answered the question of what socialism is and how to build it, and creatively responded to the question of what kind of Party to build and how to build it. These ideas later led to the formation of the important thought of "Three Represents". In 2002, the 16th Party Congress established the "Three Represents", together with Marxism-Leninism, Mao Zedong Thought, and Deng Xiaoping Theory, as the guiding ideology that our Party must adhere to in the long run. This is another step forward in the Party's guiding philosophy.

Since the 16th Party Congress, the Central Committee of the CPC, with Comrade Hu Jintao as its General Secretary, has led the entire Party and the people of all ethnic groups in continuing to explore the problems of what socialism is and how to build it, what kind of Party to build and how to build it, and has creatively answered the question of what kind of development to achieve and how to develop, opening up a new realm of localizing Marxism. The 17th Party Congress took the Scientific Outlook on Development as an important guideline for China's economic and social development and as a key strategic idea that must be adhered to and implemented in the development of socialism with Chinese characteristics and wrote it into the Party Constitution.

The 17th Party Congress summarized the major strategic ideas, such as Deng Xiaoping Theory, the "Three Represents", and the Scientific Outlook on Development, which were developed by the Party in practice since the reform and opening up of China, as an organic and unified whole named "the theoretical system of socialism with Chinese characteristics". The Party Congress further pointed out that the theoretical system of socialism with Chinese characteristics is open and constantly developing. In contemporary China, to adhere to the theoretical system of socialism with Chinese characteristics is to truly adhere to Marxism. Practice never ends, and innovation never ends.

The Theoretical System of Socialism With Chinese Characteristics Is Endowed With the Valuable Quality of Localizing Marxism

The formation and development of the theoretical system of socialism with Chinese characteristics reveals its distinctive practicality, salient openness, and strong national character. These three qualities are the most important ones that enabled the theoretical system of socialism with Chinese characteristics to localize Marxism.

Distinctive Practicality: The Engine of Localizing Marxism

Since the Third Plenary Session of the 11th Party Congress, the Party has broken through the shackles of dogmatism and formulated the basic line of "one central task and two basic points" in accordance with the theme of peace and development of the times and opened up the road to building socialism with Chinese characteristics. The fundamental reason why the theoretical system of socialism with Chinese characteristics is completely correct and can lead to China's continuous development and progress is that it not only adheres to the basic principles of Marxism but also pays attention to the actual situation in China. It grasps the basic national conditions of China and the characteristics of each phase of the country's economic and social development and reflects the new requirements of China's social progress and the new expectations of the people, which is Marxism in practice.

Salient Openness: The Booster of Localizing Marxism

The theoretical system of socialism with Chinese characteristics is the result of the CPC's members' combination of the basic principles of Marxism with the great practice of China's reform and opening up and socialist modernization, and their theoretical innovations on the basis of absorbing and drawing on all the achievements of civilization of human society. Openness is the salient feature of the theoretical system of socialism with Chinese characteristics.

Strong National Character: The Passport to Localizing Marxism

The theoretical system of socialism with Chinese characteristics not only adheres to the basic principles of scientific socialism but is also deeply rooted in Chinese reality. The system absorbs the achievements of traditional Chinese culture and is committed to the great rejuvenation of the Chinese nation, which displays a strong national character and exhibits a unique Chinese style, Chinese outlook, and Chinese characteristics, being the Marxism of contemporary China. The strong national character of the theoretical system of socialism with Chinese characteristics is a passport, leading to a Marxism that is rooted in the national soil, draws on national nutrients, and serves national aspirations.

The Theoretical System of Socialism With Chinese Characteristics Elevates the Localization of Marxism to a New Level

The birth of the theoretical system of socialism with Chinese characteristics is the result of the combined effect of many elements since the reform and opening up. It reflects the ability of the Communist Party of China to take stock of the situation, expand new horizons, sum up new experiences, and respond to new realities in the new historical period of reform and opening up.

The Scientific Judgment of the International Situation Provided a New Vision for the Localization of Marxism in China

In the late 1970s, as peace and development became the theme of the times, and as multi-polarization and economic globalization were in full development, competition in terms of comprehensive national power was increasingly fierce. After the Cold War, various forces in the world continued to restructure, and new divisions and combinations of powers emerged. The overall strength of the vast number of developing countries gradually increased, and the international environment tended to be moderate. Having experienced two world wars, people of all countries generally aspired to an international environment of peace, development, and cooperation. Economic globalization has generated closer and closer ties between different countries in the world, which grew to be inextricably linked to each other. The competition for markets, capital, and resources among countries was more complex, and the competition in terms of comprehensive national power between countries was increasingly fierce. The new scientific and technological revolution and the widespread application of the key inventions it has brought about have driven unprecedented and profound changes worldwide in the ways of production, lifestyles, and the way people think. In the face of the far-reaching changes triggered by the changes of the times, the Communist Party of China must continue to innovate its thinking and theories in order to grasp the pulse of the times, keep pace with the development of society, solve new problems and meet new challenges, and create a new situation in the development of socialism with Chinese characteristics, so as to guide the scientific development of practice. The theoretical system of socialism with Chinese characteristics, from Deng Xiaoping Theory to the important thought of "Three Represents", and then to the Scientific Outlook on Development and other major strategic ideas, are all formulated and developed on the basis of our Party's assessment of the new situation of world development.

Reflections on the Positive and Negative Experiences of Building Socialism Provided New Visions for the Localization of Marxism in China

The Third Plenary Session of the 11th Central Committee of the CPC drew a profound lesson from the Cultural Revolution, seriously summed up the positive and negative experiences of the Party in the cause of socialist construction, rejected the blind adherence to Mao's instructions, re-established the Marxist ideological line of seeking truth from facts, and made the historic decision to shift the work focus of the Party and the State onto economic construction and implement reform and opening up. At the same time, the CPC also drew lessons from the experiences of other socialist countries, especially the Soviet Union and Eastern Europe, which provided important lessons for the better development of socialism with Chinese characteristics.

The Basic National Conditions of the Primary Phase of Socialism Provided a New Basis for the Localization of Marxism in China

After the Third Plenary Session of the 11th Central Committee of the CPC, the Party, on the basis of summing up the historical experience since the founding of PRC, conducted a new exploration of the historical stage of socialism in China and gradually made the scientific conclusion that China is still in the primary stage of socialism and will remain so for a long time, which accurately grasped the basic national conditions of China. The scientific judgment of the basic national conditions is the fundamental starting point for our Party to carry out theoretical innovation and formulate correct policies and guidelines.

The 13th Party Congress systematically expounded the theory of the primary phase of socialism, stressing the need to fully understand the protracted nature, difficulty, and complexity of socialist construction, and the need to constantly enhance the awareness of always starting from this reality. The 15th Party Congress further elaborated on the characteristics of the primary stage of socialism. The 17th Party Congress also made an in-depth analysis and generalization of the characteristics of the new stage of China's development in the new century from eight aspects and clearly pointed out that the basic national condition that China is still in the primary stage of socialism and will remain so for a long time did not change, and the main social contradiction remained to be one between the people's growing material and cultural needs and the backward social production. It is because the theoretical system of socialism with Chinese characteristics is grounded firmly on the basic national conditions of the primary stage of socialism and its corresponding characteristics that it has been able to innovate the Marxist theory and serve the new realities of reform and opening up in China.

The Vivid Practice of Reform and Opening Up Provided a New
Script for the Localization of Marxism in China

Reform and opening up is a new great revolution led by the CPC under the new conditions of the times, and its direction is very clear. First, from the perspective of productive forces, the aim is to liberate and develop productive forces, build a modernized country, make people's lives prosperous, and ultimately achieve the great rejuvenation of the Chinese nation. Second, from the perspective of institutional construction, the aim is to facilitate the self-improvement and development of China's socialist system, so that socialism can truly reflect the pulse of the times and national character and socialism with Chinese characteristics can be built and perfected. Finally, from the perspective of Party building, the aim is to combine the great cause of socialism with Chinese characteristics with the new great project of the Party building, to strengthen and improve Party building while leading the development and progress of contemporary China, and to ensure that the Party is always at the forefront of the times. The Communist Party of China and the Chinese people have been tenacious and progressive and have been constantly innovating and putting theories into practice, which resulted in a historic change in the image of the Chinese people, socialist China, and the Communist Party of China.

Since the Third Plenary Session of the 11th Central Committee of the CPC, the theoretical system of socialism with Chinese characteristics has been continuously enriched and developed under the impetus of practice, which constantly reflects new features of the times and practical requirements. Practice is the source of theoretical innovation, while every innovation of the Party's theory has also driven the practice of reform and opening up into a new realm. The course of reform and opening up is the process of the Party's practical exploration and theoretical innovation in the new period, as well as the formation and development of the theoretical system of socialism with Chinese characteristics.

*People's Initiative in the New Era Provided Inexhaustible Impetus
for the Localization of Marxism in China*

The Marxist view of the masses emphasizes that people are the main body of practice and the source of wisdom, the fundamental driving force for historical progress and social development, and thus the true makers of history. Since the reform and opening up, many major theoretical innovations have been put forward one after another on the basis of respect for the people's pioneering ideas. Comrade Deng Xiaoping said, "Many things in the reform and opening up are proposed by the masses in practice".[1] Comrade Jiang Zemin said, "Good solutions do not fall from the sky, nor are they inherent in our minds, but can only come from people's creativity and the practice of reform and opening up".[2] Comrade Hu Jintao also pointed out that

> the great practice of the greatest number of people in transforming the world and creating a happy life is the driving force and source of theoretical innovation. Without the practice of the people, theoretical innovation will be water without a source, and will not be able to have an appeal to the people and play a guiding role in practice.[3]

Since the Third Plenary Session of the 11th Central Committee, from Xiaogang Village to the household joint production responsibility system, from the rise of township enterprises to the radical reform of state-owned enterprises, from the construction of new socialist countryside to the promotion of urbanization, all the events fully demonstrated the wisdom and creativity of the people in the practice of reform and opening up. The CPC members have always been people-oriented, respecting the people's initiative and doing their utmost to mobilize the wisdom and power of the masses to develop socialism with Chinese characteristics. Therefore, we can also say that the theoretical system of socialism with Chinese characteristics is formulated and developed by our Party's adherence to the principle of developing for the people, relying on the people for development, actively mobilizing the people, giving full play to the people's initiative, and gathering strength and wisdom from the people.

The Unceasing Exploration of Three Key Topics

The Unceasing Exploration of "What Socialism Is and How to Understand Socialism"

An Innovative View on the Nature of Socialism

In the 1992 Southern Talks, Deng Xiaoping made a classic explanation of the nature of socialism, stating that "the nature of socialism is to liberate and develop the productive forces, eliminate exploitation and polarization, and ultimately achieve common prosperity".[4] This new theoretical overview condensed the nature of socialism from its myriad characteristics into a brief one and interpreted "what is socialism" at a deeper level. First of all, he summarized the liberation and development of productive forces as the nature of socialism, which was an innovation of Deng Xiaoping. This changed the past approach, which talked about socialism in abstract terms without considering productive forces and tried to promote the development of productive forces by merely changing production relations. At the same time, he highlighted the liberation of productive forces in the socialist period, believing that only by continuously liberating productive forces could we better develop them. Second, it emphasizes the elimination of exploitation and polarization, which manifests the value of socialism in achieving common prosperity. Marxism believes that achieving free and comprehensive human development is the ultimate goal of social development. Deng Xiaoping combined this basic understanding of Marxism with the basic conditions of the primary stage of socialism and made the realization of common prosperity the fundamental goal of the primary stage of socialism, reflecting the combination of Marxism and contemporary Chinese reality. He also pointed out that the elimination of exploitation and polarization is a long-term dynamic process, in which the socialist public ownership system and the labor-based distribution system are the basis that ensures the realization of common prosperity.

After the Fourth Plenary Session of the 13th Party Congress, the CPC members represented by Comrade Jiang Zemin made a deeper interpretation of the nature of socialism in the important thought of "Three Represents", proposing that the all-round development of human beings is also the essential requirement of socialist society. In 2001, Jiang Zemin made it clear in his speech at the conference celebrating the 80th anniversary of the founding of the Communist Party of China,

> We build socialism with Chinese characteristics of the various undertakings. All the work we carry out not only focuses on the people's real material and cultural needs but also improves the quality of the people, which means promoting the all-round development of people. This is the essential Marxist requirement for building a new socialist society. We must develop the material and spiritual civilization of socialist society on the basis of constantly promoting the all-round development of people.[5]

After the 16th Party Congress, the CPC members represented by Comrade Hu Jintao have developed a deeper understanding of the nature of socialism and pointed out that social harmony is also the essential attribute of socialism with Chinese characteristics. This is an important conclusion reached by the Party at a new stage in history. In the face of new changes and challenges of the times, the Party summarized the historical experience of socialist construction at home and abroad, especially in China, and deepened the understanding of the nature of socialism.

After the 18th Party Congress, General Secretary Xi Jinping profoundly elaborated on the Chinese Dream of the great rejuvenation of the Chinese nation, which is an important strategic thought put forward by the Party at the important strategic stage of deepening reform, building a moderately prosperous society and pushing forward the cause of socialist modernization to a deeper level. It also adheres to and develops the theory of scientific socialism, grasping the nature of socialism completely and accurately in the new period. Chinese Dream reflects Chinese people's good wishes and the historical destiny of the Chinese nation, clarifying the common goal of struggle for the whole Party and the Chinese people of all ethnic groups.

An Innovative View on the Primary Stage of Socialism

Deng Xiaoping pointed out at the beginning of the reform and opening up that China's realities were a weak foundation, a large population, and backward production. A Chinese modernization must be based on Chinese characteristics. In 1981, the Sixth Plenary Session of the 11th Party Congress put forward for the first time that China's socialism was still in its primary stage. The report of the 12th Party Congress put forward the assertion that "our socialist society is still at the primary stage of development", with "underdeveloped material civilization" as the basic characteristic of this stage. The 13th Party Congress comprehensively and systematically expounded the theory of the primary stage of socialism and put forward the basic policy of "one central task and two basic points".

The 14th Party Congress reaffirmed that China was still in the primary stage of socialism, emphasizing that it would be a long historical stage of at least 100 years. The 15th Party Congress reemphasized the primary stage of socialism, pointing out that being in the primary stage of socialism is the "greatest reality" in China. On this basis, the 15th Party Congress formulated the basic program of the Party in the primary stage of socialism, further unifying the thinking of the whole Party and the whole nation.

At a time when the life of Chinese people generally reached a moderately well-off level, the 16th Party Congress in 2002 once again pointed out that China was at the primary stage of socialism and would remain so for a long time, and that the general moderately well-off level reached now was still a low, incomplete, and unbalanced one, and that consolidating and improving such a level would call for a long period of hard struggle. The 17th Party Congress further pointed out that in the new period, China was still in the primary stage of socialism and would remain so for a long time, and the main social contradiction between the growing material and cultural needs of the people and the backward social production remained unchanged. The 18th Party Congress proposed the "three unchanged" on the basis of "two unchanged" in the 17th Party Congress and added "China's international status as the world's largest developing country remains unchanged", which deepened the understanding of the primary stage of socialism.

An Innovative View on Socialist Market Economy

At the beginning of the reform and opening up, Deng Xiaoping proposed that

> socialism also has a market economy, while capitalism also has plans to exert control. Don't think capitalism means no control and absolute freedom. Most Favored Nation is a means of control! Don't think developing some market economy is the road to capitalism. It isn't the case. We need both the plan and the market. If we don't have a market, we won't even know the information in the world. Then we are resigned to the state of lagging behind.[6]

In 1981, the Sixth Plenary Session of the 11th Party Congress adopted *The Resolution on Several Historical Issues of the Party Since the Founding of the People's Republic of China*, which put forward the policy of "planned economy as the mainstay, market regulation as a supplement". In October 1984, *The Decision of the Central Committee of the Communist Party of China on Economic Reform* adopted at the Third Plenary Session of the 12th Party Congress put forward the new concept of "planned commodity economy on the basis of public ownership", affirming that the full development of the commodity economy is an unavoidable stage of socialist economic development and a necessary condition for the realization of China's economic modernization. The 13th Party Congress proposed that the system of socialist planned commodity economy should be "an inherently unified system of planning and market" and that "the scope of planning and market is supposed to cover the whole society". In 1987, Deng again stressed that both planning and market were means, both of which could be used if they benefitted the development of productive forces. In 1992, he clearly pointed out in his Southern Talks,

> Planned economy is not equal to socialism, for capitalism also has plans. Market economy is not equal to capitalism, for socialism also has markets. Plan and market are economic means. The proportion of planning and market is not the essential difference between socialism and capitalism.[7]

In this way, the concept that planned economy and market economy are attributes of socialist or capitalist systems has been removed. The erroneous idea that planned and market economy correspond to specific social systems has been corrected, which laid a solid foundation for the formation of the theory of socialist market economy.

The 14th Party Congress set the establishment of a socialist market economy system as the goal of China's economic system reform, which is a major breakthrough in Marxism of our Party, indicating the establishment of Deng Xiaoping's theory of socialist market economy.

The Third Plenary Session of the 14th Party Congress adopted *The Decision of the Central Committee of the Communist Party of China on Several Issues Concerning the Establishment of a Socialist Market Economy System*, which further clarified its basic framework: establishing a modern enterprise system, fostering and developing a market system, establishing a sound macroeconomic control system, and establishing a reasonable personal income distribution and social security system. The CPC members represented by Comrade Jiang Zemin put forward the idea of combining the socialist market economy with the socialism as the basic social system, which solved the problem of whether and how to combine socialism and market economy in theory.

The Third Plenary Session of the 16th Party Congress put forward clear goals and tasks to improve the socialist market economy system. The 17th Party Congress, based on the economic development goals to be achieved in the new historical period, put forward the requirement to make significant progress in improving the socialist market economy system, to better play the essential role of the market in the allocating resources, and to formulate a macroeconomic control system conducive to scientific development. The 18th Party Congress report clearly pointed out that the core issue of economic system reform is to deal with the relationship between the government and the market and must respect the laws of the market and better bring the role of the government into play. The Third Plenary Session of the 18th Party Congress emphasized that the reform of the economic system is the focus of deepening reform comprehensively. The core issue is how to deal with the relationship between the government and the market, so that the latter can play a decisive role in the allocation of resources and better bring the role of the government into play. From the evolution of these terms, we can see that our Party's understanding of the definition and operation laws of socialist market economy has been deepening and maturing.

The Unceasing Exploration of "What Kind of Party to Build and How to Build It"

Stage One (1978–1989): The theoretical results of the exploration of "what kind of party to build and how to build it" at this stage are mainly reflected in Deng Xiaoping Theory. After the Third Plenary Session of the 11th Party Congress, the CPC members with Comrade Deng Xiaoping as the main representative realized that the CPC was a party leading socialist construction in a country that was economically and culturally backward. Deng Xiaoping gave comprehensive and in-depth thoughts on the questions of "what kind of party should the ruling party be, what qualities should the members of the ruling party have, and how can the party be regarded as good at leadership".[8] He pointed out, "We should build our party into a fighting Marxist party and a strong core to lead the people in the construction of socialist material and spiritual civilization".[9] Concerning how the Party should be built, he proposed that we should strive to build the Party into a dynamic one which is willing to reform, a disciplined one that upholds justice and integrity, and an effective one that selects the best persons to serve the people. He also proposed to adhere to the unity of upholding and improving the Party's leadership. Concerning the improvement of the Party's working methods, he proposed to adhere to the ideological line of emancipating the mind and seeking truth from facts, and to the mass line of trusting the masses, relying on them, "from the people and to the people". These ideas provide the ideological guidelines for the CPC to clarify its historical orientation, grasp its new historical mission, and lead the cause of socialist modernization and reform and opening up more effectively and concretely in the new period of reform and opening up.

Stage Two (1989–2002): The theoretical results of the exploration of "what kind of Party to build and how to build it" at this stage are mainly reflected in the important thought of "Three Represents". After the Fourth Plenary Session of the 13th Party Congress, the CPC members with Comrade Jiang Zemin as the main representative led the Party to further promote the new great project of Party building, emphasizing the need to build the Party into a Marxist Party that is armed with Deng Xiaoping Theory, steadfast in ideology, politics, and organizations, and able to serve the people wholeheartedly, withstand all kinds of risks, always take the lead in the times, and lead the people to build socialism with Chinese characteristics.

Since the late 1980s, owing to the new circumstances at home and abroad and within the Party, the status and environment of the CPC and the historical tasks of the Party underwent many significant changes. Jiang Zemin pointed out in the report of the 16th Party Congress,

> Through revolution, construction and reform, our Party has changed from a Party that led the people in their struggle to seize national power to one that leads the people to take control of national power and govern for a long period, from a Party that led national construction under external blockade and planned economy to one that led national construction under the conditions of opening up to the outside world and developing a socialist market economy.[10]

It is on the basis of the scientific understanding of these new changes that, after the Fourth Plenary Session of the 13th Party Congress, the CPC members mainly represented by Comrade Jiang Zemin founded the "Three Represents" important thought on the basis of Deng Xiaoping's thought on party building. In February 2000, Jiang pointed out during his visit to

Guangdong that as long as our Party always represents the development requirements of China's advanced productive forces, the direction of China's advanced culture, and the fundamental interests of the broadest number of Chinese people, our Party will always be invincible and will always be sincerely supported by the people of all ethnic groups and lead them forward.[11] In July 2001, Jiang, in his speech at the conference commemorating the 80th anniversary of the founding of the Party, put forward the idea of strengthening and improving the Party's construction, always maintaining the Party's advanced nature and purity in accordance with the Three Represents.

In November 2002, the 16th Party Congress established the Three Represents, together with Marxism-Leninism, Mao Zedong Thought, and Deng Xiaoping Theory, as the guiding ideology that the Party must adhere to in the long term and wrote it into the Party Constitution. In 2004, Three Represents was included into the Constitution of the PRC.

Stage Three (2002–2012): The theoretical results of the exploration of "what kind of party to build and how to build it" at this stage are mainly seen in the Scientific Outlook on Development. Under the new situation, the Party Central Committee with Comrade Hu Jintao as the General Secretary proposed to build the Party according to the requirements of the Scientific Outlook on Development, emphasizing the need to adhere to the "two imperatives" proposed by Mao Zedong and to strengthen the Party's ruling capacity and advanced nature. In his speech to celebrate the 90th anniversary of the founding of the Party, he mentioned the "four insistences", namely, first, we must insist on emancipating the mind, seeking truth from facts, and advancing with the times, always maintaining the Party's pioneering spirit; second, we must insist on "for the people and relying on the people", always maintaining the Party's close ties with the people; third, we must insist on a strict standard in selecting competent cadres, always maintaining the vivacity of the Party; fourth, we must insist on the Party's strict administration of itself, always maintaining its integrity. Hu Jintao also put forward "five musts", namely, we must adhere to the emancipation of the mind, to seeking truth from facts, and to advancing with the times; we must appoint competent cadres regardless of their backgrounds; we must adopt the people-oriented concept of governance; we must treat the symptoms and look for their roots, take a comprehensive perspective in administrating the Party, and combine punishment and prevention with a focus on the latter; we must use the system to regulate power, affairs, and personnel. These are the strategic plans to improve the scientific Party construction under new historical conditions. All these reflect the maturity of the Scientific Outlook on Development, which allows our Party can see a clearer direction for the better and more effective promotion of more new great projects during the new historical period of reform and opening up.

The Unceasing Exploration of "What Kind of Development to Achieve and How to Develop"

The Innovations in Development Theory by the CPC Members Represented by Comrade Deng Xiaoping After the Third Plenary Session of the 11th Party Congress

First, regarding the development path, Deng Xiaoping put forward the theory of building a development path of socialism with Chinese characteristics. The 13th Party Congress put forward the basic line of "one central task and two basic points" for the primary stage of socialism, i.e., to treat economic construction as the central task, to insist on the four basic principles, and on reform and opening up, which set a baseline for China's development in the new period of reform and opening up from a macro perspective. In 1992, Deng Xiaoping emphasized in his Southern Talk that

> planned economy is not equal to socialism, for capitalism also has plans. Market economy is not equal to capitalism, for socialism also has markets. Plan and market are economic means. The proportion of planning and market is not the essential difference between socialism and capitalism.[12]

The erroneous idea that planned and market economies correspond to specific social systems has been corrected, which puts up a signpost for development at the crossroads. On the correct understanding of the relationship between socialism and capitalism, he proposed, firstly, we should accept the coexistence of the two systems and make use of capitalism in the modernization of socialism. Second, he emphasized the need to abandon capitalism as we learn from it and to uphold socialism while using capitalism. In this way, to a certain extent, the obstacles of ideas on the road to development are cleared.

Second, regarding the driving force of development, Deng Xiaoping believed that revolution could liberate the productive forces, and so could reform. The comprehensiveness and profundity of reform triggered a series of far-reaching adjustments in economy, social life, working style, and mental state. It is not only conducive to the liberation of productive forces, but also to their development. He pointed out that "without reform and opening up, without economic development, and without improving people's lives, China would only come to a dead-end".[13]

Third, on the development strategy. First, the "three-step" strategy. Deng Xiaoping designed a grand blueprint for the basic realization of modernization in three steps. The first step was to double the gross national product (GNP) from 1981 to 1990 and reach US$500 per capita to solve the problem of food and clothing. The second step was to double GNP again from 1991 to the end of the 20th century and reach US$1,000 per capita to reach the well-off level. Second, the idea of "two overall situations". Deng put forward the idea of "two overall situations" in 1988, saying

> the coastal areas should speed up the opening up to the outside world so that the vast area with 200 million people can develop faster first, which can promote the better development of the inland. This is a matter of the overall situation. The mainland should take into account the overall situation. In turn, when development reaches a certain point, the coastal areas should contribute more to help the development of the inland, which is also a matter of the overall situation.[14]

Finally, the strategy of "grasping two links at the same time". In early 1992, Deng pointed out in the Southern Talks, saying "we should pursue the process of reform and opening up and at the same time fight crime. We should grasp both aspects and be determined in combating all kinds of criminal activities and eliminating all kinds of hideous phenomena".[15] These preliminary strategic ideas clarified in a more systematic way the manner to develop contemporary China.

The Innovations in Development Theory by the CPC Members Represented by Comrade Jiang Zemin After the Fourth Plenary Session of the 13th Party Congress

First, on the development path

[1] The idea of comprehensive development of a socialist society was put forward. At the 14th Party Congress, Jiang Zemin pointed out that "we should focus on economic construction, strengthen socialist democracy, legal system, and spiritual civilization, and promote overall social progress".[16] This idea emphasizes that economic development and social development should be coordinated with each other and that the 12 relationships should be properly handled as well as the unity of current development and sustainable development.

[2] Jiang put forward the idea of the all-round development of people. In his speech on July 1, 2001, he proposed that

> we build the cause of socialism with Chinese characteristics. All the work we are carrying out should not only focus on the people's real material and cultural needs but also promote the improvement of the quality of the people, that is, to strive to promote the all-round development of people.[17]

[3] The idea of the coordinated development of socialist economy, politics, and culture.

Second, on the impetus of development. Jiang put forward the strategy of "reinvigorating the country through science and education" at the National

Science and Technology Conference held in May 1995, which is the inheritance and application of the idea of "science and technology is the primary productive force" proposed by Deng in the new period. At the same time, it was pointed out that innovation is the soul of a nation's progress. All these reflect that after the Fourth Plenary Session of the 13th Party Congress, the CPC members represented by Comrade Jiang Zemin have deepened their understanding of the dynamics of social development.

Third, on the development strategy. On the basis of the "three-step" development strategy proposed by Deng, Jiang proposed the strategies of "reinvigorating the country through science and education", "sustainable development", and "large-scale development of the western region", which are coordinated with the country's economic and social development and realized the innovation of Marxist social development theory.

The Proposal of the Scientific Outlook on Development by the CPC Members Represented by Comrade Hu Jintao After the 16th Party Congress

The 17th Party Congress report made a complete and comprehensive summary of the Scientific Outlook on Development: its principle is development, its core is people-orientation, its basic requirement is comprehensive, coordinated, and sustainable development, and its fundamental approach is to be holistic and balanced

1 The principle of the Scientific Outlook on Development is development. Marxism believes that productive forces are the ultimate determining power of human social development. As the ruling party, only by continuously promoting development can we meet the expectations of the people and understand the key to socialist modernization, thus making development the key to our Party's governance and the country's prosperity.

2 The core of the Scientific Outlook on Development is being people-oriented. People-oriented is to take into account the fundamental interests of the broadest number of people. People are the main body and the basic force to promote development, so we should seek development and promote development for the fundamental benefits of the broadest number of people. The purpose of the Communist Party of China is to serve the people wholeheartedly and adhere to the concept of being people-oriented. We must always realize, maintain, and develop the fundamental interests of the people and take these efforts as the starting point of all the work of the Party and the State. We should respect the principal position of the people, give full play to people's initiative, and promote the overall development of people so that development is for the people and by the people, and its fruits are shared by the people.

3 The basic requirement of the Scientific Outlook on Development is comprehensive, coordinated, and sustainable development. We should

adhere to the path of civilized development where developed production, affluent livelihood, and good ecology are pursued, where the development speed, structure, quality, and efficiency are unified, and where economic development, population, resources, and environment are coordinated, enabling people to live and work in a good ecological environment, and achieving sustainable economic and social development.

4 The fundamental approach of the Scientific Outlook on Development is holistic and balanced. We should integrate urban and rural development, development of different regions, economic and social development, the harmonious development of humans and nature, domestic development and opening up to the outside world, integrate central and local relations, integrate individual and group interests, local and overall interests, current and long-term interests, and fully mobilize the enthusiasm of all parties.

In short, the Scientific Outlook on Development is the concentrated expression of the Marxist worldview and methodology on development, the guidepost for China to move forward in the right direction in the new period of reform and opening up, and a major strategic idea that must be adhered to and implemented in building socialism with Chinese characteristics.

New Developments in the Theoretical System of Socialism With Chinese Characteristics

On "Chinese Dream"

On November 29, 2012, Xi Jinping pointed out during his visit to the exhibition "The Road to Rejuvenation", saying

> everyone has ideals and pursuits, and they all have their own dreams. Now, everyone is discussing the Chinese dream, and I think that achieving the great rejuvenation of the Chinese nation is the greatest dream of the Chinese nation since modern times. This dream is the long-cherished wish of several generations of Chinese people, reflecting the overall interests of the Chinese nation and the Chinese people, being the common expectation of every Chinese people.[18]

Looking back at the development of the Chinese nation, our ancestors, with ideals and beliefs, created glorious achievements that attracted international attention, and the Chinese nation once had a glorious page in the history of the world. However, the situation had shifted where China had undergone great changes since modern times. Under foreign invasion and domestic dictatorship, the country's fate was in decline and the Chinese nation was facing an unprecedented crisis. From that moment on, the Chinese people have always taken it as their duty to achieve national rejuvenation and have tied their fate to that of the nation. In the new era, Xi, when talking about the fate of individuals and the country, stressed that

> the future and destiny of each individual is closely linked to those of the country and the nation. Only when the country and the nation are prosperous can everyone will be fine. Achieving the great rejuvenation of the Chinese nation is a glorious and arduous undertaking that requires the concerted efforts of generations of Chinese people.[19]

As the navigator of the new generation of the Chinese nation, he is well aware of the enormity and long-term nature of the great rejuvenation of the nation, for which he said,

> Empty talk harms the country, while hard work makes it flourish. We, the CPC members of this generation, must build up our Party, unite all Chinese people to build up our country and develop our nation, and continue to march towards the goal of the great rejuvenation of the Chinese nation.[20]

On March 17, 2013, at the first session of the 12th National People's Congress, Xi explained in detail the connotation of the Chinese Dream. He pointed out that

> the goal of achieving a moderately prosperous society, building up a rich, strong, democratic, civilized and harmonious socialist modern state, and the Chinese dream of achieving the great rejuvenation of the Chinese nation are to bring about prosperity, national renewal, people's happiness, which not only deeply reflects the ideals of Chinese people today but also the glorious tradition of our ancestors' relentless pursuit of progress.[21]

In this way, the core of the Chinese Dream of the great rejuvenation of the Chinese nation has been summarized, namely, prosperity, national renewal, and people's happiness.

Prosperity means being prosperous and powerful. The former requires a more developed national economy, more dynamic social factors of production, and people's better livelihood. The latter means that the driving force of science and technological innovation in economic development grows stronger and that politics is more democratic, culture more thriving, society more harmonious, and ecology more pleasant. In a word, the cause of socialism with Chinese characteristics is further developed and perfected.

National renewal is reflected in two aspects, namely, internal and external. The internal aspect refers to the inheritance and development of past economic achievements, excellent culture and other achievements of Chinese civilizations, and the continuous development and improvement of our own cultural treasure. The external aspect means to share the achievements of our own civilization with the world as part of the progress of human civilization, so as to influence and change the world, and in the process, restore the glory of the Chinese nation among all nations of the world.

People's happiness is reflected in the development of everyone, the common opportunity to live a brilliant life, to make dreams come true, and to grow and progress with the motherland and the times, which ultimately means that people's rights are more fully protected. The Chinese Dream is the dream of the country, the dream of the nation, and also the dream of every Chinese people, with the three intertwined and interconnected. This dream of the nation and the state is there for each Chinese person to better build, pursue, and fulfill their own dreams. Meanwhile, with the realization of each person's dreams, the dream of the nation and the state will gradually come true.

When talking about the principles that need to be grasped in order to realize the Chinese Dream, Xi emphasized the "three musts":

"To realize the Chinese dream, we **must** take the Chinese path".[22] The Chinese path is the road of socialism with Chinese characteristics. This path is the result of our Party's ultimate choice based on a review of history and the consideration of reality. We have learned to take the way of self-improvement in the great practice of reform and opening up for over 40 years. We have learned to take the way of self-reliance in the 70 years of continuous exploration since the founding of the People's Republic of China. We have learned to take the way of self-respect in assessing the development of the Chinese nation for over 170 years since the early modern times. We have learned to take the way of self-awareness in inheriting the 5,000-year-long civilization of the Chinese nation. The road to socialism with Chinese characteristics is the result of our self-awareness, self-respect, self-reliance, and self-improvement. Self-awareness means knowing our own traditions, self-respect not fearing foreign aggression, self-reliance not relying on foreign forces, and self-improvement perfecting and developing ourselves. The Chinese nation consists of a group of creative people. In the new era, we must continue to improve and take the path of development that suits China's national conditions. We should have confidence in our theory, path, system, and culture, and unswervingly advance along the correct Chinese road.

"To realize the Chinese dream, we **must** carry forward the Chinese spirit".[23] The Chinese spirit is the national spirit with patriotism as the core, and the spirit of the times with reform and innovation as the center. The Chinese nation has built up a strong national spirit in its long history, in which patriotism is the core. Since the Third Plenary Session of the 11th Party Congress, the Chinese nation has experienced a history of reform and opening up, which had endowed our nation with the spirit of the times with reform and innovation as its core. Reform and innovation have provided intellectual support and spiritual impetus for the development of our reform and opening up. The realization of the Chinese dream requires every patriot to carry forward the spirit of reform and innovation in the new era of reform and opening up and to redouble their efforts to achieve the great rejuvenation of the Chinese nation.

"To realize the Chinese dream, we **must** unite Chinese power".[24] The power of China is the unified power of the people of all ethnic groups. Every Chinese person is a part of the big family of China, shouldering the mission of personal happiness as well as the responsibility of contributing to the glory of the country. Let us unite closely with a unified mind and strength under the leadership of the Communist Party of China and strive for the realization of our common dream. In the new era, the realization of the Chinese Dream cannot be achieved without the united efforts of the Chinese people. The power of countless people will converge into that of the nation so that the cause of socialism with Chinese characteristics can be pushed forward continuously and the Chinese Dream of the great rejuvenation of the Chinese nation can be realized.

Through the elaboration of the Chinese path, Chinese spirit, and Chinese power, Xi finally put the realization of the Chinese Dream on the people, pointing out that "the Chinese Dream is ultimately the people's dream, which must be realized by relying closely on the people for the benefit of the people".[25] Achieving the great rejuvenation of the Chinese nation is a glorious and arduous undertaking, which requires generations of Chinese people to work hard for it. Meanwhile, as the dream of national rejuvenation, the Chinese Dream is also of every Chinese person, and every one of us will build, pursue, and realize the dream of socialist modernization. The "dream of national rejuvenation" and the "personal dream" are intertwined together into the Chinese Dream in the new period. In this sense, each of us also advances, practices, and develops the theoretical system of socialism with Chinese characteristics. We should respect the people's initiative and their status as the makers of history, so as to realize human development in all aspects and provide a constant source of motivation for further innovation of the socialist theoretical system with Chinese characteristics.

At the critical stage of building a moderately prosperous society, Comrade Xi Jinping's systematic elaboration of the Chinese Dream is a thoughtful consideration of history and reality, a scientific grasp of the laws of economic and social development, a rational response to the characteristics of the times and the expectations of the people, and the Party's advancement with the times in its theoretical understanding. The introduction of the Chinese Dream marks a new stage of localizing Marxism.

On Chinese Path

*The Nature of Socialism With Chinese Characteristics
Being Socialism*

Adherence to and development of socialism with Chinese characteristics is the key to the socialist modernization led by the Party since the reform and opening up, which is also the theme of all the theories and practices of the Party. A series of important speeches by Comrade Xi Jinping made in-depth, thorough, and comprehensive elaborations on this theme. In the new period, adhering to and developing socialism with Chinese characteristics provides the theoretical guide for a series of practical issues such as deepening reform and building a moderately prosperous society in an all-round way.

General Secretary Xi pointed out that

> socialism with Chinese characteristics is the dialectical unity of the theoretical logic of scientific socialism and the historical logic of China's social development, which is scientific socialism rooted in Chinese soil, reflecting the will of the Chinese people and adapting to the requirements of development and progress of China and the times, and is the only way to build a moderately prosperous society, speed up socialist modernization and achieve the great rejuvenation of the Chinese nation.[26]

This remark is a scientific interpretation of the meaning of socialism with Chinese characteristics. Through a deep understanding of its meaning, it is easy to understand that the reason why scientific socialism is scientific rather than idealistic lies in the combination of the basic principles of scientific socialism with the reality of each country and the characteristics of the times, in opposition to the mechanical application of dogmas and classical texts. What makes socialism with Chinese characteristics socialism is CPC's success in combining Marxism with Chinese reality and flexibly applying the basic principles of scientific socialism to build socialism based on the spirit of seeking truth from facts. It not only adheres to the basic principles of scientific socialism but also endows it with Chinese genes according to China's actual practice and the characteristics of the times. It opposes both the mechanical reproduction of Marxism and the erroneous idea of detaching from the basic system of socialism.

Correct Understanding of the Two Historical Periods Before and After the Reform and Opening Up

General Secretary Xi pointed out,

> In our Party's leadership of people in socialist construction, there are two historical periods before and after the reform and opening up, which are interrelated and significantly different. However, both are essentially the practical exploration of our Party's leadership of people in socialist construction.[27]

The latter historical period cannot be used to negate the former one, nor can the former be used to negate the latter. General Secretary Xi's remarks on "two historical periods" are of great significance for our scientific understanding of the history of the People's Republic of China in the new period, guiding us to take a rational perspective in viewing the characteristics of different development periods, to correct certain misconceptions, and to unify the thinking of the whole Party and the whole nation.

In the historical period before the reform and opening up, the CPC members represented by Comrade Mao Zedong made unremitting explorations of the cause of socialist construction and achieved a series of results. It was that generation that created New China and established the basic system of socialism. It was also that generation that provided much of the institutional framework for today's socialist construction. Of course, we do not deny that mistakes were made and detours were taken during that period of socialist exploration, but we should measure that on a large historical scale and should not downplay the historical achievements made then merely because there had been mistakes.

Over the past 40 years of reform and opening up, our country's comprehensive national power has increased significantly with booming social development and more prosperous life for the people. General Secretary Xi pointed out that "reform and opening up is the key that determines the fate of contemporary China",[28] which reflects that despite certain problems in the process, the achievements are still dominant. Problems can only be solved by continuing to promote reform and deepening reform comprehensively.

The two historical periods before and after the reform and opening up witnessed certain achievements in exploring the construction of socialism with Chinese characteristics, but both of them are not perfect, and their accomplishments are unified in the process of exploring the great practice of socialism with Chinese characteristics. For the two periods, a correct attitude is to affirm the achievements made in the exploration at first, and we shall not use the achievements of one period to negate the other period for the latter's mistakes. The correct understanding of these two historical periods is not only a historical issue but also a political one. The conception of this issue helps us to unify our thinking, form a consensus on reform, engage in construction wholeheartedly, and seek development with determination.

Taking a Perspective of Development in Socialism With Chinese Characteristics

General Secretary Xi Jinping pointed out that

> we must take a perspective of development as we adhere to Marxism and socialism. The more our cause advances and develops, the more unseen circumstances and new problems will emerge, so do the risks, challenges, and the unpredictable we will face. We must enhance our vigilance and get prepared for danger in times of peace.[29]

This remark provides a theoretical guide for us to grasp the laws of socialist modernization and adhere to and develop socialism with Chinese characteristics in the new era.

We should adhere to and develop socialism with Chinese characteristics, with an emphasis on the latter, namely unifying our adherence to and development of it. At present, China is still in the primary stage of socialism. We are still facing many new problems in the development. There is no ready-made experience to solve some of the emerging problems, so we need to have the tenacity to adhere to the principles and also the courage to pioneer, innovate, and make new attempts. The history of China's socialist construction is a chronicle of the courage to practice, try, and make breakthroughs and innovations in exploration rather than stick to the dogmas. Therefore, comprehensively deepening reform and building a moderately prosperous society also requires us to adhere to the basic principles of socialism with Chinese characteristics with the perspective of development. We should stick to the principles, solve new problems, and formulate new theories in the course of development.

On Reform and Opening Up

At the gathering to celebrate the 40th anniversary of reform and opening up, General Secretary Xi Jinping delivered an important speech. In the speech, he summarized the great achievements and valuable experience of the Party and the state in the past 40 years of reform and opening up, spoke highly of the outstanding contribution of the Chinese people to the cause of reform and opening up, solemnly declared the confidence and determination to carry out reform and opening up to the end, and clearly put forward the goal of steadfastly deepening reform in all aspects, expanding opening up and continuously promoting reform and opening up in the new era, which is a document of Marxist platform. Xi Jinping's important speech is of great significance and guiding value to deeply understand the historical necessity and practical importance of comprehensively deepening reform, to scientifically understand its urgency and difficulty, to systematically grasp it's inner laws and key tasks, to promote the realization of the Two Centenary Goals, and to realize the Chinese Dream of the great rejuvenation of the Chinese nation.

Four "Based-on": The Interpretation of the Background and Reason for Reform and Opening Up

Xi Jinping pointed out,

> Our Party made the historic decision to carry out reform and opening up based on a grasp of the future destiny of the Party and the country, based on an in-depth summary of the practice of socialist revolution and construction, based on an insight into the trend of the times, and

based on an in-depth understanding of the expectations and needs of the people.[30]

This is a profound analysis and precise grasp of the law of the historical development of socialism with Chinese characteristics, a generalized summary of the origin and historical necessity of the cause of reform and opening up. As he pointed out in his speech,

> Historical development has its own laws, but people are not completely passive in it. As long as we grasp the momentum of historical development, seize the opportunity of historical change, work hard and forge ahead, human society will be able to move forward better.[31]

The generalization of "four based-on" is a new overview of our Party's historical decision standing at a new historical starting point, with a historical consciousness that serves as a more realistic guide for the cause of reform and opening up today.

"Great Awakening", "Three Milestones", and "Three Tremendous Transformations": A Summary and Definition of the Historical Status and Significance of Reform and Opening Up

Xi Jinping pointed out that "reform and opening up is a great awakening of our Party, and it is this great awakening that gave birth to the great creation of our Party from theory to practice".[32] At the same time, from the perspective of history, he proposed that

> The founding of the Communist Party of China, the founding of the People's Republic of China, and the pursuit of reform and opening-up and socialism with Chinese characteristics were the milestones on the way toward great national rejuvenation in modern times. They represent three historic events that took place after the May Fourth Movement in 1919.[33]

In addition, he also used three "Great Leaps" to point out that

> The Chinese nation has achieved a tremendous transformation from standing up, growing rich to becoming strong! Socialism with Chinese characteristics has achieved a tremendous transformation from establishment, development to improvement! The Chinese people have achieved a tremendous transformation from the days of scarcity to a life of moderate prosperity![34]

This is the most highly historical evaluation of reform and opening up made by our Party so far.

The "Ten 'Insist On'" Is the Latest Achievement of Localizing Marxism in China

General Secretary Xi Jinping's speech profoundly explained the historical implications of the 40 years of reform and opening up and the basic laws of development, namely the "Ten 'Insist On'". He pointed out,

> "Over the past 40 years, we have always insisted on emancipating the mind, seeking truth from facts, and advancing with the times, being pragmatic, on the guiding position of Marxism without faltering, and on the basic principles of scientific socialism without wavering"; "We have always insisted on focusing on economic construction, and constantly liberating and developing social productive forces"; "We have always insisted on the path of political development of socialism with Chinese characteristics"; "We have always insisted on the development of advanced socialist culture"; "We have always insisted on securing and improving people's livelihood during development"; "We have always insisted on protecting the environment and conserving resources, and on promoting ecological civilization"; "We have always insisted on the absolute leadership of the Party over the military"; "We have always insisted on promoting the peaceful reunification of the motherland"; "We have always insisted on an independent and peaceful foreign policy"; "We have always insisted on strengthening and improving the leadership of the Party.[35]

The "Ten Insist On" not only clarifies the consistency of history and logic but also sorts out the unity of theory and practice, revealing the root for the success of China's reform and opening up and showing how our Party inherited and developed Marxism, socialism, and socialism with Chinese characteristics in this great process. It is not only the wisdom from historical experience but also the concentrated reflection of theoretical innovation. It has both rich political significance and theoretical implications, being the latest achievement in localizing Marxism.

"Nine Pieces of Precious Experience" Peculiar to the Characteristics of Reform and Opening Up

General Secretary Xi Jinping's speech provided an in-depth summary of the historical experience of the splendid achievements over the past 40 years, namely the "Nine Pieces of Precious Experience". He pointed out,

> First, we must see that the Party exercises leadership over all work and keeps enhancing and improving its way of leadership. Second, we must adhere to a people-oriented approach and keep delivering on the aspirations of the people for a better life. Third, we must uphold Marxism

as our guiding ideology and explore theoretical innovations based on practice. Fourth, we must stay on the path of socialism with Chinese characteristics, and uphold and develop socialism with Chinese features. Fifth, we must improve and develop the system of socialism with Chinese characteristics to harness and enhance the advantages of our system. Sixth, we must continue to take development as the top priority and enhance our composite national strength. Seventh, we must stay committed to reform and opening-up and promote joint efforts to build a community with a shared future for mankind. Eighth, we must exercise full and rigorous governance over the Party to strengthen its capacity to innovate, power to unite, and energy to fight. Ninth, we must maintain the worldview and methodology of dialectical and historical materialism to strike a balance between reform, development and stability.[36]

The historical experience demonstrated in the past 40 years is of great practical significance for us to understand the historical inevitability of reform and opening up more deeply, grasp the laws of it more proactively, and shoulder the historical responsibility of comprehensively deepening reform more firmly.

Looking back on the past 40 years, from Comrade Deng Xiaoping guiding our Party to make the great decision of reform and opening up, to the 14th Party Congress establishing the goal of building the socialist market economy, to the Third Plenary Session of the 16th Party Congress emphasizing scientific development, to Comrade Xi Jinping's important speech at the gathering celebrating the 40th anniversary of reform and opening up, history shows that our Party has an increasingly deep and clear understanding of the laws of constructing socialism with Chinese characteristics. The theories of reform grow to be more extensive and sophisticated, and the thinking on reform had been maturing. Comrade Xi Jinping's speech at the gathering celebrating the 40th anniversary of reform and opening up has enriched our Party's theory of reform and opening up and provided the basic guidelines for comprehensively deepening reform in the new period. In the new era, we should deeply understand, comprehensively study, and consciously apply the spirit of Comrade Xi Jinping's important speech at the gathering celebrating the 40th anniversary of reform and opening up into the whole process of socialist modernization construction.

Notes

1 Central Literature Research Office of the Communist Party of China. *Selected Important Documents Since the 18th National Congress of CPC*: vol. 2. Beijing: Central Literature Publishing House, 2016, p. 41.
2 Central Literature Research Office of the Communist Party of China. *Jiang Zemin's Remarks on Socialism with Chinese Characteristics (Excerpts by Topics)*. Beijing: Central Literature Publishing House, 2002, p. 649.

3 Central Literature Research Office of the Communist Party of China. *Selected Important Documents Since the 16th National Congress of CPC*: vol. 2. Beijing: Central Literature Publishing House, 2005, p. 365.

4 Central Literature Research Office of the Communist Party of China. *Selected Important Documents Since the Reform and Opening Up*: vol. 2. Beijing: Central Literature Publishing House, 2008, p. 635.

5 Jiang Zemin. *Selected Works of Jiang Zemin*: vol. 3. Beijing: People's Publishing House, 2006, p. 294.

6 Jiang Zemin. *On Socialist Market Economy*. Beijing: Central Literature Publishing House, 2006, pp. 1–2.

7 Central Literature Research Office of the Communist Party of China. *Selected Important Documents Since the Reform and Opening Up*: vol. 2. Beijing: Central Literature Publishing House, 2008, p. 659.

8 Deng Xiaoping. *Selected Works of Deng Xiaoping*, vol. 2, 2nd ed. Beijing: People's Publishing House, 1994, p. 276.

9 Central Literature Research Office of the Communist Party of China. *Selected Important Documents Since the Reform and Opening Up*: vol. 1. Beijing: Central Literature Publishing House, 2008, p. 312.

10 Central Literature Research Office of the Communist Party of China. *Selected Important Documents Since the Reform and Opening Up*: vol. 2. Beijing: Central Literature Publishing House, 2008, p. 1245.

11 Central Literature Research Office of the Communist Party of China. *Selected Important Documents Since the 15th Party Congress*: vol. 2. Beijing: Central Literature Publishing House, 2001, p. 1206.

12 Central Literature Research Office of the Communist Party of China. *Selected Important Documents Since the Reform and Opening Up*: vol. 2. Beijing: Central Literature Publishing House, 2008, p. 659.

13 Deng Xiaoping. *Selected Works of Deng Xiaoping*: vol. 3. Beijing: People's Publishing House, 1993, p. 370.

14 Deng Xiaoping. *Selected Works of Deng Xiaoping*: vol. 3. Beijing: People's Publishing House, 1993, pp. 277–278.

15 Ibid., p. 378.

16 Jiang Zemin. *Selected Works of Jiang Zemin*: vol. 1. Beijing: People's Publishing House, 2006, p. 224.

17 Central Literature Research Office of the Communist Party of China. *Selected Important Documents Since the Reform and Opening Up*: vol. 2. Beijing: Central Literature Publishing House, 2008, p. 1183.

18 Xi Jinping. *The Governance of China*. Beijing: Foreign Languages Press, 2014, p. 36.

19 Xi Jinping. *The Governance of China*. Beijing: Foreign Languages Press, 2014, p. 36.

20 Xi Jinping. *The Governance of China*. Beijing: Foreign Languages Press, 2014, p. 36.

21 Ibid. p. 39.

22 Xi Jinping. *Speech at the First Session of the 12th National People's Congress*. Beijing: People's Publishing House, 2013, p. 3.

23 Xi Jinping. *Speech at the First Session of the 12th National People's Congress*. Beijing: People's Publishing House. 2013, p. 4.

24 Xi Jinping. *Speech at the First Session of the 12th National People's Congress*. Beijing: People's Publishing House. 2013, p. 4.

25 Xi Jinping. *Speech at the First Session of the 12th National People's Congress*. Beijing: People's Publishing House, 2013, p. 5.

26 Xi Jinping. *The Governance of China.* Beijing: Foreign Languages Press, 2014, p. 21.
27 Xi Jinping. *The Governance of China.* Beijing: Foreign Languages Press, 2014, p. 22.
28 Ibid., p. 71.
29 Xi Jinping. *The Governance of China.* Beijing: Foreign Languages Press, 2014, p. 23
30 Xi Jinping. *Speech at the Gathering Celebrating the 40th Anniversary of Reform and Opening up* (December 18, 2018). http://www.xinhuanet.com/2018-12/18/c_1123872025.htm.
31 Xi Jinping. *Speech at the Gathering Celebrating the 40th Anniversary of Reform and Opening up* (December 18, 2018). http://www.xinhuanet.com/2018-12/18/c_1123872025.htm.
32 Xi Jinping. *Speech at the Gathering Celebrating the 40th Anniversary of Reform and Opening up* (December 18, 2018). http://www.xinhuanet.com/2018-12/18/c_1123872025.htm.
33 Xi Jinping. *Speech at the Gathering Celebrating the 40th Anniversary of Reform and Opening up* (December 18, 2018). http://www.xinhuanet.com/2018-12/18/c_1123872025.htm.
34 Xi Jinping. *Speech at the Gathering Celebrating the 40th Anniversary of Reform and Opening up* (December 18, 2018). http://www.xinhuanet.com/2018-12/18/c_1123872025.htm.
35 Xi Jinping. *Speech at the Gathering Celebrating the 40th Anniversary of Reform and Opening up* (December 18, 2018). http://www.xinhuanet.com/2018-12/18/c_1123872025.htm.
36 Xi Jinping. *Speech at the Gathering Celebrating the 40th Anniversary of Reform and Opening up* (December 18, 2018). http://www.xinhuanet.com/2018-12/18/c_1123872025.htm.

4 Localize Marxism With Fine Traditional Chinese Culture

Bai Yang

The localization of Marxism in China includes not only the combination of Marxism with Chinese practice but also the integration of it with fine traditional Chinese culture. The realization and development of the localization of Marxism lie not only in our insistence on the combination of Marxism with the practice of revolution, construction, and reform in China but also in our emphasis on its adaptation in the field of culture and on deepening the localization of Marxism in China in its continuous integration with the fine traditional Chinese culture.

Fine Traditional Chinese Culture Provides the Conditions for Localizing Marxism

There are many reasons why Marxism, a German idea, triumphed in this ancient oriental nation which was relatively backward in economy, politics, and technology at that time. However, it is undeniable that the long-standing and profound Chinese culture has provided the necessary conditions for the occurrence and development of the localization of Marxism.

The Salient Features of Traditional Chinese Culture Make It Possible to Localize Marxism Culturally

The Chinese nation has a long history, with an uninterrupted civilization of more than 5,000 years, which nurtures a profound and sophisticated Chinese culture. From a diachronic perspective, Chinese culture has undergone many changes in regimes and developments through the times but has always remained coherent and uninterrupted, which is rarely seen among the cultural systems in the world today. From a synchronic perspective, Chinese culture contains the elements of the Han Chinese and many ethnic minorities. Though it endured many foreign cultural invasions, its nature never changed, providing the basic cultural genes for the integration and development of the Chinese nation. Chinese culture is a cohesive one with strong tolerance, cohesion, and the ability to inherit, which makes it possible to localize Marxism.

DOI: 10.4324/9781003356042-5

China, with its vast territory, diverse ethnic groups, and large population, has long been at the forefront of world culture in its long history of civilization, which can be attributed to the strong tolerance, cohesion, and the powerful ability to pass on of Chinese culture. The Chinese culture has been able to tolerate and actively absorb the advanced aspects of other cultures when multiple coexisting civilizations are impacting each other. While integrating foreign elements into the large Chinese system, Chinese culture manages to retain its own cultural core and continuously enrich specific cultural elements. This constant progress and improvement of the cohesive cultural development path further strengthen the Chinese nation's identification with its own culture, thus giving it a strong ability to pass on its culture. As a result, Chinese culture gains a steady vitality.[1]

This cohesive approach to cultural development determines that every time Chinese culture integrates foreign cultures, it does not simply copy them but puts an emphasis on localizing them. Whether it was the invasion of nomadic cultures or the spread of Buddhist culture, whether it was during the boom or the decline of a regime, this mode of cultural development of cohesion is carried on. It is for this reason that Chinese culture did not collapse under the impact of modern capitalist colonial expansion, but selected Marxism in the process of borrowing foreign cultures and testing them in practice, and blazed the trail of socialism with Chinese characteristics in the process of localizing Marxism. It can be said that without this inherited cohesive cultural development path, it is impossible to localize Marxism culturally. It is this outstanding feature of Chinese culture that allows the localization of Marxism.

The Value Orientation of Traditional Chinese Culture Provides the Cultural Impetus for the Localization of Marxism

The strong tolerance, cohesion, and ability to pass on peculiar to traditional Chinese culture provide the possibility for the localization of Marxism. However, further motivating factors are needed to support the choice of and belief in Marxism. China's specific practical needs play a decisive role in the occurrence and development of Marxism's localization, but if the value orientation of traditional Chinese culture is diametrically opposed to that of Marxism, the localization of Marxism will lack a critical cultural impetus. The reason why Marxism is widely spread and accepted in China and become the spiritual belief and pursuit of the people is that the value orientation of traditional Chinese culture has provided the driving force for it.

Since the early Qin Dynasty, traditional Chinese culture had a strong practical dimension. Driven by the reality of saving the nation from subjugation and destruction, this practical dimension grew increasingly salient in early modern times. In the late 19th and early 20th centuries, when faced with many different theories and doctrines, the learned people of the Chinese nation decided upon Marxism, which aimed to transform the world and was closely related to the prevailing cultural values of patriotism and preserving the nation and the race among intellectuals at that time. The faith in Marxism of the early Chinese Marxists, including Li Dazhao, Mao Zedong, Zhou Enlai, and Deng Zhongxia, originated from the value of saving the Chinese nation from distress and fighting for the rise of China. If the value orientation of traditional Chinese culture resembles that of the Buddhist culture, which focuses on spiritual cultivation and transcendence of the self, then Chinese intellectuals would not feel the mission of saving the country from peril and hardship, and would not have the pursuit of changing reality and transforming China. In this way, Marxism, a powerful tool for transforming the world, would not be in line with the cultural psychology and value orientation of the Chinese nation, and would not have been widely circulated or localized in China. Therefore, it can be said that the value orientation of traditional Chinese culture determines the intention of our choice of Marxism, providing the motivation for its localization.

The Fine Content of Traditional Chinese Culture Provides the Cultural Soil for the Localization of Marxism

Traditional Chinese culture involves the comprehensive way of life and thinking of the Chinese nation, which offers the basic value scale to the established society and provides the broadest cultural identity for people. The excellent content of traditional Chinese culture is not the cultural concepts, attitudes, and orientations of a few people, but the cultural genes shared by the majority of the Chinese nation, which act as the soul and blood of the nation and the spiritual homeland of the people. If any new ideology or culture is to be accepted and developed by the people of a certain nation or region, it must be combined with their social life and cultural traditions, which is a basic law for the spread of human thinking. The fact that Marxism was quickly accepted by the early Chinese Marxists and eventually localized and popularized is due to, from the perspective of culture, the inherent compatibility or similarity between Marxism and the excellent tradition of Chinese culture. As Zhang Dainian and Cheng Yishan said,

> The Chinese people's acceptance of Marxism is closely related to the traditional Chinese culture, which has long nourished materialism, atheism, dialectics, democracy, humanism, historical materialism, and the ideal of a perfect society, so that Marxism can easily take root in Chinese soil.[2]

Traditional Chinese culture glitters the light of simple materialism, which provides the soil for the adaption of the Marxist materialistic view of history. The materialistic view of history is the core achievement of Marxist philosophy and an important contribution to human philosophical thought, whose creation has triggered a great change in the view of social history and marked the birth of Marxist philosophy. The inherent ideological elements of the materialist historical view of traditional Chinese culture are undoubtedly very important for the localization of Marxism. In terms of social ideals, the ancient Chinese philosophers attacked the assumption that the world is without a proper way and pursued a world with the Way, viewing the Way as a sign of perfection, harmony, and order. In the chapter "Ceremonial Usages" of the Confucian classic *The Book of Rites*, it is recorded that this pursuit is specified in the social ideal of the Great Union, where "a public and common spirit ruled all under the sky",

> men did not love their parents only, nor treat as children only their own sons. A competent provision was secured for the aged till their death, employment for the able-bodied, and the means of growing up to the young. They showed kindness and compassion to widows, orphans, childless men, and those who were disabled by disease, so that they were all sufficiently maintained. Males had their proper work, and females had their homes. They accumulated articles of value, disliking that they should be thrown away upon the ground, but not wishing to keep them for their own gratification. They labored with their strength, disliking that it should not be exerted, but not exerting it only with a view to their own advantage.
>
> (trans. James Legge)

With regard to the concept of social development, Kang Youwei, a scholar of the Qing Dynasty, proposed in his book *The Book of Great Union* that human history must develop in three stages, namely, Chaos (*juluan*), Prosperity (*shengping*), and Great Peace (*taiping*). Although these ideas are a utopian view of society based on small-scale peasant production, which is fundamentally different from the communist ideal, they do have similarities. In addition, in terms of the relationship between material and spiritual life, there are a lot of ancient Chinese ideas that contain elements of the materialistic view of history, for example, "One can only know etiquette and manners with a full granary and sufficient food and clothing" (from *Guanzi*),

> In the hungry years, people do not even entertain their youngest brother. During the good year, people even receive unfamiliar guests. It is not because people alienate their family members and care about unfamiliar guests. It is the result of the abundance or deficiency of food
>
> (from *Hanfeizi*)

Although these remarks are quite far from the complete theory of the materialistic view of history, they identify the decisive role of material conditions in social development to a certain extent and undoubtedly reflect the glittering of the materialistic view of history. Here are some remarks familiar to Chinese people. For example, "Do not worry about scarcity, but worry about inequality. Do not worry about poverty, but worry about instability", "The world will be in order if people love each other. If they hate each other, the world will be in chaos", "Overworked are the people and happiness shall they enjoy", "People are the foundation of the state. When the foundation is consolidated, the state will be in peace", "Nothing is more valuable than people in the universe", etc. These opinions have many similarities with the Marxist materialistic view of history. Although these remarks in traditional Chinese culture are somewhat idealistic and subjective, these ideologies have, to a certain extent, lowered the cognitive barriers to the Chinese people's acceptance of the materialistic view of history and laid the psychological foundation for their recognition of Marxism.

The simple dialectics in traditional Chinese culture provided the soil for the localization of Marxist dialectics. The tradition of dialectics in Chinese culture began in the pre-Qin era, with Confucius calling it "discerning confusion", Lao Tzu calling it "observing time and again", Zhuang Tzu calling it "repetitive disorderliness", *The Book of Changes* calling it "transformation", and Xun Tzu calling it "removing the block", which all contained the flavor of dialectics.[3] The basic elements of their dialectical thinking include the holistic view reflected in the idea of "the unity of heaven and man", the concept of development represented in "the infinite birth and rebirth of life", "heaven in its motion gives the idea of strength, and the noble man, in accordance with this, nerves himself to ceaseless activity", and "the operation of heaven and earth renews every day", the view of the unity of opposites seen in "*yin* and *yang* is called the Way" and "the complementary relationship between existence and non-existence, between difficulty and simplicity, between length and shortness, and between height and depth". The theory of the universe's birth, the Five Elements (metal, wood, water, fire, and earth) and *yin* and *yang*, and the unity of opposites constitute the backbone of ancient dialectical thinking.[4] The tradition of dialectics in Chinese culture has been passed down through the Qin Dynasty, the Song Dynasty, the Ming Dynasty, and then the late Qing Dynasty. Although it was prevented from full development by feudal dictatorship, the tradition was still inherited through numerous twists and turns. In the long process of development, the Chinese dialectics presented very unique national characteristics. First of all, Chinese dialectics does not focus on natural matters and does not exist abstractly and independently but concentrates on social issues and is demonstrated in the form of political and ethical thoughts. On the one hand, this feature restricts the systematization of Chinese dialectics and prevents it from being a science. However, on the other hand, Chinese dialectics is thus equipped with practical significance, which is ready to be applied by the mass of Chinese people, resulting in a more general way of thinking and laying the foundation for the localization and popularization of Marxism, especially Marxist dialectics. Second, Chinese dialectics involves the basic law of the unity of the opposites, which is one of the core principles of Marxist dialectics. The ancient concepts of "reverse", "subdue", "confront", "fight", "revenge", "divide", etc. are very similar to what we call the confrontation of contradictions today. The old notions of "oneness", "harmony", "peace", "birth", "completion", etc. are comparable to what we call identity in contradictions. The worldviews of "division and union", "duality into oneness", and "be opposite yet complementary" resemble our description of the confronting yet identical relationship between contradictions.[5] These concepts and categories describing the unity of opposites play a direct role in promoting our acceptance of its counterpart in Marxist dialectics. In addition, Chinese dialectics emphasizes a worldview that sees matters in connections and from the perspective of development, and grasps issues in a holistic and systematic way, which is very consistent with the Marxist dialectical approach to understanding and solving problems. Of course, dialectical thinking in traditional culture is simple and spontaneous, which does not appear in a rigorous scientific form. However, this dialectical spirit has a long history and is deeply rooted in people's hearts, which provides a fertile intellectual soil for us to accept Marxist dialectics and use it to reform the original one.

There are many other similarities between traditional Chinese culture and Marxism. For example, between the traditional Chinese culture's advocacy of practice (*gongxing*) and the Marxist doctrine of practice, between the emphasis on "the rise and fall of the nation is the concern of every citizen" and the Marxist aim of transforming the world, between the people-oriented political pursuit reflected in the sayings "the people can carry the boat and also overturn it" and "the people are more valuable than the sovereign" and the Marxist idea of serving the people. We can clearly see the compatibility between traditional Chinese culture and Marxism in these connections. Therefore, the triumph of Marxism in China is not accidental, because the excellent content of traditional Chinese culture allows the occurrence and development of the localization of Marxism, and the profound traditional Chinese culture provides fertile soil for its blossoming.

The National Character of Traditional Chinese Culture Provides the Cultural Style for the Localization of Marxism

The national character of traditional Chinese culture is reflected not only in its cultural content but also in the form of culture. The form and content of a mature and long-standing national culture are inseparable as body and soul. Due to the different economic, political, cultural, and social backgrounds, there does not exist a sole correct theoretical form and cultural style for Marxism. In the process of localizing Marxism, the excellent content of traditional Chinese culture supplies the soil, while the national character offers a Chinese style and manner.

Marxism, as a Western theoretical form that originated in Europe and developed in Russia, has a distinctive Western style in its original form of expression. The success or failure of Marxism's localization, popularization, and modernization depends on whether its expression can be transformed into a national form that the Chinese people are pleased to accept. As the mainstream culture that has been nourishing the Chinese nation for thousands of years, traditional Chinese culture is familiar and popular to the masses, and its way of thinking and expression has long been immersed in their minds. Therefore, the process of localizing Marxism requires that Marxism must be combined with traditional Chinese culture, which can be achieved by means of a certain national form. Only by embedding a cultural style in line with the characteristics of Chinese national culture into Marxism can it have a stronger leading power and appeal.

In localizing Marxism, the members of the Communist Party of China combined Marxism with traditional Chinese culture, inherited and promoted the national form, and thus created a unique cultural style. Mao Zedong Thought, as an excellent example of the localization of Marxism, created a new form of Marxism with the style of traditional Chinese culture, transforming Marxism from a European format to a Chinese one, which is a high-level development of the new national, scientific, and popular culture created by the CPC. During the construction of socialism with Chinese characteristics, generations of CPC members, taking into account the specific characteristics of Chinese society, inherited and carried forward the traditional Chinese culture, and further promoted the historical process of localizing Marxism. As a result, the Chinese characteristics in the crystallization of Marxist ideas and theoretical views are growing stronger, and the theoretical system of socialism with Chinese characteristics is thus developed and established. The remarkable achievements of the localization of Marxism are closely related to the inheritance and development of the national form of traditional Chinese culture, which has given Marxism a unique national style, thus contributing to the immense influence and popularity of Chinese Marxism.

Combining With Fine Traditional Chinese Culture, the Localization of Marxism Has Reaped Considerable Achievements

Since the beginning of the 20th century when Marxism began to spread in China, Marxism has initiated its localization. Throughout this process, Chinese Marxists have always insisted on combining Marxism with China's concrete reality. On the basis of adhering to the guiding position of Marxist theory, they inherited and carried forward the positive elements of traditional Chinese culture and created Marxist theoretical achievements with Chinese style and manners, thus pushing forward the pace of localizing Marxism.

Creating a Model of Localized Marxism by Combining It With Fine Traditional Chinese Culture

The CPC members, in the process of localizing Marxism, have always been attaching importance to inheriting the excellent traditions of national culture. The earliest Chinese Marxists, such as Li Dazhao and Chen Duxiu, all studied and explored the approach to combining Marxism with Chinese culture while studying and spreading Marxism. Throughout the history of localizing Marxism, Comrade Mao Zedong, the major founder of the Communist Party of China, the Chinese People's Liberation Army, and the People's Republic of China, and the great leader of the Chinese people of all ethnic groups, genuinely insisted on the close integration of Marxism with traditional Chinese culture, creating an excellent example of Marxism's localization, i.e., Mao Zedong Thought, which transformed Marxism from European to Chinese form and realized the first historical leap of localizing Marxism.

As we all know, traditional Chinese culture always occupied an important position in Mao's upbringing, education, and knowledge structure, which deeply influenced his manner, values, and way of thinking. Whether in the early period of the Communist Party of China, in the construction of revolutionary bases, or in the War of Resistance against Japanese Aggression and the Liberation War, Mao always attached importance to the study of Chinese history and culture. After the founding of the PRC, apart from reading Marxist-Leninist works, Mao also spent a lot of time reading books concerning Chinese culture. Among Mao's representative works, there are numerous allusions to the ancient Chinese texts. According to statistics, the four volumes of *Selected Works of Mao Zedong* contain more than 30 quotes from *The Commentary of Zuo*, 20 to 30 quotes from *The Analects*, *Mencius*, *The Historical Records*, *Book of Han*, and *Philosophical Writings of Zhu Xi*, and numerous other references to *The Great Learning*, *Doctrine of the Mean*, *Strategies of the Warring States*, *Book of Later Han*, *Records of the Three Kingdoms*, *The Art of War*, *Book of Poetry*, *Book of Jin*, *Book of Documents*, *Lao Tzu*, *Book of Changes*, *Discourses of the States*, etc.[6] Mao's familiarity and mastery of traditional Chinese culture are evident. In the process of studying and applying Marxism-Leninism to analyze and solve China's problems, he never departed from the Chinese cultural context. Instead, he always attached importance to the inheritance and development of national styles in proposing his thinking, thus creating a new style for the localization of Marxism. Comrade Mao Zedong was a great Marxist who insisted on studying and implementing Marxism-Leninism, but it should also be recognized that he was also the inheritor and promoter of the traditional culture and excellent traditions of the Chinese nation. A great deal of his thinking came directly from the traditional culture of the Chinese nation. For example, in military thinking, Mao drew on the useful ideas in ancient texts such as *The Art of War*, *The Commentary of Zuo*, *Records of the Three Kingdoms*, and even *Heroes of the Marshes* (a Chinese popular fiction), and created many outstanding strategic ideas and tactical policies such as "do not rush to the forefront", "retreat when necessary", "reciprocal treatment", armed struggle of workers and peasants, guerilla war, etc. In the three representative documents, "The Strategic Problems of Chinese Revolutionary War", "The Strategic Problems of Anti-Japanese Guerrilla War" and "On the Protracted War", we can clearly see how deeply Mao's military thought was influenced by ancient Chinese military culture. Another example is that the idea of independence, which is one of the living souls of Mao Zedong Thought, does not come directly from Marxism-Leninism or the thought of the Communist International at that time, but from the national cultural tradition and spirit of the Chinese nation of self-improvement and self-reliance. It can be said that without the national spirit of independence, the CPC could not have survived and the Chinese nation would not have achieved the great victory of the Chinese revolution and construction, let alone the localization of Marxism.

Mao Zedong Thought is a special manifestation of Marxism in China, which is also nourished by Chinese culture, being the crystallization of the excellent culture of the Chinese nation, and the supreme expression and the best theoretical overview of Chinese national wisdom. Mao Zedong Thought is the excellent results achieved in localizing Marxism by combining it with Chinese culture.

Promoting the Development of Marxism in China by Inheriting Excellent Cultural Traditions

The theoretical system of socialism with Chinese characteristics, which is based on Deng Xiaoping Theory, the important thought of "Three Represents" and the Scientific Outlook on Development, inherits the excellent tradition of the Communist Party of China, adheres to the policy of critical inheritance and innovative development of traditional Chinese culture, and promotes the excellent traditional culture of the Chinese nation in combining it with the concrete reality of China, which is a new development of the localization of Marxism in the important historical period of reform and opening up.

In the new period of socialist modernization, as the chief engineer of reform and opening up, Deng Xiaoping paid special attention to the combination of Marxism and the specific reality of China, actively advocated the inheritance of the excellent traditional culture of the nation, and endowed Marxism with distinctive Chinese characteristics. Although Deng did not quote much from traditional Chinese texts in his speeches and drafts, the profound fine traditional Chinese culture glitters in the specific contents of Deng Xiaoping Theory. As for the proposal of "Chinese characteristics", Deng grasped the core requirement of localizing Marxism in the practice of socialist construction, namely the need to adhere to the combination of

Marxism and Chinese reality, where the reality includes not only the actual situation of China's reform practice but also that of Chinese history and culture. Deng proposed the construction of socialism with Chinese characteristics, which is emphasizing absorbing and developing the excellent part of the national culture on the basis of grasping China's reality so that China's socialist modernization is effective with Chinese style. In the 1980s, Deng proposed to achieve the goal of a "moderately prosperous" (*xiaokang*) society by the end of the 20th century. The word *xiaokang* originated from the ancient Chinese text *The Book of Rites*, which refers to a social development one level lower than the Great Harmony, in which people's life is in a more relaxed condition between subsistence and affluence. Deng used applied this old concept to the present, and vividly illustrated the milestones of China's modernization with the image of a moderately prosperous society, which greatly mobilized the whole nation to build socialism with Chinese characteristics. Like Mao Zedong Thought, Deng Xiaoping Theory also carries strong national cultural characteristics and sets an example for the localization of Marxism.

From the late 1990s to the convening of the 16th Party Congress, the third generation of the Party's central leadership, with Comrade Jiang Zemin at its core, accurately grasped the new situation and new trends in domestic and international social development and put forward the important thought of "Three Represents", which summarized the fundamental direction, guidelines, and basis for all the work of our Party. The Three Represents entails that the CPC should always represent the development requirements of China's advanced productive forces, always represent the direction of China's advanced culture, and always represent the fundamental interests of the broadest number of Chinese people. Among them, the second item means that the Party's theories, lines, programs, guidelines, policies, and work must strive to reflect the requirements of developing a modern, world-oriented, future-oriented, national, scientific, and popular socialist culture, promoting the continuous improvement of the thinking and moral quality as well as the scientific and cultural quality of the whole nation and providing spiritual impetus and intellectual support for China's economic development and social progress. The specific requirements put forward by the "Three Represents" in the construction of socialist culture are not only the inheritance of Mao Zedong's new democratic cultural thought but also have distinctive characteristics of the times. In the process of modernization, cultural construction cannot be separated from the foundation of national culture. The more national a culture is, the more popular it would be. Only a distinct national character can align a culture with national needs and characteristics, and only then can it be scientific. Traditional Chinese culture is the source and foundation of advanced culture, and advanced culture is the inheritance and transcendence of fine traditional Chinese culture. Meanwhile, in the process of promoting the ideological and moral quality and scientific and cultural quality of the whole nation, the Three Represents proposes to vigorously carry forward the national spirit, emphasizing that the national spirit is the spiritual support for the survival and development of a nation. The national spirit of the Chinese nation includes the fine tradition and the spirit of the times formed by the CPC during its long-term revolution, construction, and reform and also the national spirit on which the survival and development of the Chinese nation have been depending for 5,000 years, such as patriotism, industriousness, bravery, and self-reliance. Therefore, we believe that the Three Represents important thought is a further development of the theory of socialism with Chinese characteristics, which inherits and carries forward the excellent cultural traditions of the Chinese nation on the basis of adhering to the guiding position of Marxism.

Since the 16th Party Congress, the Party Central Committee with Comrade Hu Jintao as the general secretary grasped the new issues and contradictions facing our country's development based on the basic national conditions of China's primary stage of socialism, used the Marxism in development to guide the new practice, and put forward the important strategic thought of implementing the Scientific Outlook on Development, which was a new leap in the localization of Marxism. In the Scientific Outlook on Development, its principle is development, its core is people-orientation, its basic requirement is comprehensive, coordinated, and sustainable development, and its fundamental approach is to be holistic and balanced. In-depth implementation of the Scientific Outlook on Development requires us to proactively build a harmonious socialist society, continue to deepen reform and opening up, and effectively strengthen and improve the Party's construction. To understand the scientific meaning of the Scientific Outlook on Development, we must acknowledge that it is very closely related to traditional Chinese culture. Traditional Chinese culture contains much thinking in people-orientation, advocating the political value of "the people are more important than the ruler" and "people are the foundation of the state. When the foundation is consolidated, the state will be in peace". The Scientific Outlook on Development emphasizes people-orientation, which reflects the inheritance and promotion of traditional Chinese thinking. Considering the numerous ideas on "harmony" in Chinese history, we can even argue that the goal and ideal pursuit of Chinese culture is harmony, which can be summarized as the worldview of the unity of heaven and human, the dialectics of harmony generating vitality, the value of harmony in diversity, and the stress on harmony as the basis for interpersonal relationships. "Harmony" is the inherent spirit and distinctive feature of Chinese culture,[7] so the proposal of building a socialist harmonious society is based on the correct understanding and inheritance of Chinese cultural traditions, which endowed the Party's Marxist theoretical views and policy measures with a more robust Chinese style.

From Deng Xiaoping Theory to the Three Represents important thought, and then to the Scientific Outlook on Development, the Party has been constantly exploring and summarizing experience in the practice of socialist construction, establishing the theoretical system of socialism with Chinese characteristics and further combining Marxism with the fine traditional Chinese culture, which opened up a broader development prospect for the cause of socialism with Chinese characteristics.

Promoting the Fine Traditional Chinese Culture and Creating a New Prospect of Localizing Marxism

Since the 18th Party Congress, the Party Central Committee with Comrade Xi Jinping as its core has adhered to Deng Xiaoping Theory, the important thought of the "Three Represents" and the Scientific Outlook on Development as its guidance. They adhere to and develop socialism with Chinese characteristics, and put forward many new ideas, new viewpoints, and new requirements under the new historical conditions, enriching and developing the Party's scientific theory. It finally gives birth to Xi Jinping Thought on Socialism with Chinese Characteristics for a New Era, the latest achievement of localizing Marxism, which created a new situation of localizing Marxism. Xi Jinping Thought on Socialism with Chinese Characteristics for a New Era consists of a series of theoretical, practical, and strategic innovations, which are rich in content and cover a wide range of topics. This theoretical system contains important instructions on adhering to and developing socialism with Chinese characteristics, as well as in-depth explanations on achieving the great rejuvenation of the Chinese nation. Specific instructions on deepening reform and promoting scientific development are provided, so are detailed discussions on the confidence in our path, theory, system, and culture. Strategic guidance on foreign policy is seen, so are strict requirements on Party building. Ideological work is emphasized, so are core socialist values. This theoretical system profoundly answers a series of major theoretical and practical questions about the development of the Party and the country under new historical conditions. It is a great theoretical system formed by combining the basic principles of Marxism with the actual development of Chinese society and the splendid culture of Chinese civilization for 5,000 years.

Cultural confidence is an important issue in Xi Jinping Thought on Socialism with Chinese Characteristics in the New Era. Xi attaches great importance to cultural confidence, emphasizing that cultural confidence is a more basic, broader, and deeper confidence among the "four confidences", and also a more basic, deeper, and more lasting power, which are profound elaborations on cultural confidence from the overall situation of the socialist cause with Chinese characteristics. Xi pointed out that "history and reality have shown that a nation that abandoned or betrayed its own history and culture was not only unlikely to develop itself but also likely to stage a historical tragedy".[8] The excellent traditional culture of the Chinese nation has preserved our deepest spiritual pursuit, representing the most unique spiritual identity of the Chinese nation, which is the cultural root of cultural confidence in the new era. "Fine traditional Chinese culture is our deepest cultural soft power and the fertile cultural ground where socialism with Chinese characteristics is rooted".[9] Xi pointed out that to achieve the Two Centenary Goals and to realize the Chinese Dream of the great rejuvenation of the Chinese nation, it is necessary to make full use of the great wisdom accumulated by the Chinese nation for thousands of years. Xi vigorously promotes the fine traditional Chinese culture with a view to consolidating confidence and achieving the creative transformation and innovative development of Chinese culture. In other words, it is to "create our new situation with the principles of the ancients".

The importance attached to traditional Chinese culture by the leadership of the CPC Central Committee with Comrade Xi Jinping at its core is also highlighted in the work of cultivating and promoting core socialist values. During the collective study of the Political Bureau of the CPC Central Committee on the cultivation and promotion of core socialist values and the promotion of traditional Chinese virtues, Xi spoke highly of the fine traditional Chinese culture. He said,

> the profound and sophisticated fine traditional Chinese culture is the foundation for us to stand firmly in the midst of the world's intense cultural exchanges. The Chinese culture has a long history, which preserves the deepest spiritual pursuit of the Chinese nation and represents our unique spiritual identity, providing rich nutrients for the growth and development of the Chinese nation."[10]

Xi clearly put forward the correct attitude and approach to traditional culture and traditional virtues that we should uphold. He said,

> By remembering the past can we open up the future. Good inheritance facilitates better innovation. Facing the history and culture, especially the values and moral norms passed down by the ancestors, we should insist on the principle of making the past serve our present-day needs, bringing forth the new through the old, treating it with discrimination, and inheriting it selectively. We should try to use all the spiritual wealth created by the Chinese nation to educate and cultivate people.[11]
>
> We should earnestly draw on the essence of the fine traditional Chinese culture on thinking and morality, vigorously promote the national spirit with patriotism as its core and the spirit of the times with reform and innovation as its core, and excavate and expound the contemporary values of the excellent traditional Chinese pursuit of benevolence, people-orientation, integrity, justice, harmony, and a better society, so that the fine traditional Chinese culture can be an important source that nurtures core socialist values. We should deal with the relationship between inheritance and creative development well, focusing on creative transformation and innovative development.[12]

We must promote core socialist values by drawing on the rich nutrition from the fine traditional Chinese culture, or it will lose its vitality and influence. The core socialist values of "prosperity, democracy, civility, harmony, freedom, equality, justice, rule of law, patriotism, dedication, integrity, and friendship" reflect the genes of China's excellent traditional culture and the ideals and beliefs established by the Chinese people through all the hardships they have gone through since the modern times. Therefore, we should firmly establish core socialist values throughout the society and enable the Chinese nation to stand more confidently with greater strength in the world.

Fine traditional Chinese culture is a significant source of Xi's ideas on the governance of China. He emphasized the importance of traditional culture on many occasions, in the form of signature articles and keynote speeches, which were always full of elements of fine traditional Chinese culture. The localization of Marxism makes new achievements under the new conditions of the times while inheriting and promoting fine traditional Chinese culture. Practice proved that to promote the further development of the localization of Marxism, it is necessary to inherit and carry forward the fine traditional Chinese culture, and fully utilize the great wisdom accumulated by the Chinese nation for thousands of years, so as to realize the creative transformation and innovative development of Chinese culture, and help achieve the Two Centenary Goals.

Challenges and Opportunities of Localizing Marxism in the Current Ideological and Cultural Context

How to Face the Diversified Values and Hold on to Marxism as Our Ideological Position in China?

Whenever history enters a period of great transition, the conflict of values will be relatively prominent with the complication of social problems. At present, China's society is in a critical period of system transition and social transformation. Many serious problems in social development exist while great progress is made. In the field of ideology and culture, the diversification of values, loss of faith, and moral misconduct are major issues. In the development of market economy, the diversification of economic components, social organizations, material benefits, employment patterns, distribution methods, and lifestyles result in the diversification of people's values and ways of thinking. At the same time, China's traditional culture can no longer play as strong a role as before in guiding values in the face of a constantly developing and changing social environment, while the new value system supporting people's spiritual world has not matured. In such a social reality with diversified values, if the core values, ideological beliefs, and moral norms recognized by the masses are absent, the development of the society will be uncertain and dangerous. In such a context, the theoretical research on Chinese Marxism has long lacked sufficient scientific guidance for the domestic reality and sufficient understanding of the needs of the people, resulting in the fact that the theoretical development of Chinese Marxism fails to make timely and effective responses to the reality and that the cultural achievements of Chinese Marxism fail to catch up with the times and influence the common people. In other words, it does not function effectively enough to cultivate and guide people's values.

Since the 18th Party Congress, our Party has vigorously promoted the construction of core socialist values, laying emphasis on inheriting and carrying forward the fine traditional Chinese culture and virtues, carrying out education campaigns on core socialist values, and actively guiding people to respect and abide by moral norms, which are positive responses to the real problems in China's ideological and cultural context. Only when the core socialist values become the mainstream value orientation of our society, the guiding position of Chinese Marxism can be maintained and developed to further facilitate the steady progress of the great practice of socialism with Chinese characteristics.

How to Deal With the Relationship Between Chinese Culture, Western Culture, and Marxism and Realize the Comprehensive Innovation in Localizing Marxism?

After decades of practical summary and theoretical research, academia has a relatively clear conclusion on the direction of the development of Marxist localization. Wholesale Westernization is not acceptable, nor the conservative approach of reviving Confucianism should be adopted. A comprehensive and innovative approach should be taken to develop Chinese Marxism. The theory of comprehensive innovation advocates the idea of "applying the past to the present, the foreign elements to the Chinese context, critical inheritance, and comprehensive innovation", and believes that

> the classical traditional Chinese culture should be used as a maternal culture with a long history, the modern Western culture as an exotic culture to stimulate modernization, and the socialist culture under the guidance of Marxism as a mainstream culture with its leading role.[13]

Under the guidance of Marxism, the theory proposes to draw on the essence of Chinese and Western cultures and create a new type of socialist culture with Chinese characteristics.

The key to realizing the comprehensive innovation of Marxism in China lies in how to correctly handle the relationship between Chinese culture, Western culture, and Marxism. First of all, we believe that Chinese culture is the inexhaustible driving power of the Chinese nation to survive and unite. We should comprehensively and objectively understand and evaluate the traditional culture of the Chinese nation, take the essence and remove the dross, and make it compatible with the construction of contemporary socialism with Chinese characteristics. The key questions here are two: first, what are the criteria for judging the essence and the dross; second, how to make traditional culture compatible with modern civilization and play the role of guidance for practical life. Besides, Western culture is a special product of the particular historical environment and cultural background of Western society, which played a great role in the process of modernization of Western society. In dealing with Western culture, we often propose to learn from it critically, but what are the standards for our judgment? How can we avoid the negative influence of Western culture and maintain the independence of cultural development in the process of learning from it? Finally, when it comes to Marxism, as the guiding ideology of the construction of socialism with Chinese characteristics, how can it draw nutrients from the soil of traditional Chinese culture, while absorbing the beneficial supplements of Western culture? How can Marxist theory play a guiding role in the process of localizing Marxism? The direction of dealing with the relationship between Chinese culture, Western culture, and Marxism has already been determined, but specific principles, methods, and practical measures need to be further clarified. Only by actively responding to these fundamental questions and challenges can the comprehensive innovation of Chinese Marxism be realized.

How to Meet the Challenges From the New Media and Enhance the Say of Marxism in China?

With the reform and opening up and the development of mass media, multiple ideologies and ideas are colliding with each other and constantly impacting people's minds. The battle of different ideas for having a greater say has intensified. In the 21st century, the popularity of Internet media increases significantly, and cultural industries featuring film and drama embrace unprecedented development. However, at the same time, the Internet and cultural environment in China have not yet developed into a state where order and freedom can coexist, and where all people can consciously abide by the law under the regulation of law. Information true or false abounds on the Internet with all sorts of voices in conflict. Utilizing the advanced technology of media, Western societies have been spreading Western thinking and culture, diluting the importance of ideology, and clamoring that Marxism is out of date. The individualism, money-worshiping, and hedonism promulgated by American blockbusters, Japanese animation, and Korean entertainment programs are rife and rampant. Meanwhile, as the reform enters the hard stage, special interest groups are taking advantage of their dominant position in the new media platform to maintain their own interests and control the discourse, excluding the disadvantaged groups in the distribution of benefits and shaping public opinion, which further intensifies the underlying turbulence of social ideology.

Against such context, channels and forms for spreading the theoretical achievements of Chinese Marxism have not been expanded or enriched. Marxism is still mainly disseminated and propagated through official channels in official languages. At the same time, traditional media (e.g., newspapers, periodicals, radio, and television) have not been able to explain the profound achievements of Chinese Marxism in simple language and in a way welcomed by the people. Therefore, it is at the risk of losing its say and being marginalized. The lack of experience in the use of new media greatly compresses the space for Marxist discourse, so its appeal and power of Marxist fade to a certain extent. However, as we often believe, opportunities go along with challenges, and where there are crises, there is also a way out. In the process of localizing Marxism, on the one hand, we must continue to regulate the cultural order and Internet environment; on the other hand, we must actively respond to the challenges from the media in the new environment, to explore the possibilities of new media, to enrich the channels and forms of disseminating Chinese Marxism, and to take the initiative in the battle for more say, so as to bring into play the positive energy of fostering correct ideas and guiding public opinion.

Further Deepen the Combination of Marxism and Fine Traditional Chinese Culture

The localization of Marxism must be rooted in the soil of Chinese culture, and the construction of socialism with Chinese characteristics can only be realized through the combination with the fine traditional culture of the Chinese nation. From the perspective of the development of socialism with Chinese characteristics and deepening the localization of Marxism, we must always adhere to the correct guidance of Marxism, establish a high degree of cultural awareness and cultural confidence, correctly understand, inherit, and promote the fine traditional culture of the Chinese nation. In today's particular national conditions, while deepening the localization of Marxism by combining it with the fine traditional culture of the Chinese nation, we should pay attention to the specific attitude and method of treating traditional culture and correctly deal with its relationship with Western modern civilization. Taking comprehensive innovation as the core, we should constantly meet the practical needs of China's current social development and always aim to achieve the great rejuvenation of the Chinese nation.

To Deepen the Localization of Marxism by Combining It With Chinese Culture, We Should Adopt a Correct Attitude and Approach to Traditional Chinese Culture

Marxism never advocates the severance of tradition, and it is itself born and developed on the basis of the critical inheritance of excellent human thought and culture. From this point of view, one of the criteria for judging whether a country or a political party adheres to Marxism is how it treats history and traditional culture. Chinese Marxists have always insisted on inheriting traditional culture in the process of localizing Marxism. In their long-term revolutionary, construction, and reform practices, they gained a deeper understanding of the value, status, and role of traditional Chinese culture and accumulated richer experience in how to inherit and carry forward fine traditional culture. The report of the 17th Party Congress emphasized that we should have a comprehensive understanding of the traditional culture of our motherland, take its essence and remove the dross, adapt it to contemporary society and modern civilization, and maintain its national character while making it catch up with the times. The report of the 18th Party Congress further pointed out that culture is the legacy of the nation and the spiritual home of the people. Building a prosperous nation with a blooming socialist culture entails an excellent inheritance system of traditional culture in order to promote the fine traditional Chinese culture.

The major content of traditional Chinese culture, which was formed during the feudal society, has played a very important role in maintaining the stability and development of that society. In order to deepen the localization of Marxism, we must use Marxist positions, views, and methods to analyze and evaluate Chinese culture scientifically. We shall notice the incompatibilities between traditional Chinese culture and China's modernization and get alert to the negative and corrupt elements of traditional culture that may have adverse effects on socialist construction. Meanwhile, we must inherit and promote the essence of traditional culture and push forward the sustainable development of national culture. We should use Marxism as a surgeon to perform "surgery" on traditional Chinese culture, removing the falsehoods and the dross, based on whether it is conducive to the construction of socialism with Chinese characteristics and the great rejuvenation of the Chinese nation, with a view to the healthy development of traditional culture. Critical inheritance of traditional culture under the guidance of Marxism will not damage the value and role of traditional Chinese culture. On the contrary, it is the only way for traditional Chinese culture to gain a foothold and play a positive role in the construction of modernization.

To Deepen the Localization of Marxism by Combining it With Fine Traditional Chinese Culture, We Should Proactively Absorb the Outstanding Achievements of Other Modern Civilization

In the process of localizing Marxism, we should not only fully explore and apply the essence of traditional culture but also proactively absorb the excellent achievements of modern civilization, treat foreign culture with an open mind and scientific attitude, and coexist peacefully and develop together with other outstanding civilizations in a culturally diversified world. As General Secretary Xi Jinping pointed out when reviewing and summarizing the historical experience of reform and opening up, our cause is about opening up and learning from the world, and we should neither belittle ourselves nor boast of ourselves wildly. Instead, we should pay more attention to learning and absorbing the excellent achievements of civilization created by people all over the world, studying from each other and drawing on each other's merits. Only by fostering the ability to absorb and accommodate on the basis of cultural awareness can Chinese Marxism continue to develop in the historical stage of interaction of a variety of civilizations.

Localizing Marxism is fundamentally different from the narrow nationalism. Marxism always attaches importance to learning and borrowing from different national cultures, and it is not the Marxist attitude to reject or copy the results of other nationalities without analysis. Localizing Marxism implies the integration of Marxism with Chinese national culture, but it does not mean negligence of other cultures. On the contrary, in order to promote the development of the modernization of Chinese society, Chinese Marxism has always adhered to the policy of facing modernization, the world, and the future, understanding and respecting other cultures, and fully absorbing the best achievements of other modern civilizations. On the basis of respecting the leading status of Marxism and the maternal status of traditional Chinese culture, and through scientific analysis and independent localization, Chinese Marxism has established a relationship with other cultures in which it draws on other culture's merits, coexists with them peacefully, and develops together. As global connections grow closer and diversified cultural development coexists, we must enhance cultural awareness and cultural confidence in the process of localizing Marxism, actively draw on the beneficial achievements of human civilization, especially the fine elements of modern Western civilization, and build a socialist cultural system with Chinese characteristics that is guided by Marxism, has a national style, and fully absorbs the best cultural achievements of all sorts.

To Deepen the Localization of Marxism by Combining It With the Fine Traditional Chinese Culture, We Should Take Comprehensive Innovation as the Core of Development

In the process of localizing Marxism, it is necessary to inherit and carry forward the fine traditional Chinese culture and also to study and borrow from the achievements of modern Western civilization. However, it is far from enough to realize the localization of Marxism by merely drawing on thinking and culture of all sorts. The Marxist cultural view regards comprehensive innovation as the key to the power of culture, and the proper relationship between inheriting, studying, and innovating as the key to cultural development. Innovation is the soul of a nation's progress, the inexhaustible power of a country's prosperity, and the source that keeps culture alive.[14] Whether for the fine traditional Chinese culture or for the modern Western civilization, it is necessary to constantly adapt to the needs of the times and integrate new elements and transform themselves in practice. Only under the banner of comprehensive innovation can the localization of Marxism maintain the quality of keeping up with the times and achieve one victory after another in social practice.

To deepen the localization of Marxism with comprehensive innovation as the core of development is to require us to, on the basis of inheriting and learning from the best cultural achievements of ancient and modern China, adhere to the Marxist worldview and methodology as the guide, to focus on our practical needs, to carry out scientific integration and innovative development of Chinese Marxism, traditional Chinese culture, and the achievements of Western civilization, and to establish a system of thinking and culture with Chinese characteristics. It also requires us to base ourselves on the practice of reform and opening up and socialist modernization, to scientifically analyze the new changes in the world, the nation, and the Party, to summarize the new experiences created by the people in practice, and to thoroughly study and solve the new issues of reform and opening up and modernization, so that the CPC will continue to innovate and keep pace with the times in practice and make our thinking and actions compatible with the development of times. We are also required to combine the construction of socialism with Chinese characteristics with the world trend and the theme of the times, focus on the development frontier of the world in science and culture, grasp the new trends, and always stand at the forefront of the development of the times.

Deepening the Localization of Marxism by Combining It With the Fine Traditional Chinese Culture Helps Meet the Needs of Current Social Development of China

As mentioned above, in the trend of economic globalization, diversification of cultures, and information networking, various interest groups are playing against each other, and multiple cultures coexist, ushering in the digital era of "information explosion" in human society. Meanwhile, China's society is in a critical period of institutional transformation and social transition. Social development made great progress while serious problems abound, particularly the diversity of values, the lack of faith, and moral misconduct. Against such a background, cultivating and promoting the core socialist values, and inheriting and carrying forward the fine traditional Chinese culture and virtues become an urgent task for the Party in the respect of thinking and culture. To deepen the localization of Marxism by combining it with the fine traditional culture of the Chinese nation, we should meet the practical needs of our current social development.

The Chinese culture has a long history and rich content, providing cultural guarantee and value support for the survival and development of the Chinese nation for a long time. The profound fine traditional Chinese culture is the foundation for us to get a foothold among world civilizations. The fine traditional Chinese culture has contemporary values, such as its emphasis on benevolence, people-orientation, integrity, justice, harmony, and a better society, which are important sources for nurturing core socialist values. Against the today's background of diversified values, advocating the inheritance and promotion of Chinese traditional culture requires us to draw on the essence of traditional culture, which provides cultural nourishment and fosters popular recognition for the cultivation and promotion of core socialist values, thus improving the vitality, cohesiveness, and appeal of core socialist values. The cultivation of moral qualities of all people is as important as economic development in the market economy. As the essence of Chinese culture, traditional Chinese virtues provide valuable resources for us to define moral norms and improve moral quality. The CPC clearly points out that we should inherit the traditional virtues, respect and abide by them, and pursue noble moral ideals, which basically meets the needs of the current social development and the people, injecting inexhaustible impetus for the localization of Marxism. Only by deepening the localization of Marxism through combining it with fine traditional Chinese culture, and only by constructing and developing socialist culture, can we grasp the development direction of socialism with Chinese characteristics, and gain spiritual impetus and intellectual support for it.

Deepening the Localization of Marxism by Combining It With the Fine Traditional Chinese Culture Helps Achieve the Great Rejuvenation of the Chinese Nation

Culture is the lifeblood of the nation and the spiritual home of the people. The 5,000-year history of China's splendid civilization would not have existed without the fine traditional Chinese culture. The Chinese nation will lose the foundation of national unity and the fundamental national identity. As the construction of socialism with Chinese characteristics cannot be separated from the framework of the nation state, the localization of Marxism cannot be detached from the foundation of national culture. The combination with the fine traditional Chinese culture to deepen the localization of Marxism aims to achieve the great rejuvenation of the Chinese nation. The rejuvenation of the nation not only includes the rise of a country in the economic field, but also the overall improvement of the spiritual outlook and moral quality of the whole nation, which means that the ideology, culture, and values of the nation have considerable attraction and influence on other nations. The rejuvenation of the Chinese nation is a comprehensive one that involves prosperity of the state, political democracy, social harmony, and the inheritance and promotion of national culture. In the process of localizing Marxism, inheritance of the fine traditional Chinese culture helps maintain the continuity and development of national culture and can promote the great rejuvenation of the Chinese nation in the cultural field.

Due to the differences in natural environment, historical development, and national characteristics, traditional Chinese culture is fundamentally different from Western culture in many aspects, such as way of thinking, ethical norms, and value orientations. Western culture played an outstanding role in promoting the development of productive forces and modernization of social production. However, with the abundance of material, problems such as the anxiety for quick success, hollowness and impatience, moral misconduct, and alienation of human nature by material interests are pervasive, while Western culture does not have the innate ability to adjust the imbalance. Traditional Chinese culture, which emphasizes ethics and inner cultivation and pursues harmonious social development, has unique insights and significant regulatory functions in dealing with the relationship between human beings, between human beings and society, and between human beings and nature. Inheriting and carrying forward the fine traditional Chinese culture and giving full play to its unique social functions are important and meaningful for solving many problems in the process of modernization and satisfying people's growing needs for a better life. The significance of deepening the localization of Marxism by combining it with the fine traditional Chinese culture is not only to promote the localization, modernization, and popularization of Marxism with traditional culture but also to revive the Chinese national culture. As economic construction witnesses new progress and material development reaches new high, the combination with the fine traditional Chinese culture to deepen the localization of Marxism strengthens the country's cultural soft power and helps achieve the great development and prosperity of socialist culture. It also continues to enrich the spiritual world of the people, enhances the national mental strength, and helps achieve a great leap in national spiritual construction and realize the goal of building a socialist cultural power. It also helps the Chinese culture with national style go global and makes Chinese culture exert its due and irreplaceable international influence on the international stage.

Combining with the fine traditional Chinese culture to deepen the localization of Marxism is a long-term and arduous historical task. At present, China's great cause of reform and opening up enters a critical period, facing unprecedented development opportunities as well as risks and challenges. In the face of the profound changes in the world, the country, and the Party, we must summarize our experience in the process of localizing Marxism, grasp the requirements of the times, respond to the aspirations of the people, relentlessly explore and master the laws of socialism with Chinese characteristics, establish a high degree of cultural awareness and cultural confidence in the creative practice of the Party and the people, deepen the localization of Marxism in the process of combining it with the fine traditional Chinese culture, stride forward toward the grand goal of building a socialist cultural power, and open up broader development prospects for the cause of socialism with Chinese characteristics.

Notes

1 Sun Daiyao. Understanding the Three Dimensions of the "Three Confidence": Study Note No. 20 of Learning General Secretary Xi Jinping's Series of Important Remarks. *Frontline*, 2013;12.
2 Zhang Dainian, Cheng Yishan. *Chinese Culture and Debates on Culture*. Beijing: China Renmin University Press, 1990, p. 186.
3 Wei Jianlin. The Tradition of Dialectics in Chinese Culture Has Great Significance in Reality. *Chinese Social Sciences Today*. November 22, 2011.
4 Li Zonggui. A Brief Discussion on the Characteristics of Traditional Chinese Philosophy. *Academic Forum*, 5, 1988.
5 Sun Mingzhang. On the Development and Features of Ancient Chinese Dialectics. *Journal of Xiamen University (Arts & Social Sciences)*, 1985;6.
6 Li Rui. *Mao Zedong: A Life of Reading*. Shenyang: Volumes Publishing Company, 2005, p. 234.
7 Guo Jianning. "Harmony" Does Not Equal to No Conflict or Struggle. *People's Tribune*, 2013;16.
8 Xi Jinping's Remarks on Cultural Confidence Since the 18th Party Congress. October 13, 2017. http://www.xinhuanet.com/politics/2017-10/13/c_1121796384. htm.
9 Xi Jinping Stressed During the 18th Collective Study of the Political Bureau of the CPC Central Committee that We Should Remember Historical Experience, Lessons, and Warnings, which Supply Useful References for the Modernization of National Governance Capacity. October 14, 2014. http://politics.people.com. cn/n/2014/1014/c1001-25826596.html.
10 Xi Jinping. *The Governance of China*. Beijing: Foreign Languages Press, 2014, p. 164.
11 Xi Jinping. *The Governance of China*. Beijing: Foreign Languages Press, 2014, p. 164.
12 Xi Jinping. *The Governance of China*. Beijing: Foreign Languages Press, 2014, p. 164.
13 Zhang Dainian and Wang Dong. The Modern Rejuvenation and Comprehensive Innovation of the Chinese Civilization. *Teaching and Research*, 1997;5.
14 Guo Jianning. Adapting Marxism to Chinese Conditions and Constructing a Shared Spiritual Homeland. *Journal of Peking University (Philosophy & Social Sciences)*, 2010;4.

5 Localize Marxism With Theoretical Innovation

Liu Ying

The localization of Marxism in China contains two basic dimensions: theoretical innovation and practical exploration, and its essence in theoretical form is theoretical innovation. In the historic practice of revolution, construction, and reform, contemporary Chinese people, oriented by the problems of the times, combine the basic tenets of Marxism with China's reality, with Chinese traditional culture as well as the practical experience. Meanwhile, contemporary Chinese people move with the times to promote theoretical innovation.

Theoretical Innovation Is the Essential Requirement and the Source of Vitality of Marxism

In the 170 years since its birth, Marxism has maintained its vitality despite its ups and downs. From the 19th century to the 20th century, Marxism turned from a specter hovering over Europe into a realistic social system, creating the socialist movement, the most far-reaching social reform movement in history. Although the socialist movement experienced setbacks in the Soviet Union and Eastern Europe from the end of the 20th century to the 21st century, Marxism still proved its vitality in the process of revolution, reform, and construction in China once again. It has become a powerful spiritual drive to guide and promote the building of socialism with Chinese characteristics.

Why has Marxism remained vibrant and evergreen? One of the important reasons is that it has maintained continuous theoretical innovation, which is derived from the practicality, development, and creativity of Marxism, which is the requirement of Marxism and the source of its vitality.

Marxism is practical. The view of practice is the primary view as well as the theoretical foundation of Marxism. Marxism believes that practice is the material activity of man to transform the world actively. We can only understand the fundamental characteristics of human activity and the nature of human cognitive and theoretical activities from practice. Practice is the basis for the occurrence and development of human cognition, meanwhile, cognition depends on practice, setting it as the criterion. Human cognition

DOI: 10.4324/9781003356042-6

and theory come into being under certain socio-historical conditions, which in turn restrict cognition and theory. However, due to the subjective initiative of man, they have transcendence and leading force. Inheriting the advanced ideological and cultural achievements of mankind in the past and considering the problems and characteristics of the times, human cognition and theory can form the "essence of the spirit of the times" and develop continuously with the unfolding of social history. It is because of this that "Marxism is not purely a theoretical study, but a guide to action based on social practice."[1] The practical point of view on the one hand requires that the content of Marxism should not be separated from the reality, on the other hand, it requires that Marxism should be constantly enriched with new content according to the changes in practice and constantly discard the conclusions that have been proved to be historically limited.

Marxism has a developmental nature. Engels once said: "Our theory is a developing theory, not a dogma that must be memorized and regurgitated."[2] The reason why Marxism is so vigorous is that it is not a static, closed theoretical system. It never sees itself as a system of ultimate truth, but as a system that constantly evolves with the development of practice "which provides a starting point and a method for further research rather than ready-made dogma."[3] A true Marxist is not a defender of dogma, but a thinker and a doer who constantly applies Marxist positions, views, and methods to solve real problems.

Marxism is creative. This creativity is manifested as the constant discovery of new problems, the formulation of new ideas, and the formation of new theories in practice. Marx and Engels themselves have been constantly enriching and perfecting their theories in the light of the problems arising in the development of capitalism and the communist movement. Consequently, their successor must also promote the creative development of Marxist theories in practice. The basic tenets of Marxism are universal, but the practice and development of Marxism are national, regional, and up-to-date. Moreover, Marxism must be inherited in creation. Lenin developed Marxist theory by combining it with the practice of the Russian revolution and found the correct path for the Russian revolution; Mao Zedong combined Marxist-Leninist theory with the practice of the Chinese revolution with the vital Mao Zedong Thought as its product; Deng Xiaoping, by combining Marxism-Leninism and Mao Zedong Thought with the practice of contemporary Chinese socialist modernization, found the correct path to realizing Chinese socialist modernization and created the theoretical system of socialism with Chinese characteristics, which has tremendous vitality.

The practicality, development and creativity of Marxism are the concrete manifestation of its scientific nature. As a scientific social theory, Marxism is not an absolute truth that is fixed and static. Rather, it must be combined with the reality of a country, a place, and an era and constantly develop and innovate with the reality and the problems of the times. Therefore, in China,

Marxism must also require continuous theoretical innovation, and this is the essence of localizing Marxism.

As early as October 1938, Mao Zedong pointed out that "any talk about Marxism apart from China's specific characteristics is only Marxism in the abstract, Marxism in a vacuum."[4] Deng Xiaoping once said, "When everything has to be done by the book when thinking turns rigid and blind faith is the fashion, a party or a nation can't make progress. Its life will cease and that party or nation will perish."[5] Jiang Zemin has also proposed, "If we dogmatically cling to words said by authors of Marxist classics despite the changes in historical conditions and present realities, then we will damage the vitality of Marxism."[6] Hu Jintao pointed out that

> we must not lose the good traditions of our ancestors, but we must also say something new. The basic tenets of Marxism must be adhered to, but they also should be continuously developed and improved in practice. Moreover, the localization of Marxism should be actively promoted.[7]

Xi Jinping stressed that "theoretical innovation pioneers the way for innovation in practice, and for comprehensively deepening the reform we must renew our theory first"[8] and proposed

> to promote theoretical innovation, we must adhere to the basic tenets of Marxism without wavering. This is the basis and starting point for the development of Marxism, otherwise, it will lose its way and go astray. At the same time, we must continue to enrich the development of Marxism with the development of practice, and constantly give Marxism a new vitality to better uphold Marxism.[9]

Only with theoretical innovation can Marxism exist and develop. On the one hand, we must insist the cardinal principles, the basic standpoint, views and methods of Marxism, otherwise it is bound to lead to confusion and loss of direction. At the same time, Marxism is also an open system, which develops continuously with practice. The greatest respect and most faithful adherence to Marxism lie only in the theoretical innovation based on inheritance.

Localizing Marxism: Theoretical Innovation and Its Achievements

Theoretical Innovation of the Party

When the Communist Party of China was founded with only 50 members, it was facing an old China that was torn apart and in deep disaster. Today, with more than 90 million members, the CPC is leading an increasingly powerful new China on the path to socialist modernization. For more than 90 years, the Communist Party of China has been able to develop and grow, leading the Chinese people to create great achievements in national independence and development. One of the fundamental reasons is that it has always adhered to the guidance of scientific theory, always insisted on taking the changing trend of time as the historical basis for the theoretical innovation of the localization of Marxism, always insisted on combining the cardinal principles of Marxism with the specific realities of China's revolution, construction and reform, and advance the localization of Marxism through theoretical innovation.

The history of the Party for more than 90 years is not only a "history of struggle" in which the Party has led the people of all ethnicities to make unremitting efforts for national rejuvenation, but also a "history of innovation" in which the basic principles of Marxism have been combined with the specific realities of China and the characteristics of the times. Since its establishment, the Communist Party of China has made two major theoretical leaps and produced two major theoretical innovations: Mao Zedong Thought and System of Theories of Socialism with Chinese Characteristics, which includes such major strategic ideas as Deng Xiaoping Theory, the Theory of Three Represents, the Scientific Outlook on Development and Xi Jinping Thought on Socialism with Chinese Characteristics for a New Era. Among them, Mao Zedong Thought mainly answers the question of how to realize the new democratic revolution and socialist revolution in a large semi-colonial and semi-feudal Eastern country. The theoretical system of socialism with Chinese characteristics mainly answers the questions of what kind of socialism and party should we build, how to build such socialism and party, and what kind of development should we develop as well as how to develop in a large developing country with a population of more than one billion people. In the theoretical system of socialism with Chinese characteristics, Xi Jinping Thought on Socialism with Chinese Characteristics for a New Era is a new leap in localizing Marxism, answering a series of major questions like what kind of socialism with Chinese characteristics should be upheld and developed in the new era and how to uphold and develop socialism with Chinese characteristics.

Theoretical Innovation by Marxist Theoreticians

The Party leaders and the collective leadership have undoubtedly made important contributions to the theoretical innovation of localizing Marxism. With rich practical experience, they are often the creators and founders of innovative theories, the pioneers of ideological emancipation, as well as the leading core and organizers of theoretical innovation, and the earliest promoters and implementers of innovative theories. Focusing on solving practical and theoretical problems in the process of revolution and construction, their achievements were mainly theory, line, principles, and policies that guide the Chinese revolution and construction.

In addition, scholars and theoretical workers are indispensable and irreplaceable in localizing Marxism. Since modern times, many scholars have made significant contributions to the dissemination and development of Marxist classics and their basic tenets in China. More importantly, in the face of the new issues raised by the great practice of the Chinese revolution, construction, and socialism with Chinese characteristics, carrying the sense of mission that "everyone should be responsible for the prosperity of the country," they promote the theoretical innovation of localizing Marxism and seek solutions to the problems of times with their profound theoretical accumulation and professional advantages. They have provided theoretical and intellectual support for the Party and the state. Marxist scholars and theoreticians tend to pay attention to social practice but maintain a relatively indirect connection with it and a careful distance from it that can allow them to be reflective, so that they can see more than the present and transcend the limitations of specific practices, leading theoretical problems arising from reality to great depth. Scholars' awareness of problems and theoretical exploration have laid a profound theoretical foundation for the Party's theoretical innovation and have made important contributions to the elaboration, deepening, and popularization of the Party's theoretical innovation.

Commitment to Translation and Dissemination: Laying the Foundation for Localizing Marxism

When Marxism was introduced to China, it was translated and spread by advanced intellectuals and became the way to save the country. Intellectuals and scholars have always been the main force in the translation, exposition, and dissemination of Marxism. Although the work of translation and dissemination cannot be regarded as theoretical innovation in the strict sense, it is still significant for laying the foundation for the theoretical innovation of the localization of Marxism. Without such preliminary and fundamental work, the localization of Marxism and its theoretical innovation would be impossible.

We often say that the salvo of the October Revolution brought us Marxism-Leninism. However, before that, Marxism had already been mentioned and introduced as a school of thought of European socialism. The invasion of foreign powers and the decline of the Qing Dynasty in modern times prompted many people with lofty ideas to pursue social revolution and strengthen the country, and Marxism was introduced to China as a social trend to save the country and the people. In the 20 years before and after the Revolution of 1911, students in Japan became the main force in translating and spreading Marxism to China. Among them, Liang Qichao, Zhu Zhixin, Zhang Ji, Liu Shipei, and other students in Japan translated and introduced the life of Marx, classical papers like the *Communist Manifesto*, and part of the basic tenets of Marxism. In the spring of 1899, the monthly magazine

The Review of the Times sponsored by the Christian Literature Society for China published the first three chapters of *Social Evolution* by the British evolutionist Benjamin Kidd, translated by T. Richard and written by Tsai Erkang, in which the names of Marx and Engels were mentioned several times—this must be the first time that Chinese people knew the name of Marx. In the early 20th century, there were a lot of articles introducing Marx and socialism in the press. For example, from 1902 to 1904, Liang Qichao published several articles introducing Marx and socialism in The New People's Gazette. In 1905, Min Bao published Zhu Zhixin's *A Short Biography of the German Social Revolutionaries* and introduced in detail the life of Marx and Engels, the basic content of the Communist Manifesto, and the doctrine of surplus value and capital accumulation.

In the late 19th and early 20th centuries, Marxism as a social trend had already entered the vision of Chinese intellectuals, but it was not until the October Revolution in Russia that it was widely propagated and became the way to save the country. After the October Revolution, advanced intellectuals, represented by Li Dazhao and Chen Duxiu, spread Marxism in China, and the pattern of "Southern Chen and Northern Li" was formed for a while. The explanation of Marx's materialistic conception of history made by Li Dazhao, the analysis of Chinese society based on Marxist political economy presented by Chen Duxiu, the "materialism of dialectics" proposed by Qu Qiubai and the systematic study of Marxism by Li Da are representative of researches on Marxism since the 1920s. At that time, the dialectical materialism was popular throughout the country, and as Ai Siqi said at that time,

> Scholars recognized it as the basis of all learning... Any stubborn old scholars, as long as they were not willing to fall into decline, could not help but look at the Marxist canon, and any sharp thinkers who dared to be original had to turn to *Capital*.[10]

With the famous "Question and Doctrine" debate between Li Dazhao and Hu Shi and the discussion on socialism between Chen Duxiu and Liang Qichao, Marxism was gradually transformed from an academic trend to a guiding ideology for social transformation in China.

Before the Yan'an period, the translation and dissemination of Marxist works were mainly in the form of opinions, chapters, fragments, or individual articles. The year 1938 witnessed the establishment of the Marxist-Leninist Institute in Yan'an. The compilation department of the Institute compiled and published two major series and two major anthologies, namely, the Marx-Engels Series and the Anti-Japanese War Reference Series, the Selected Works of Lenin and the Selected Works of Stalin, and the two volumes of the Selected Works of Marx. After the founding of New China, under the leadership of the Party's Central Committee, the Central Compilation and Translation Bureau and the People's Publishing House were established one after another, providing organizations for the translation and publication of classic Marxist works. The most important result was the official publication of Marx/Engels Collected Works, Lenin Collected Works, and Collected Works of I.V. Stalin. The first edition of the Marx/Engels Collected Works was published from 1956 to 1985 (all 50 volumes), and the second edition was re-edited from the Russian and German versions in 1995. After the publication of the complete works, the Central Compilation and Translation Bureau selected and edited the Selected Works of Marx and Engels, Selected Works of Lenin, and Selected Works of Stalin on this basis. In addition, many important works of Marx, Engels, Lenin, and Stalin were also published in single volumes, and some collections and compilations of special remarks were also selected and compiled to facilitate the systematic study of the classical writers of Marxism on a certain aspect of the subject. The publication of these basic documents provides an important textual basis for scholars' research and the Party's theoretical innovation.[11]

In parallel with the translation, teachers and researchers in the philosophical and social science of colleges, universities, party schools, and the social science academy system have made contributions to the interpretation and dissemination of localizing Marxism.

Theoretical Support: Promoting the Party's Theoretical Innovation

Scholars and theoreticians provided rich theoretical support to promote the Party's theoretical innovation with their theoretical advantages, which makes a great contribution to localizing Marxism. The early advanced intellectuals made initial thinking and accumulated valuable experience about how to innovate and theoretically adapt Marxism to the Chinese Context. Marxist scholars such as Li Dazhao, Chen Duxiu, Li Da, Yun Daying, Deng Zhongxia, Li Hanjun, Cai Hesen, and Qu Qiubai, who were both revolutionaries and theorists, began their theoretical thinking, research, and dissemination based on the question of "China's future." They were already aware of the need to study how to put their theories into practice. For example, Li Dazhao once explicitly said, "We should carefully study how Marx's materialistic view of history can be applied to the political and economic situation in contemporary China."[12] Moreover, they were aware of the need to consciously apply the method of analyzing social history provided by the materialistic view of history in actions to observe and analyze Chinese social problems. In Li Da's *Marxism and China* published in 1923, he proposed that serious consideration should be given to how the Chinese Communists could use Marx's doctrine to transform Chinese society, and how the Chinese proletariat should prepare for solving Chinese problems. Yun Daying also said, "Our task is to find a policy that is suitable to the national conditions and compatible with communism."[13] This means that from the very beginning, the early Marxist scholars put forward the conscious demand for localizing Marxism and actively promoted the integration of Marxism with Chinese reality and Chinese problems.

After the founding of the Communist Party of China, during the initial exploration of the new democratic revolution and the socialist construction, theoreticians made positive contributions to the enrichment and development of Marxist theory and the theoretical innovation of the localization of Marxism. During the Yan'an period, "Adaptation to the Chinese context" had become a consensus among scholars, and theoreticians represented by Ai Siqi and He Peiyuan argued for localizing Marxism from different perspectives. For example, in 1938, Ai Siqi wrote "The Present Situation and Tasks of Philosophy," proposing the idea that we should adopt a philosophy to the Chinese context and make it more practical. Moreover, he pointed out that the localization

> is to draw philosophical nutrients from the experience of mobilization in various sectors of the war effort and develop philosophical theories. We should enrich and develop our theories according to the experience of each period, and not take the fixed philosophical theories as to the formulas that govern everything.[14]

All these made him the first scholar in the academic field to propose the "adaptation of Marxist philosophy to the Chinese context." After Mao Zedong put forward the proposition of the localization of Marxism, Ai Siqi also wrote, *China's Peculiarities* (1940), *How to Study Dialectical Materialism* (1940), *Review of Several Important Philosophical Ideas since the War of Resistance* (1941), and other articles, which systematically argued the meaning, necessity, possibility, basic tenets, and specific ways of localizing Marxism.

In addition, intellectuals in Yan'an also began to pay attention to the relationship between Marxism and traditional Chinese culture. For example, Chen Boda used dialectical materialism to study ancient Chinese philosophy and proposed that materialism and dialectics could find their roots in the Chinese philosophical tradition. Later, he published "The Beginning of Ancient Chinese Philosophy," "The Philosophical Thought of Lao Tzu," "The Philosophical Thought of Confucius," and "The Philosophical Thought of Mo Tzu" in *Liberation* and *Chinese Culture* to explore the materialistic and dialectical thoughts in ancient Chinese philosophy.

Mao Zedong's ideas on the localization of Marxism were undoubtedly influenced by the intellectuals around him in Yan'an. One of the examples is that in writing the two works on the systematic expression of the localization of Marxist philosophy, "On Practice" and "On Contradiction," he absorbed and drew on some of the research results of Marxist philosophers, especially Li Da's *Outline of Sociology* and Ai Siqi's *Popular Philosophy*.

During the transition period and the period of socialist construction after the founding of New China, with the establishment of the basic system of socialism,

> the Party's path, guidelines, and policies in different periods objectively promoted the evolution and changes of Marxism in terms of theoretical themes, forms of expression and even basic categories. For example, the Party's judgment on the basic nature and basic contradictions of socialism, and the formation of The political line, to a large extent, constitute the political and theoretical theme of the new Chinese Marxism, and other issues are centered on such themes.[15]

The main issues of academic discussions and theoretical exchanges focused on class contradictions and class struggles during the period of socialist construction, productivity and relations of production in the people's commune movement, internal contradictions of the people during the socialist period, and revolutionary issues during the socialist period. The "Left" thinking of the Party leaders on the major issues of social construction at this stage dominated and influenced the academic world to a certain extent. During the "Cultural Revolution" period, due to the extreme development of the political line of "taking class struggle as the key link," Marxism was reduced to a vulgar philosophy of struggle, and the theoretical research and innovation on the localization of Marxism suffered a major setback.

With the establishment of Deng Xiaoping Theory and the socialist market economy system and the new development of the path of socialism with Chinese characteristics since the 21st century, scholars have made new contributions to the theoretical innovation of Marxism in China.

Among them, the typical events and innovations are, first of all, the two great discussions at the early stage of reform and opening up. One of them was the debate about the criterion for testing truth. As the ideological and theoretical starting point of the reform and opening up, it was directly aimed at the "two whatevers" argument that still dominated the Party after the end of the Cultural Revolution, and its first diatribe was the well-known "Practice Is the Sole Criterion for Testing Truth." The first draft of this article was an article submitted to *Guang Ming Daily* by Hu Fuming, a teacher in the philosophy department of Nanjing University, on the subject of the standard of practice. After being revised by experts from the Party School of the CPC Central Committee and the editorial department of *Guang Ming Daily*, and reviewed and finalized by Hu Yaobang, the article was published on May 10, 1978, in the 60th issue of *Theoretical Trend* and on May 11, 1978, in *Guang Ming Daily*. The article was later reprinted in *People's Daily*, *PLA Daily*, and other national newspapers at all levels, triggering a nationwide discussion on the issue of practice and standards of truth. The Third Plenary Session of the 11th Central Committee of the Communist Party of

China affirmed this theoretical discussion from the perspective of ideology and political line, and since then, the academic and theoretical world has been discussing this proposition more deeply and for several years. The topics covered whether the practice is the sole criterion for testing truth, how to understand the criterion of practice and how practice tests truth, the subject-object elements and the principle of the subjectivity of practice, and the relationship between logical proof and the criterion of practice, which laid a solid ideological foundation for the re-establishment of the Party's ideological line of seeking truth from facts at a crucial historical moment and also consolidated and expanded the real political effect of this theoretical innovation point.

The second is the great discussion on human nature, humanism, and alienation. This discussion addressed the status of human beings in Marxism, the essence and nature of human beings, the relationship between Marxism and humanitarianism, and the questions of whether alienation applies only to capitalist societies and whether alienation exists in socialism, which is related to the essence of socialism. This discussion has given a profound impetus to the historical rethinking of the Cultural Revolution and has played an important role in establishing the human-centered ideological core of socialism with Chinese characteristics and clarifying the basic nature of socialism.

Over the past 40 years of reform and opening up, theoreticians have closely cooperated with the adjustment of the national development strategy, conducted an in-depth analysis of the socialist market economy, launched theoretical discussions on the basic nature of the socialist economy and the direction of reform, and made positive contributions to the Party's theoretical innovation and the introduction and implementation of lines, guidelines, and policies.

Before the Third Plenary Session of the 11th Party Congress in 1978, "many economists had made academic discussions on the issue of economic laws, and the crucial theoretical article, 'Act in Accordance with Economic Laws to Accelerate the Realization of the Four Modernizations', published by Hu Qiaomu on October 6, 1978 had aroused people's general attention."[16] Since then, extensive discussions had been carried out throughout the academic circles, focusing on the relationship between socialist planned economy and commodity economy, and between planning and market. At last, the academic circles had reached a basic consensus that socialist economy is the unity of planned economy and commodity economy. After the Third Plenary Session of the 12th Party Congress set the direction of socialist commodity economy, market-oriented economic system reform has been vigorously carried out. Before the socialist market economic system was established as the goal of economic system reform in the Report of the 14th Party Congress, there was a debate about whether the market economy was pertaining to capitalism or socialism and whether China should implement the market economy or not. After the 14th Party Congress, with the establishment of the goal of socialist market economy system and the proposal of relevant planning, scholars discussed and clarified the basic concepts and basic relations around the relationship between socialist commodity economy and socialist market economy and the difference between socialist economy and capitalist economy. Theories of many scholars provided important support for the theoretical innovation of the Party at that time, such as Liu Guoguang's "compatible theory of socialist market and planning," Yu Zuyao's theory holding that "socialist economy is a special market economy," and "the combination theory of the market economy and social basic system" raised by Su Xing. At the same time, scholars have made explorations on the specific directions and approaches of economic system reform. For example, Wu Jinglian put forward the competitive market system; Li Yining proposed joint-stock reform; Gao Shangquan raised the concept of labor market; Liu Guoguang proposed to pay attention to social equity in the field of distribution, etc., all of which made positive contributions to the establishment and development of socialist market economy for the central leadership's decision-making.

Scholars responded to a series of major issues in the theoretical exploration of socialism with Chinese characteristics. For example, scholars have actively explored the theory of the primary stage of socialism on the basis of analyzing and demonstrating the basic contradictions and class conditions of the socialist society and further clarifying the ideological confusion. The discussion on the meaning, basis of classification, basic characteristics, objectives, and tasks of the primary stage of socialism has made an important contribution to the theory of the primary stage of socialism clearly stated in the 13th Party Congress. Since then, scholars have discussed the features of the primary stage of socialism after entering the new century, laying a foundation for further elaboration of the general basis of socialism with Chinese characteristics in the reports of the subsequent Party Congresses.

Under the background of the primary stage of socialism, scholars input energy into the theoretical innovations, especially some key proposals, in the previous Party Congresses. They have put forward constructive suggestions on how to strengthen Party building by referring to the changes experienced by a series of ruling parties around the world such as the Soviet Communist Party and to the complex situation of Party building in China. In the new century, when China has entered a period of strategic opportunities, scholars put forward some suggestions on strengthening top-level design, adjusting economic structure, avoiding middle-income trap, building socialist consultative democracy, and so on, actively searching for solutions. Considering the intensifying international soft power competition and the imbalance among economic, political, and cultural development, scholars raised the constructs of cultural awareness, cultural confidence, and cultural self-improvement, and proposed strengthening socialist cultural building with Chinese characteristics and cultivating socialist core values. At its 18th National Congress, the Party set forth the path of socialism with Chinese characteristics, an overall plan for promoting economic, political, cultural, social, and ecological progress, as well as the overall goal of socialist modernization and the great rejuvenation of the Chinese nation. At its 19th National Congress, the Party put forward Xi Jinping Thought on Socialism with Chinese Characteristics for a New Era. Since then, scholars have carried out further understanding and in-depth research from their respective disciplines.

Promote the Innovation of Basic Theories and Build a Modern Academic System

The development of theoretical innovation of localization of Marxism in China is inseparable from the basic theoretical research achievements made by scholars in professional academic studies. These achievements, based on research views from different disciplines, have explored Marxist classics, the basic principles and history of Marxism, and various problems encountered in the development of socialist revolution, which provide fundamental support to localize Marxism in terms of the legitimacy, historical process, and historical law. Among them, representative achievements include:

First, the textbook system reform of the philosophy of Marxism. The early Marxism textbook system in China was basically a transplant of Soviet textbook system. Since the 1950s, some scholars have raised different views, especially criticizing the views that Marxist philosophy is a "combination" of dialectical materialism and historical materialism, and that historical materialism is a "generalized" product of dialectical materialism in the social and historical field. Driven by the extensive discussion on practice and truth, the reform of textbook system was carried out deeply, among which Gao Qinghai's "outline of Marxist philosophy" and Huang Nansen's "materialist dialectic system" were the most prominent. In the late 1980s, textbook reform began to focus on academic discussions of "practical materialism," although the academic world is still divided on its detailed understanding, which essentially freed Marxist philosophy from the traditional Soviet textbook system, makes practice become the basis of the whole Marxist philosophy, and also restores the active subjectivity aspect of Marxist philosophy, thus laying an ideological foundation for the reform and opening up of contemporary China from the philosophical foundation.

Second, the establishment of neo-Marxist economics. As the realistic problems in the development of economy were becoming more and more specific and complicated, while the western economics was sweeping across the country, the mainstream position of Marxist political economy in contemporary Chinese economic research was weakened. Our Marxist economists have constantly responded to the realistic problems and the challenges of western economics and promoted the reform of Marxist political economics. Some scholars represented by the "Shanghai School of Economics" were committed to the establishment of the comprehensive school of neo-Marxist economics and other theoretical types, so as to rebuild China's socialist economics.

Third, undertake the tasks for the time and adhere to the path of socialism. In the 1990s, under the background of the Revolutions in 1989 in Eastern Europe and the low tide of the world socialist movement, scholars represented by Gao Fang thoroughly analyzed the lessons of the dramatic changes in Eastern Europe. Under the international background of the post-war world pattern and the third scientific and technological revolution, they devoted themselves to study the relationship and futures of capitalism and socialism and discussed the development of the current situation of capitalism and the prospects of socialism around the world, which made outstanding contributions for the Party and the country to have a clear understanding of the world situation and firm up the socialist path and faith.

At the beginning of the 21st century, the Marxist academic circle as a whole has formed the characteristics of "transformation from political ideological research to academic ideological research, from closed research to open research, from phased research to overall research, from theory-centered research to research centered on China's practical problems."[17] Many research results have been adopted by the CPC Central Committee and even written into Party documents. In addition, many experts and scholars have been invited to attend study activities organized by the Political Bureau of the CPC Central Committee to give lectures to Party and state leaders, providing ideological material and reference basis for their theoretical innovation.

The innovation of basic theory needs the guarantee of modern academic system. With the deepening of the localization of Marxism in China, in 2004, the CPC Central Committee decided to carry out the project of Marxist theory research and construction, which included five aspects: first, to strengthen the research on the theoretical innovation and major practical problems of the localization of Marxism to China's conditions; second, to strengthen the compilation and study of Marxist classics; third, to build the basic theory of Marxism and a discipline system of philosophy and social science with the features of the times; fourth, to compile textbooks of philosophy, political economy, science, socialism, political science, sociology, law, history, journalism, literature, and other key subjects that reflect the latest theoretical achievements of Marxism in contemporary China and form a textbook system of philosophy and social science; fifth, to train teacher teams in combination of the old, the middle-aged, and the young in the leadership to study and teach Marxist theories. In 2005, the Academic Degrees Committee of the State Council and the Ministry of Education added one first-level discipline of Marxist theory and five second-level subjects, including the localization of Marxism. The academic circle has carried on the continuous and in-depth discussion on the significance, basic connotation and characteristics, research content, discipline system, and discipline construction. The development of this discipline system itself also laid an important foundation for theoretical innovation.

Directly Participate in the Party's Theoretical Innovation and
Undertake the Task of Document Writing and Publicity

The Communist Party of China attaches great importance to Marxist theorists with the direct participation of a large number of excellent theoretical researchers in the Party's theoretical innovation. In this important process, Party leaders and the collective leadership usually play a guiding role while theorists inside and outside the Party often directly participate in the drafting of research documents, editing works, and publicity of these issues.

For example, in the process of reform and opening up, Xue Muqiao and other economists directly participated in the drafting of essential reports such as *Preliminary Opinions on Economic Restructuring*. Later, some scholars from the Chinese Academy of Social Sciences submitted research reports to the State Council, such as *The Great Thoughts, Principles and Framework of the Socialist Market Economy* and *Theoretical Thoughts and Policy Choices on the Construction of the Socialist Market Economy System*, many of which were adopted by the Party and the government. As a manifesto, *Emancipate the Mind, Seek Truth from Facts, Unite and Look Forward* was outlined by Deng Xiaoping, discussed by Hu Yaobang and Yu Guangyuan and others, and at last drafted by Lin Jianqing along with other researchers.[18] The systematization of the Party's theoretical innovation achievements was inseparable from the theorists' painstaking efforts. For instance, Hu Qiaomu and Tian Jiying have participated in the editing of Selected Works of MAO Zedong; Gong Yuzhi, Zheng Bijian, and Pang Xianzhi have jointly edited Selected Works of Deng Xiaoping.

The drafting of the Party Congress Report is a typical example of the even broader participation of the people in politics. As a crucial platform for the Party's theoretical innovations, reports to all previous Party Congresses have been formed on the basis of soliciting opinions from vast number of theorists. For the report of the 14th CPC National Congress, more than 3000 people from 119 localities and departments across the country participated in the discussion of the 11 drafts of the report. For the report of the 15th CPC National Congress, about 4000 people from 135 units across the country participated in the discussion. For the report of the 16th CPC National Congress, more than 3100 people from 178 units across the country participated in the discussion. For the 17th CPC National Congress, the number is 5560. For the report of the 18th CPC National Congress, the Central Committee organized 46 units to carry out research on 15 key topics, and 57 research reports were formed. The drafting group of the report formed 7 research groups, which went to 12 provinces, autonomous regions, and municipalities to carry out special research. After the draft of the report was formed, 4511 people were solicited opinions. For the report of the 19th CPC National Congress, in accordance with the 21 major theoretical and practical issues laid down by the CPC Central Committee, 59 departments and units formed 80 research groups, conducted field investigations in 1817 community-level units, held 1501 symposia and seminars, attended and interviewed 21532 people, and produced 80 special research reports. At the same time, 25 national pilot units for the construction of high-end think tanks submitted 65 reports on major theoretical and practical issues emerging in the development of the Party and the country, which provided references for the drafting team. After the draft was formed, more than 4700 people's opinions were solicited.

The Experience and the Scope of Development of Theoretical Innovation

The achievements of Chinese revolution, construction, and development in the past 100 years are inseparable from the theoretical innovation of the localization of Marxism. These precious achievements guided China's socialist revolution and construction to future and victory. With the experience provided, the practice of socialist construction with Chinese characteristics and the new challenges of the time require the theoretical innovation to keep pace and advance continuously.

The Basic Experience of Theoretical Innovation of Localizing Marxism in China

Emancipate the Mind and Seek Truth from Facts to Properly Handle the Dialectical Unity of Inheriting and Carrying Forward

Marxism is never an abstract academic theory, but one that critique the society and create history, and closely related to the great cause of liberating the working class and even all humankind. On one hand, Marxism is significant in terms of epistemology and methodology, on the other, it is an ideal and belief, which means that Marxism itself is the unity of instrumental and value rationalities, and

> in terms of theoretical form, it is not only a relatively independent theoretical system reflecting the specific historical conditions and the changes of the characteristics of the time, but also a unified ideological system conveying the time requirements of the proletarian liberation.[19]

Therefore, we should adhere to its relatively constant value pursuit and ideological principles in order to unite people and form a joint force; at the same time, we need to adapt to reality and historical conditions to promote theoretical innovation.

It can be said that

> the core issue of theoretical innovation of Marxism is the relationship
> of inheriting and carrying forward, which makes the theory come into
> being and play a guiding role in response to the needs of practice and is
> constantly innovated by dynamic practice.[20]

Therefore, the key to the theoretical innovation of the localization of Marxism lies in that, while adhering to the basic principles of Marxism, it develops and innovates in the process of persistence and inheritance according to the dynamic changes of practical problems, rather than simply updating knowledge and logical deduction.

> It is precisely under the 'force' of the development of reality that the
> Communist Party of China has learned three truths: the first is that no
> fixed or static theory will always adapt to the development of reality; the
> second is that the success in reality is the best theory which no abstract
> dogma can argue with; the third is that any scientific theory is a two-
> way interaction of inheriting and carrying forward.[21]

General Secretary Xi Jinping pointed out that "the vitality of theory lies in innovation" and "theoretical innovation can only start from problems; in a sense, the process of theoretical innovation is the process of finding problems, selecting problems, researching problems and solving problems."[22] Every major theoretical innovation in China over the past 100 years has been achieved by creatively applying Marxist theory to study major problems encountered in revolution, construction, reform, and development in close connection with reality and in response to practical needs. The Party firmly but not rigidly adheres to the practical-problem-oriented way, emancipates the mind, and seeks truth from facts, which is the necessary premise to realize theoretical innovation. The key to the Party's adherence to Marxism under different historical conditions is to timely solve the new challenges encountered in practice and provide scientific guidance.

People First: Start From the Fundamental Interests of the Broadest Masses

The nature, purpose, and ultimate goal of the CPC determine that it must put people first. Faithfully representing and expressing the interests of the masses is the inexhaustible source for the Party's theoretical innovation, with its basic starting point and foothold lying in realizing the interests of the masses.

General Secretary Xi Jinping stressed,

> why is the question concerning human beings a fundamental and prin-
> cipled issue in the research of philosophy and social sciences? For whom

do Chinese philosophy and social science scholars write books and speak? Is it for the few or for the majority? These are the questions that must be clarified.

"If philosophy and social sciences in China want to make achievements, they must adhere to the people-centered research orientation."[23] In the process of academic theoretical innovation, in particular, the reflection and correction of the historical problems deviating from Marxism, such as ignoring human nature, the obsession with class struggle, and being wrongly official-oriented instead of people-oriented, are also constantly verifying the core position of human in Marxist theory. It is demonstrated that the fundamental position of Mao Zedong Thought and socialism with Chinese characteristics lies in guiding the Chinese people to fight against oppression and exploitation, strive for national independence and liberation, run the country as masters, get rid of poverty, improve living standards, narrow the gap between rich and poor, and finally realize the prosperity of the country and the great rejuvenation of the Chinese nation, which reflects the fundamental interests of the people. In consequence, the localization of Marxism and the path of socialism with Chinese characteristics under the leadership of the Communist Party of China have gained legitimacy on a realistic level and are full of vigor and vitality in the past, present, and future.

Learn and Think, Insist on the Benign Interaction Between Political and Academic Discourses

In the theoretical innovation process of the localization of Marxism, the central collective leadership of the Party is the main leader, organizer, and promoter. Marxist scholars and theorists also play an irreplaceable role. At the same time, some Party leaders themselves are theoreticians, which makes it difficult to simply distinguish them completely.

The benign interaction between political and academic discourses, their mutual influence, complement, and promotion for each other, is the important motivation for the Party to keep pace with the times in theory and practice, and the important reason for the harvest of theoretical innovation achievements. The innovation of Marxist theory in contemporary China must attach great importance to scholars and theorists, further strengthen the study of Marxist theory, further enhance the academic level and academic level of philosophy and social science research, and ensure the legitimacy and credibility of theoretical innovation by more standardized academic discussion. The leading collective of the Party should always pay attention to the theoretical development of the academic circle, learn from the research achievements of theorists, arm the minds of party members and cadres with the achievements of theoretical innovation, and improve the ideological and theoretical level of the whole Party. Theorists should also shoulder the historical responsibility of promoting the theoretical innovation and constantly enrich philosophy and social sciences academic ideological and theoretical system. For theorists, efforts should be made to form an academic discourse system with Chinese characteristics and Chinese style to provide solid theoretical support for promoting the development of socialism with Chinese characteristics, the exactly contemporary Chinese Marxism.

China Position, World View: The Unity of National and Global Perspectives

Essentially, to localize Marxism is to combine the basic principles of Marxism with the concrete reality of China, which must be based on China and reflect the national characteristics. Marxism, as Lenin said, provided only general guiding principles, and the application of these principles was, specifically, different in England from France, different in France from Germany, and different in Germany from Russia.[24] The existing theoretical innovation achievements are undoubtedly Marxism rooted in China, based on China's national conditions and realistic problems. The achievements are also the basic direction that future theoretical innovation must adhere to.

At the same time, the existing theoretical innovations also include the achievements of scientific analysis of the international environment and features of the time. For example, Party leaders, experts, and scholars have made numerous overseas visits to objectively evaluate the gap in economic development between China and the West, and on this basis analyze the achievements made in building socialism with Chinese characteristics and the direction of its future development; the Central Committee has sponsored a research project on the historical lessons of the collapse of some long-ruling parties in the world and the current situation of the Communist Party in various countries and the international situation, which provided direct theoretical resources for the Party building in this new period; The Party's overall consideration of international economic, political, and cultural soft power competition is also the direct motive force and reason for carrying out the Scientific Outlook on Development, building a harmonious society, building socialist culture with Chinese characteristics, condense and carry out the socialist core values and other theoretical innovations.

In the future, facing the changing international situation and the pressure from the western developed countries in such aspects as economy, technology, and culture, while basing our theoretical innovations on China's practical conditions, we should continue to observe the international environment closely from a broad perspective. We should not only learn from the excellent achievements of all other civilizations but also pay attention to constructing a discourse system with Chinese characteristics and adhere to the dialectical unity of national and global perspectives.

The Task of the Time Facing China and the Future of Theoretical Innovation

The theoretical innovation of the localization of Marxism should always be problem oriented. At this new historical starting point, "the environment at home and abroad is undergoing extensive and profound changes. China is facing a series of urgent problems and challenges in its development, and there are still many difficulties and problems ahead."[25]

In terms of the current international environment we are facing, China's deepening integration into the world and the increase of economic ties and common interests have made the external environment stable on the whole. However, with the rise of China, unstable factors are also increasing and external pressure is mounting. This is mainly reflected in the facts that the United States and other countries began to show a comprehensive containment posture against China in terms of economy, politics, information, and cultural security; the situation in neighboring countries is unstable; and disputes over territory and territorial waters still exist. In terms of soft power, China is under increasing pressure in the international soft power competition. Although we should have the best say in interpreting China's practice and formulating China's theory, "in fact, China's philosophy and social sciences still have a relatively small voice in the international community, that is, what is true cannot be said and what is said cannot be spread."[26]

Reform in China has now entered a deep-water zone where challenges and problems are tough and complex, with many institutional obstacles hindering scientific development. In terms of economy, with an unsatisfying independent innovation capacity, the industrial structure urgently needs to be adjusted, where the low-end industry has excess capacity, while the high-end industry is in the middle and lower reaches of the international industrial chain. The traditional development mode of high input, high consumption, and low benefit needs to be changed. The relationship of population, resources, and the environment is increasingly strained, and the ecological environment demands prompt improvement. Environmental problems such as haze and water pollution have become major issues affecting people's health and livelihood. Domestic consumption is seriously insufficient, failing to release the huge energy driving economic development. The relationship between government control and the market needs to be further clarified. The long-standing GDP-dominant mindset in the past led to an imbalance between national wealth and the welfare of the people. In terms of politics, the channels and mechanisms of public interest articulation need to be improved. The government should take action to establish stronger trust in the public. The anti-corruption situation is still serious, and public power needs more effective supervision and restraint. In terms of culture, various social trends of thought are complex and diverse, value orientation is increasingly diversified, and the development of network information technology and other factors bring more severe challenges to ideological construction. In terms of society, the gap between the rich and the poor has widened, and factors of instability have increased. The urban-rural dual structure caused the imbalance of resource allocation. Inequity in education, medical care, employment, housing, and other areas has persisted for a long time.

Various problems pushed socialist modernization into a new bottleneck and key stage and formed a realistic pressure on theoretical innovation. These challenges and difficulties have become the direct driving force for the new development stage of the theoretical system of socialism with Chinese characteristics.

There is no end to practical development, knowledge of truth, and theoretical innovation. In the past 100 years, through constant theoretical innovation, Marxism has developed from a branch of Western learning into a major trend in the field of Chinese thought and has become the mainstream thought leading China to prosperity and revival. In the great practice of socialism with Chinese characteristics, the Party and the vast number of theorists will continue to handle the tasks of the times from the political and academic perspectives, promote theoretical innovation, make the path of socialism with Chinese characteristics more inspiring, attractive and cohesive, and make new achievements in localizing Marxism.

Notes

1 Theoretical Bureau of the Publicity Department of the CPC Central Committee. *Ten Lectures on Marxist Philosophy.* Beijing: Learning Press, 2013, p. 36.
2 Central Compilation and Translation Bureau for Works of Marx, Engels, Lenin and Stalin. *Marx/Engels Collected Works:* vol. 10. Beijing: People's Publishing House, 2009, p. 562.
3 Ibid., p. 691.
4 Mao Zedong. *Selected Works of MAO Zedong:* vol. 2, 2nd ed. Beijing: People's Publishing House, 1991, p. 534.
5 Deng Xiaoping. *Selected Works of Deng Xiaoping:* vol. 2, 2nd ed. Beijing: People's Publishing House, 1994, p. 143.
6 Jiang Zemin. *Selected Works of Jiang Zemin:* vol. 3. Beijing: People's Publishing House, 2006, p. 337.
7 Party Literature Research Center, CPC Central Committee. *Selected Important Documents Since the 15th National Congress:* vol. 3. Beijing: People's Publishing House, 2003. p. 2213.
8 Xi Jinping. Explanatory Notes for the Decision of the CCCPC on Some Major Issues Concerning Comprehensively Deepening the Reform. *People's Daily*, November 16, 2013.
9 Xi Jinping. The Communist Party of China's 90 Years of Guiding Ideology and Basic Theory of The Times and Historical Enlightenment. *Study Times*, June 27, 2011.
10 Ai Siqi. *Twenty-two Years of Chinese Philosophical Thought.* Shanghai: Fudan University Press, 1989, p. 396.
11 Hu Weixiong. One Hundred Years of Translation and Dissemination of Marxist Works in China. *Journal of China Executive Leadership Academy Yan'an,* 2013;2.

12 China Li Dazhao Research Association. *The Collected Works of Li Dazhao*: vol. 3. Beijing: People's Publishing House, 1984, p. 711.

13 Yun Daiying. *Collected Works of Yun Daiying:* vol. 1. Beijing: People's Publishing House, 1984, p. 258.

14 Ai Siqi. *The Complete Works of Ai Siqi.* Beijing: People's Publishing House, 2006, p. 491.

15 Fang Songhua, Chen Xaingqin, Jiang Youfu. *Outline of Academic History of Marxism in China.* Shanghai: Academia Press, 2011, pp. 73–74.

16 Fang Songhua, Chen Xaingqin, Jiang Youfu. *Outline of Academic history of Marxism in China.* Shanghai: Academia Press, 2011, p. 224.

17 Xu Qingpu and Shi Jialiang. *On the Research Trend of Sinicized Marxism in Modern Times.* Studies on Marxism, 2007;3.

18 Li Nan and Zhou Jianhua. On the Subject of Theoretical Innovation of Contemporary Adaptation of Marxism to Chinese Conditions. *Jianghan Tribune*, 2010;5.

19 Hou Huiqin. *Thirty Years of the Theoretical Innovation of the Adaptation of Marxism in Chinese Conditions (1978–2008).* Beijing: China Social Sciences Press, 2008, p. 8.

20 Hou Huiqin. *Thirty Years of the Theoretical Innovation of the Adaptation of Marxism in Chinese Conditions (1978–2008).* Beijing: China Social Sciences Press, 2008, p. 8.

21 Chen Jin. *The Communist Party of China and the Theoretical Innovation.* Studies on Mao Zedong and Deng Xiaoping Theories, 2013;5.

22 Xi Jinping. *Speech at the Symposium on Philosophy and Social Sciences (May 17, 2016).* Beijing: People's Publishing House, 2016, p. 20.

23 Xi Jinping. *Speech at the Symposium on Philosophy and Social Sciences (May 17, 2016).* Beijing: People's Publishing House, 2016, p. 12

24 Central Compilation and Translation Bureau of the Works of Marx, Engels, Lenin and Stalin. *Collected Works of Lenin,* vol. 2, 2nd ed., Beijing: People's Publishing House, 1995, pp. 274–275.

25 Xi Jinping. *Note on the Decision of the CPC Central Committee on Some Major Issues concerning Comprehensively Deepening Reform.* People's Daily, November 16, 2013.

26 Xi Jinping. *Speech at the Symposium on Philosophy and Social Sciences (May 17, 2016).* Beijing: People's Publishing House, 2016, p. 24.

6 Outlook of Localization of Marxism

Liu Ying

A great era calls for great theories, and a great era breeds great theories. The practice of socialism with Chinese characteristics has entered a new era, giving birth to the thought of socialism with Chinese characteristics in the new era. Using the Marxist position, viewpoint, and method, Xi Jinping Thought on Socialism with Chinese Characteristics for a New Era focuses on the call of the times and answers the major questions of what kind of socialism with Chinese characteristics we should uphold and develop in this new era as well as how we should go about achieving these tasks in the new era. The 19th Party Congress established Xi Jinping Thought on Socialism with Chinese Characteristics for a New Era as the guiding ideology that the Party must adhere to for a long time and wrote it into the Party Constitution, ensuring that the Party's guiding ideology is kept pace with the times.

Socialism With Chinese Characteristics Has Entered a New Era

The 19th Party Congress solemnly declared that socialism with Chinese characteristics has entered a new era, making a major political judgment on the new historical orientation of China's development. The "newness" of the new era lies in the fact that we are at a new stage of development, moving from the "underdeveloped" period to the "developed" period and facing a new social conflict. The new era also lies in the fact that the Chinese nation has achieved a tremendous transformation from standing up and growing prosperous to becoming strong, and we are embarking on a new journey toward a new goal.

Evolution of the Principal Conflicts Facing Chinese Society

General Secretary Xi Jinping made a major political assertion at the 19th Party Congress: what we now face is the conflict between unbalanced and inadequate development and the people's ever-growing needs for a better life. This assertion is the correct conclusion reached by adhering to the world view and methodology of dialectical materialism and historical

DOI: 10.4324/9781003356042-7

materialism, the Party's line of thought of seeking truth from facts, and the analysis of history and reality, theory, and practice, which reflects the objective reality of China's social development and is a major theoretical innovation of the CPC. The history of the CPC is the history of constantly and profoundly understanding and judging the main conflicts of society and constantly solving the main conflicts of Chinese society. During the New Democratic Revolution, the CPC correctly analyzed the social conflicts of semi-colonial and semi-feudal China, firmly grasped the main social conflicts of imperialism and the Chinese nation, feudalism and the people, and their specific manifestations at different times, and formulated the general line of the New Democratic Revolution and a series of policies, which eventually achieved national independence, people's liberation, national unification, and social stability.

After the founding of New China, especially after the establishment of the basic system of socialism, the Eighth Party Congress described the main conflict of China's society for the first time:

> The main conflict in the country has been the conflict between the people's demand for the establishment of an advanced industrial country and the reality of a backward agricultural country, between the people's need for rapid economic and cultural development and the current economic and cultural failure to meet the people's needs.[1]

This was in line with the reality of China at that time. However, due to complex socio-historical reasons, this correct assertion was not adhered to later.

After the third Plenary Session of the 11th Central Committee of the Party, our Party scientifically analyzed that China is still in the primary stage of socialism, affirmed the proposition of the Eighth Party Congress, and further streamlined and refined it. The Resolution on Certain Questions in the History of Our Party, adopted at the Sixth Plenary Session of the 11th Central Committee of the Party, proposed that the main conflict to be solved is that China's underdeveloped social production was unable to meet the ever-growing material and cultural needs of the people. This has provided us with scientific guidance for the deployment of the overall work of the Party and the State.

Since the reform and opening up, the CPC has formulated and adhered to the correct lines and policies based on this major problem and has made great achievements in the construction of socialism with Chinese characteristics. After more than 40 years of arduous exploration and long-term efforts, the level of China's social productivity has increased significantly, and the overall national strength has leaped to the forefront of the world. Moreover, the economic development has entered a period of new normal, and there have been significant changes in the development pattern. People's lives have improved significantly, and the development of social undertakings has been accelerated. China's international status and influence have increased significantly, and it is increasingly moving to the center of the world stage. Along with development, new characteristics of social production and social demand have emerged, which have become the main basis for the changes in the main problems of our society.

After more than 40 years of reform and opening up, the level of social productivity in China has generally improved significantly, and the social production capacity has entered the forefront of the world in many aspects. Since 2010, China's GDP has steadily ranked second in the world, the total import and export value of both goods and services have ranked second in the world, foreign investment and foreign capital utilization have ranked second and third in the world respectively, and some areas of infrastructure construction are leading the world, with the total mileage of high-speed railways, highways, and port throughput ranking first in the world. The production capacity of industry and agriculture has increased significantly, with more than 220 major industrial and agricultural products ranking first in the world, and there is even excess capacity in iron and steel products. This shows that China's long-standing shortage economy and inadequate supply conditions have been fundamentally transformed, and it is no longer realistic to talk about "backward social production."

In addition, the people's living standard has improved significantly, and their aspiration for a better life has become stronger, with higher demands not only for material and cultural life but also for democracy, rule of law, fairness, justice, security, and environment. Since the reform and opening up, China's people's living standards continue to rise to a new level, with the per capita GDP rising from 385 yuan in 1978 to 59,660 yuan in 2017, which is an average annual growth of about 9.5%, reaching the level of upper-middle-income countries. Urban and rural residents' per capita disposable income has risen from 343.4 yuan and 133.6 yuan in 1978 to 36,396 yuan and 13,432 yuan in 2017 respectively. The rural poverty rate has dropped sharply from 97.5% in 1978 to less than 3.1% in 2017, far below the world average. The education level of residents has continued to improve, with nine-year compulsory education fully universalized and the gross enrollment rate of higher education reaching 45.7% in 2017, nearly 10 % points higher than the world average. At the same time, the health condition of urban and rural residents has improved significantly, and the average life expectancy of residents reached 76.7 years in 2017, higher than the world average. Moreover, the level of social security has improved greatly, the social security system covering urban and rural areas has been basically established, and many other aspects of livelihood protection have also improved significantly. With the continuous improvement of people's living standards, the needs of the people are diversified, multi-level, and multi-faceted, and they expect better education, more stable jobs, more satisfactory income, more reliable social security, higher level of medical and health services, more comfortable living conditions, more beautiful environment as well as more colorful spiritual and cultural life. The people's awareness of democracy, fairness, rule of law, participation, supervision, and rights is increasing. This shows that the needs of the people have gone beyond the scope and level of material culture in terms of field and focus, and only "material cultural needs" can no longer truly and comprehensively reflect the aspirations and needs of the people.

On the whole, the imbalances and inadequacies in development in China is the main factor affecting the satisfaction of people's needs for a better life. Unbalanced development mainly refers to the unbalanced development of various areas and fields in various regions. From the point of view of productive forces, China has the world's fastest high-speed rail and the most powerful spherical radio telescope "FAST" equipped with the world's largest aperture, the world's largest hydroelectric generating sets, and other world-leading techniques. However, China also has a large number of traditional, relatively backward, or even primitive productive forces. Moreover, different regions and different areas have unbalanced productivity levels. From the overall layout of the "five-sphere integrated plan," economic and social development has made significant achievements, but there are still shortcomings in culture and ecological civilization as well as other fields. From the perspective of urban-rural development, the gap between urban and rural areas, and between the development level of the eastern, central, and western regions in China is still large. From the point of view of the income distribution, although China's per capita national income has entered the world's upper-middle-class level and the vast majority of people have solved the problem of food and clothing, the income distribution gap is still large, some people in rural areas have not been out of poverty, also, there are still many people in difficulty in the city. These problems of unbalanced and inadequate development are hampering each other, bringing about many social problems, and limiting China's future development. In the future, we should be aware of the stage of China's development, in line with the people's aspirations for a better life, and centered around the people, put forward new ideas, new strategies, and new initiatives focusing on major social problems.

In the scientific understanding of the changes in the main problems in our society, General Secretary Xi Jinping pointed out that

> we must recognize that the evolution of the principal conflict facing Chinese society does not change our assessment of the present stage of socialism in China. The basic dimension of the Chinese context – that our country is still and will long remain in the primary stage of socialism – has not changed. China's international status as the world's largest developing country has not changed.[2]

On the one hand, this is reflected in the fact that although China has made remarkable achievements in the world, it is still the largest developing country in the world and still faces a series of serious challenges and many problems that need to be solved. China has become the world's second-largest economy, but the level of economic development is not the only condition that determines the stage of social development but should be comprehensively grasped from the relationship between productive forces and relations of production, economic foundation and superstructure, material civilization and spiritual civilization construction, from economic construction, political construction, cultural construction, social construction, ecological civilization construction and Party construction, and other aspects of comprehensive consideration.

On the one hand, this is reflected in the fact that although China has made remarkable achievements in the world, it is still the largest developing country in the world and still faces a series of serious challenges and many problems that need to be solved. China has become the world's second-largest economy, but the stage of social development cannot be determined solely by economic development. However, it should be comprehensively grasped from the productive forces and the relations of production, economic basis and superstructure, material civilization, and spiritual civilization construction. It should also be considered comprehensively from economic construction, political construction, cultural construction, social construction, ecological civilization construction, party construction, and other aspects.

On the other hand, the primary stage of socialism itself is a dynamic development process that is long-term and phrased. In the long-term historical process of the primary stage of socialism, the principal social conflicts will change with social development. The essence of grasping the changes in the principal conflicts of our society is to grasp more accurately the changing characteristics of the primary stage of socialism in China and to better adhere to the theory of the primary stage of socialism. Along with promoting economic development, we should promote the overall development of various undertakings, to better build the cause of socialism with Chinese characteristics.

Therefore, in recognizing and understanding the changes in the principal conflicts of our society, we must consider and study this issue in unison with the fact that our country is still in the primary stage of socialism and will remain in it for a long time, and that our international status as the largest developing country in the world remains unchanged, and understand dialectically the "to changes" and "not to change," so we would neither lag behind the times nor be out of touch with reality.

Stood Up, Grown Rich, Becoming Strong

Major General Jin Yinan once told of such a personal experience: in 2000, he was studying at Britain's Royal Academy of Military Sciences, where all officers were required to talk about their country's ideology. Among the 30 officers from 26 countries and regions who participated in the study, Jin was the only one from a socialist country. When he came on stage to give his speech, he noticed that the class suddenly fell into a deathlike silence as if no one was there—and everyone was waiting to see what this Chinese officer would say. Standing on stage, Jin showed a PowerPoint presentation with only two photos, one showing China in 1900 and the other in 2000. In 1900, the Eight-Power Allied Forces invaded Beijing, and next year the Qing government signed the Peace Protocol of 1901, which marked the failure of the "Sick Man of Asia." After 100 years, China has become a rising country, with its industry, science, technology, education, and medical care ranking among the best in the world. Over 100 years, Marxism has changed China, enabling it to find its own way to national independence and liberation.[3]

As those two photos showed, the past century witnessed great changes taken place in China under the guidance of Marxism. In his report to the 19th National Congress of the Party, General Secretary Xi Jinping pointed out that

> the Chinese nation; which since modern times began had endured so much for so long; has achieved a tremendous transformation: it has stood up; grown rich; and is becoming strong; it has come to embrace the brilliant prospects of rejuvenation.[4]

The Chinese nation is an indomitable nation, and its modern history is full of humiliation, a history of struggle from kneeling to standing up. After Britain's invasion of China in 1840, China was reduced to a semi-colonial and semi-feudal country, abused and humiliated by foreign powers, and the Chinese people were plunged into deep suffering. Dreaming to save the country, countless people with lofty ideals fought dauntlessly and explored the road of rejuvenation. The Chinese nation experienced the tragic failures of the Taiping Heavenly Kingdom, the Westernization Movement, the reform of the constitutional monarchy, and the Revolution of 1911. The Communist Party of China was born out of adversity when the nation was suffering and seeking light. It led the Chinese people in a bloody struggle, ending the history of a divided old China and founding a united new China, and "the Chinese people, who account for a quarter of the total number of mankind, have stood up ever since."[5]

Since the founding of the People's Republic of China, especially over the past four decades of reform and opening up, our Party has united the people and led them in successfully embarking on a path of socialism with Chinese characteristics. We have ensured the basic living needs of more than one billion people and, on the whole, achieved a moderately prosperous society. We will soon finish building a moderately prosperous society in all respects and bring prosperity to the Chinese people step by step. The process of "getting rich" is the process of liberating and developing productive forces, enhancing social vitality, and moving toward common prosperity. "Getting rich" started after the third Plenary Session of the 11th Party Congress in 1978 and was based on the exploration of the socialist road in the early days of this young republic. The process of "getting rich" is the process of exploring the road of socialism with Chinese characteristics, the sublation of the western road of modernization, and the success of the Chinese way of development and China's socialist system.

Under the leadership of the Communist Party of China, socialism with Chinese characteristics has entered a new era since the 18th CPC National Congress. The Chinese nation is on its way of a tremendous transformation: it has stood up; grown rich; and is becoming strong. Under the leadership of the CPC Central Committee with Comrade Xi Jinping at its core, the Party, the country, and the armed forces have undergone deep-seated and fundamental changes, made groundbreaking achievements in all areas, and taken on an entirely new look. The Chinese nation is closer, more confident, and capable of achieving the goal of rejuvenation than ever before in history. After more than 40 years of reform and opening up, especially since the 18th National Congress of the Party, the connotation of a "strong country" has become richer and its goal has become higher and higher. We have seen a success in exploring from land to sea and space, and in developing from industry and agriculture to science and technology, finance, manufacturing, transportation, culture, sports, health, and ecology. Our goals are becoming more precise, broader, and more ambitious. And even more remarkably, guided by the new vision of development, we have made coordinated efforts to promote the Five-sphere Integrated Plan, the Four-pronged Comprehensive Strategy, and the innovation-driven development strategy. We will continue to improve the Party's ability to lead and govern the country through legal means, push forward reform in an all-round way, make breakthroughs in multiple areas, and advance it in depth, and eventually make China's development more high-quality, efficient, equitable, and sustainable. By the middle of the 21st century, China will have fully developed into a great modern socialist country that is prosperous, strong, democratic, culturally advanced, harmonious, and beautiful and become a country leading in overall national strength and international influence. The Chinese nation will stand more proudly among the nations of the world at that time.

Firmly Uphold and Develop Socialism With Chinese Characteristics

As Xi Jinping pointed out, socialism with Chinese characteristics does not grow on trees. It is a fundamental achievement made by the Party along with the people after enduring untold hardships and sufferings at various costs. Only socialism can save China, and only by adhering to and developing socialism with Chinese characteristics can we realize the great rejuvenation of the Chinese nation.

Upholding and developing socialism with Chinese characteristics is the general orientation of development in contemporary China. Xi Jinping has made a comprehensive and systematic discussion on upholding and developing socialism with Chinese characteristics. He pointed out that, since the 18th CPC National Congress, we should focus on fostering stronger confidence in the path, theory, system, and culture of socialism with Chinese characteristics, pursuing with firmness of purpose the vision of innovative, coordinated, green, and open development that is for everyone, working in accordance with the overall plan for promoting all-round economic, political, cultural, social, and ecological progress and the Four-Pronged Comprehensive Strategy, and building a community with a shared future for mankind.

Four Matters of Confidence

"In today's world, if any political party, country or nation has the most reason to be confident, it must be the Communist Party of China, the People's Republic of China and the Chinese nation,"[6] Xi said at a ceremony celebrating the 95th anniversary of the founding of the Communist Party of China. Where does this confidence come from? It comes from our confidence in the path, theory, system, and culture of socialism with Chinese characteristics. To foster the "Four Confidence" is not only a theoretical problem but also a practical one that requires practice.

The root cause for all the achievements and progress we have made since the launch of reform and opening up lies in socialism with Chinese characteristics. We have blazed its path, formed its theoretical system, established its system, and developed its culture. On the path of socialism with Chinese characteristics, we have made great achievements with its theoretical system as the guide to action, its system as the fundamental guarantee, and its culture as our spiritual strength. The path, theoretical system, socialist system, and socialist culture are unified in the great practice of socialism with Chinese characteristics and constitute the fundamental symbol of socialism with Chinese characteristics.

Confidence in Our Path

The path of socialism with Chinese characteristics has answered the question of where China is heading. The history of China's revolution and development since modern times began proves that only socialism can save China and only socialism with Chinese characteristics can develop China. The past 40-plus years of reform and opening up have indisputably supported that the path of socialism with Chinese characteristics is the only way to achieve socialist modernization, bring a better life to the people, and realize the great rejuvenation of the Chinese nation. To keep to the path of socialism with Chinese characteristics, we must work under the leadership of the Party in light of China's national conditions. We will continue to take economic development as the central task, adhere to the Four Cardinal

Principles, and persist in reform and opening up. We will coordinate efforts to advance the Five-sphere Integrated Plan for economic, political, cultural, social, and ecological progress and advance the Four-Pronged Strategy for building a moderately prosperous society in all respects, deepening reform, advancing law-based governance, and strengthening Party self-governance. We will continue to unleash and develop the productive forces, realize common prosperity for all step by step, and promote all-round development of the people.

To hold the confidence of the chosen path means to believe and adhere to the path of socialism with Chinese characteristics chosen by the Party and the country amid the tide of history. First, it should be made clear that the path of socialism with Chinese characteristics is the way to realize socialism with Chinese characteristics and the practical form of the latest achievements of localizing Marxism. We must remain clear-headed and strategically focused, not be daunted by any risks and not be confused by any interference, and move forward unswervingly. Second, it should be made clear that the path of socialism with Chinese characteristics came from the great practice of reform and opening up, and that it needs to be adhered to and expanded in the course of reform and opening up. We must unswervingly advance reform and opening up and never become rigid or stagnant. Third, it should be made clear that the path of socialism with Chinese characteristics is a path of all-round development aimed at realizing socialist modernization, creating a better life for the people, and realizing the great rejuvenation of the Chinese nation. It is a path of prosperity, democracy, advanced culture, harmony, and beauty while promoting all-round development of the people and meeting the expectations of the people and step by step realizing common prosperity for all.

Confidence in Our Theory

What kind of socialism should we build? How to build socialism? What kind of party should we build? How to build the Party? What kind of development should we have? How to develop? What kind of socialism with Chinese characteristics should we uphold and develop in the new era? How to uphold and develop socialism with Chinese characteristics? The theoretical system of socialism with Chinese characteristics closely revolves around these major issues. The theoretical system of socialism with Chinese characteristics includes Deng Xiaoping Theory, the Theory of Three Represents, the Scientific Outlook on Development, and Xi Jinping Thought on Socialism with Chinese Characteristics for a New Era. It embodies the wisdom and painstaking efforts of generations of Chinese Communists to unite the people and lead them in unremitting exploration and practice and is a theoretical innovation achieved by the Party in localizing Marxism since the launch of reform and opening up. This theoretical system is rooted in the great practice of reform and opening up and socialist construction. It has formed a series of original views on the guiding principles, development path, development stage, development strategy, fundamental task, motivation, relying force, international strategy, leading force and fundamental purpose of building socialism with Chinese characteristics. It provided a guide for realizing modernization, consolidating, and developing socialism in a big developing country like China.

The confidence in theory is based on the long-term practice of the Party and the people. In 1930, Mao Zedong wrote in his work *Oppose Book Worship*: "We say that Marxism is right not because Marx himself is some sort of 'saint', but because his theory has been proved right in our practice and in our struggle. Our struggle needs Marxism."[7] Similarly, the solid foundation for our confidence in the theoretical system of socialism with Chinese characteristics lies in our practice over the past 40-plus years of reform and opening up since the beginning of this new era. Since the beginning of reform and opening up, the people are leading a more and more prosperous and healthy life, and the cause of the Party and the state has developed vigorously. All these proved that the theoretical system of socialism with Chinese characteristics is scientific and has great power. Historic changes and achievements since the 18th CPC National Congress have been made under the scientific guidance of Xi Jinping Thought on Socialism with Chinese Characteristics for a New Era. Today, to uphold Xi Jinping Thought on Socialism with Chinese Characteristics for a New Era is to truly uphold the theoretical system of socialism with Chinese characteristics and to truly uphold Marxism.

Confidence in Our System

The system of socialism with Chinese characteristics is the fundamental institutional guarantee for development in China. It is an advanced system with distinctive Chinese characteristics, obvious institutional advantages, and strong self-improvement ability. This system is reflected in all aspects of economic, political, cultural, social, and ecological progress. For example, it is reflected in the system of people's congresses as China's fundamental political system and the basic political systems of multi-party cooperation and political consultation under the leadership of the CPC, of regional ethnic autonomy, and of community-level self-governance. It is also reflected in the Chinese socialist system of laws and the basic economic system in which public ownership is the mainstay and economic entities of diverse ownership develop together, etc. Professor Han Qingxiang of the Party School of the CPC Central Committee summarized the institutional advantages of the Chinese road into eight aspects in his book What Can the Chinese Road Contribute to the World: the unity of pooling efforts to accomplish big tasks, the strict enforcement of orders and prohibitions, the efficiency of decision-making and implementation, the stability of political order, the continuity in policy formulation and implementation, the coordination of regional sector linkage, the flexibility to assess the situation and keep pace with the times, and mutual aid when disasters come.

To strengthen our confidence in our system, we should see that the socialist system with Chinese characteristics conforms to China's national conditions. It not only adheres to the fundamental nature of socialism but also draws on the achievements of institutional development, both ancient and modern, both at home and abroad. It embodies the characteristics and strengths of socialism with Chinese characteristics and does not simply copy western political models such as the model of multiple parties alternate in power, separation of the three powers, and bicameralism. It should also be noted that the system of socialism with Chinese characteristics is not perfect and fixed. We need to promptly formulate new systems and improve old ones in the light of actual conditions, actively yet prudently advance political reforming.

Confidence in Our Culture

Socialist culture with Chinese characteristics is derived from China's fine traditional culture, which was born of the Chinese civilization and nurtured over more than 5,000 years; it has grown out of the revolutionary and advanced socialist culture that developed over the course of the Chinese people's revolution, and through construction, and reform under the Party's leadership. Developing socialist culture with Chinese characteristics means developing a socialist culture for the nation—a culture that is sound and people-oriented, that embraces modernization, the world, and the future, and that promotes socialist material well-being and raises socialist cultural-ethical standards. In developing this culture, China must follow the guidance of Marxism, base its efforts on Chinese culture, and take into account the realities of contemporary China and the conditions of the present era. We must cultivate and practice core socialist values and build Chinese spirit, Chinese values, and Chinese strength.

Cultural confidence means that the Chinese nation and the CPC fully recognize and practice their own cultural values, and that have firm determination and confidence in the vitality of our own culture. Since the 18th CPC National Congress, General Secretary Xi Jinping has expounded the significance of cultural confidence from different perspectives and levels for many times. He emphasized that

> when we talk about strengthening our confidence in the path, theory, and system of socialism with Chinese characteristics, we mean, in the final analysis, strengthening our confidence in our culture. Confidence in its culture is a more fundamental and more enduring power,[8]

and "without a high degree of cultural confidence, and without a thriving culture, there will be no great rejuvenation of the Chinese nation."[9]

To strengthen confidence in the culture, we must participate extensively in dialog among other civilizations without feeling inferior or conceited and promote the creative transformation and development of fine traditional Chinese culture. We must inherit revolutionary culture, develop advanced socialist culture, and provide spiritual nourishment for the country, society, and individuals with values as the core, which will ultimately be vividly reflected in the temperament and appearance of every citizen.

Socialism with Chinese characteristics has never developed in a calm environment. However, as long as we remain firmly confident in the "four matters" of socialism with Chinese characteristics, we can hold our ground despite pressure or opposition, strengthen our confidence and enhance our strength to forge ahead, and increase our wisdom and ability to overcome risks and challenges.

The Four-Pronged Comprehensive Strategy

Since the 18th Party Congress, the CPC Central Committee has proposed and formed the strategic layout of completing the building of a society that is moderately prosperous in all respects, comprehensively expanding in-depth reform, comprehensively promoting law-based governance, and comprehensively enforcing strict Party self-governance with the overall aim of upholding and developing socialism with Chinese characteristics. Among them, completing the building of a society that is moderately prosperous in all respects is our strategic goal, comprehensively expanding in-depth reform is the driving force, comprehensively promoting law-based governance is the guarantee, and the comprehensively enforcing strict Party self-governance is the key. The "Four-Pronged Comprehensive Strategy" reflects the summary, thinking, and deployment of the CPC Central Committee with Comrade Xi Jinping at the core of the new era of governance practice, which opens up a new horizon of governance and puts forward new requirements for governance under the new situation, so that during the current and future period, the key aspects, key areas, and main directions of the work of the Party and the State in the current and future period are clearer, and the internal logic is more rigorous.

Completing the Building of a Moderately Prosperous Society in All Respects Is the Goal

To build a moderately prosperous society is a solemn promise made by the CPC to the people and history and is the common expectation of more than 1.3 billion Chinese people. This goal is the first goal of the "Two Centennial Goals," which is an important milestone on the journey of the great rejuvenation of the Chinese nation.

A moderately well-off society is the ideal social state that the Chinese people have been pursuing since ancient times. At the beginning of reform and opening up, Deng Xiaoping first proposed the concept of a "moderately well-off society" when he met with the then Japanese Prime Minister Ohira Masayoshi in 1979. Since then, Deng Xiaoping has gradually developed the "three-step" development strategy, from "meeting the most basic needs of the people" to "a moderately prosperous life" to "basic modernization." This constituted the grand blueprint of China's modernization. By 2000, China had achieved the first two steps of the "three-step" development strategy through reform and opening up and generally reached a well-off level. Since this well-off level was still incomplete and low, the 16th Party Congress held after the new century put forward the goal of "comprehensively building a higher level of well-off society benefiting more than one billion people." In the report of the 17th Party Congress held in 2007, the term "building a moderately prosperous society" was changed to "completing the building of a moderately prosperous society in all respects." The reports of the 18th and 19th Party Congresses further explained this goal and emphasized the "Two Centenary Goals," that is, to build a well-off society with more economic development, more sound democracy, more progress in science and education, more cultural prosperity, more social harmony, and more prosperous people's life by the 100th year of the founding of the CPC. Then by struggling for another 30 years, by the 100th year of the founding of New China, we will have realized modernization and built China into a modern socialist country.

Since the 18th Party Congress, the CPC Central Committee, with Comrade Xi Jinping as the core, has put forward new requirements for building a moderately well-off society in all aspects and further defined the basic connotations of building a moderately well-off society in all aspects, mainly including enhancing quality and efficiency of development, remarkable results of innovation-driven development strategy, obvious enhancement of development coordination, general improvement of people's living standards and quality, significant improvement of the overall caliber of the population and the level of civility in society, overall improvement of ecological and environmental quality, and more mature and better systems in all aspects. The main components include high-quality economic development, remarkable results of innovation drive, obvious enhancement of development coordination, general improvement of people's living standard and quality, significant improvement of national quality and social civilization, overall improvement of ecological and environmental quality, and more mature and established systems.

To build a moderately well-off society on schedule, what is more important and difficult to achieve is how to build such a society "in all respects." The term "well-off" refers to the level of development, while "in all respects" refers to the balance, coordination, and sustainability of development. General Secretary Xi Jinping has repeatedly stressed that we haven't achieved the goal if by 2020, the unbalanced, uncoordinated, and unsustainable development is more serious and the shortcomings are more prominent, although we have completed the target in terms of total volume and speed. Thus, this requires that the fields covered should be comprehensive in that we should build a moderately well-off society following the five-sphere integrated plan. The population covered should be comprehensive, in that we should build a moderately well-off society that benefits everyone. The region covered should be comprehensive, in that we should build a moderately well-off society that develops urban and rural areas coordinately. At the same time, we must also be realistic and act according to local conditions, not simply apply the relevant indicators, forcing "the same level of well-off."

The report of the 19th Party Congress puts forward that from now to 2020 is the decisive period to build a moderately well-off society in all aspects. General Secretary Xi Jinping pointed out,

> Now, with the finishing line in sight, it is time to make one final push in this journey that will traverse the first 20 years of this century. Completing this strategic task is both our historical responsibility and our greatest honor.[10]

In this period, we should closely follow the changes in the main conflicts of our society in the new era, make policies comprehensively, make efforts precisely, highlight the key points, fill the shortcomings, and especially do a good job in risk management, poverty reduction, and pollution control. At the same time, we should promote sustainable and healthy economic and social development and ensure that the final victory in building a moderately prosperous society perfect finish.

In-Depth Reform in All Respects Is the Driving Force

General Secretary Xi Jinping has stressed, "The reform and opening up is a game-changing move in making China what it is today and a game-changing move for us to achieve China's two centenary goals and its great national rejuvenation."[11] The achievements of more than 40 years have fully proved that reform and opening up is the key choice to determine the fate of contemporary China. 1978, marked by the Third Plenary Session of the 11th CPC Central Committee, China started the historical journey of reform and opening up. From the countryside to the cities, from the pilot to the extension, from the reform of the economic system to in-depth reform in all respects, the Chinese people have written a magnificent epic of national and ethnic development with their hands. Since the 18th Party Congress, the CPC Central Committee, with Comrade Xi Jinping as the core, has promoted comprehensive deepening reform with unprecedented determination and strength, made a series of major strategic plans, issued more than 360 key reform documents, and launched more than 1,500 reform initiatives. The majority of cadres and masses have actively participated in the reform and written a new chapter of reform.

After more than 40 years of great practice, China's reform and opening up have come to a new historical juncture. As the reform continues to deepen, it can be said that the easy reform has been completed, and the rest is difficult. Therefore, General Secretary Xi Jinping stressed, "Reform and opening up is an ongoing process with no end point."[12] Reform is created by problems and deepened through continuous problem-solving. The conflicts in the reform process can only be solved by the reform, and the new era requires us to carry out in-depth reform in all respects, and we must carry out the reform to the end.

In-depth reform in all respects must adhere to the correct direction. General Secretary Xi Jinping stressed,

> The purpose of promoting reform is to continuously promote the self-improvement and development of our socialist system, giving socialism a new vitality. The core of this is to adhere to and improve the leadership of the Party, and adhere to and improve the socialist system with Chinese characteristics. Deviating from this one will be the poles apart.[13]

To grasp the correct direction of in-depth reform in all respects, one should first adhere to the fundamental political direction of socialism with Chinese characteristics. The report of the 19th CPC Congress points out that the overall goal of in-depth reform in all respects is to improve and develop socialism with Chinese characteristics and to promote the modernization of the national governance system and governance capacity. These two sentences are a unified whole, the first sentence specifies the fundamental direction, and the second sentence specifies the distinctive direction of improving and developing socialism with Chinese characteristics under the guidance of the fundamental direction, only two sentences combined can be complete and comprehensive. The second is to adhere to and strengthen the overall leadership of the party. The CPC leadership is the fundamental political guarantee for the smooth progress of the difficult and complex reform work. To carry out in-depth reform in all respects comprehensively, the party must play the overall situation, coordinate the leading role of the core, and grasp the political direction and the political situation.

In-depth reform in all respects in the new era should have a focus and breakthrough. The 19th CPC Congress report highlights eight key areas and aspects of the future in-depth reform: deepening the structural reform of the supply side and setting the improvement of the quality of the supply system as the main direction, deepening the reform of the rural land system, which means extending the second round of land contract for another 30 years after it expires, deepening the reform of the financial system which means to guard the bottom line of systemic financial risks, promoting the formation of a new pattern of opening up in all respects, giving greater autonomy to the free trade zone. Moreover, we should reform the ecological and environmental regulatory system, establish the state-owned natural resources assets management and natural ecological regulatory agencies, and promote the reform of the administrative system, in the provinces, cities, and counties to explore the merging or co-location of the party and government organs with similar functions. We should also deepen the reform of the national monitoring system, the national monitoring system reform pilot rolled out, improve the assessment and evaluation mechanism of cadres, adhere to the combination of strict control and love, incentives and constraints, and so on.

The key to in-depth reform in all respects in the new era is to break through the blockades of vested interests. The 19th CPC National Congress report pointed out that the in-depth reform should "have the determination to get rid of all outdated thinking and ideas and all institutional ailments, and to break through the blockades of vested interests."[14] The breaking through the blockades of vested interests emphasized by in-depth reform in all respects is not just a general appeal for fair sharing slogans but also an emphasis on fundamentally breaking the blockades of vested interests, avoiding and preventing the formation of new vested interests through new institutional design to "develop a set of institutions that are well-conceived, fully built, procedure-based, and efficiently functioning, and do full justice to the strengths of China's socialist system." This requires starting from the issues that the people are most concerned about, that are most urgent, most needed, and most beneficial, and seizing the key areas and key links, such as accelerating the transformation of government functions, dealing with the relationship between the government and the market, deepening the reform of the income distribution system, focusing on solving the problem of excessive income disparity, promoting the reform of administrative monopolies, breaking industry monopolies and regional blockades, opening upward circulation channels, and promoting the construction of democracy and rule of law to protect the legitimate rights and interests of the people.

Comprehensive Law-Based Governance as a Guarantee

The law is of great significance to a country, and the rule of law provides an important underpinning for China's governance system and capacity. Comprehensive law-based governance is an essential requirement and important guarantee for socialism with Chinese characteristics and represents a profound revolution in China's governance. Its connotation mainly includes:

First, a comprehensive system for setting targets. To build a Chinese socialist legal system and a law-based socialist country, the general goal for promoting the rule of law was raised by the fourth plenary session of the 18th CPC Central Committee in October 2014. To achieve this, it is necessary to create a complete system of legal norms, a highly effective system for implementing rule of law, a rigorous system of scrutiny, a powerful system of legal protections, and a complete system of internal Party regulations. As of March 2018, China had more than 250 laws, 700 administrative regulations, 9000 local regulations, and 11000 administrative regulations. A socialist legal system with Chinese characteristics has been formed, but it still needs to be further improved to meet the requirements of the new era.

Second, a comprehensive work plan. The governance of the country, the exercise of power, and the work of administration must always be done according to the law. A law-based country, government, and society must be integrated in their development. The 19th National Congress of the CPC made it clear that by 2035, a law-based country, government, and society should be basically in place, institutions in all areas should be further improved, and modernization of China's governance system and capacity should be basically realized.

Third, comprehensively advancing the rule of law. Laws must be legislated scientifically and enforced strictly, justice must be impartial, and the people must be law-abiding. These are the premise, key, back line, and basis respectively.

Fourth, a comprehensive reform of the rule of law. Since the fourth plenary session of the 18th CPC Central Committee, the Party has put forward a number of important measures to reform the rule of law, covering the stability of reform and development, internal affairs, foreign affairs, national defense, and governing the Party, state, and military.

One of the key problems in advancing the rule of law in an all-round way is to deal with the relationship between the Party and law. General Secretary Xi Jinping stressed that the relationship between the Party and the law is a fundamental issue. If this issue is properly handled, the rule of law will revitalize the Party and the country. If not, the rule of law will weaken the party and the country. He sharply pointed out that the question of whether the Party or the law is superior is a false proposition. In China, the law is the unified expression of the Party's position and the people's will. The Party leads the people in formulating and implementing the Constitution and laws, and the Party must act within the scope of the Constitution and laws. The Party and the law, the leadership of the Party, and the rule of law are highly unified. China's "governing the country in accordance with the Constitution" is fundamentally different from the so-called western constitutionalism. To rule the country in accordance with the Constitution means to unswervingly uphold the CPC's leading position as defined in the Constitution and to unswervingly uphold the state system of people's democratic dictatorship and the system of people's congresses as defined in the Constitution. It is wrong, harmful, unconstitutional, and absolutely unacceptable for anyone to deny the leadership of the CPC and China's socialist system under any pretext. When we say that there is no question of whether the Party or the law is superior, this is from the perspective of the party as a whole, concerning its governing and leading position. Party and government officials at all levels must obey and abide by the Constitution and the law. They must not act in the name of the Party or use the Party's leadership as a shield to substitute their wills for the law, override the law with their power, break the law in pursuit of profit, or bend the law for personal gain. The boundary must be clearly drawn.

With this distinct premise, it is clear that adhering to the leadership of the Party is the fundamental requirement of socialist rule of law and is an integral part of advancing the rule of law in an all-round way. Party leadership is the most fundamental guarantee for realizing the overall goal of comprehensively governing the country in accordance with the law. We must always uphold the Party's core position as exercising overall leadership and coordinating the efforts of all parties and ensure that Party leadership is exercised throughout and in all aspects of law-based governance. At the same time, officials should be taken into account as the "key minority." They should set an example in respecting, observing, and applying the law. They should establish the concept of the rule of law, enhance their thinking and capacity for the rule of law, and confine their power to an institutional cage, so as to resolve the true question of whether the law or the power is greater.

Comprehensively Governing the Party With Strict Discipline as the Key

To have the courage to carry out self-reform and conduct strict self-governance has always been part of a great tradition of the CPC. General Secretary Xi Jinping once pointed out that

> the greatness of the CPC does not lie in its failure to make mistakes or to conceal its fault for fear of criticism, but in its courage to face up to problems, its courage to carry out self-revolution, and its strong ability to repair itself.[15]

As socialism with Chinese characteristics has entered a new era, Party building faces arduous tasks. First, unprecedented new challenges and requirements have appeared in the process of securing a decisive victory in building a moderately prosperous society in all respects and realizing the rejuvenation of the Chinese nation. Second, factors that threat the Party's advanced nature and weaken the Party's purity still exist. The tests the Party faces in its governance, reform and opening up, the market economy, and the external environment are long-term and complex. The dangers facing the Party of slackening our spirit, incompetence, isolation from the people, passivity, and corruption are acute and grave. Only by facing up to the problems and enforcing strict Party discipline can we ensure the vitality and combat effectiveness of the Party and provide a strong political guarantee for the development of the Party and the country.

According to the report of the 19th CPC National Congress, "effort is meant to comprehensively cover the Party's political advancement, theoretical development, organizational readjustment, work practices, discipline building, anti-corruption campaigns, and institutional arrangements, and constantly improve the quality of Party building."[16]

Political advancement is the Party's fundamental cornerstone. At the 19th National Congress of the CPC, political advancement was incorporated into the overall plan of Party building and given top priority, thus defining its strategic role in Party building in the new era. The primary task of the Party's political advancement is to hold the "Four Consciousnesses," namely maintaining political integrity, thinking in big-picture terms, following the leadership core, and keeping in alignment. We must ensure that the entire Party complies with the Central Committee and resolutely uphold its authority and centralized, unified leadership. Second, it is a must to ensure all members and officials to respect the Party Constitution, abide by the Party's guidelines on internal political conduct and its various rules, promote intraparty political culture, and create a clean and upright political environment. Finally, all Party members, especially senior leading officials, must constantly improve their political ability, that is, their ability to grasp the direction, the general trend and the overall situation, and their ability to maintain political determination, steer political situations, and guard against political risks.

Theoretical development is the basic building of the Party. The primary task of the Party's theoretical development is to firm up ideals and beliefs. Xi Jinping pointed out that ideals and beliefs are the spiritual "calcium" of communists. Without ideals and beliefs, if the ideals and beliefs are not firm, there will be "calcium deficiency" mentally, and "chondrosis" will occur. Party members and officials should earnestly study Marxist theories, especially Xi Jinping Thought on Socialism with Chinese Characteristics for a New Era, learn to apply Marxist positions, views, and methods to observe and solve problems, and base their ideals and beliefs on a correct understanding of the laws of history. Also, Party members and officials should turn a correct world outlook, outlook on life, and values into the "master switch," and consciously become firm believers and faithful practitioners of the great dream of Communism and the common ideal of socialism with Chinese characteristics.

Party officials are a central pillar of strength for the Party and the country. Improving the Party's organizational structures aims at building a team of high-caliber public servants. First, we must hold the standards of Communist Party members raised by Xi, so as to be firm in faith, serve the people, be diligent and pragmatic, dare to undertake, and be honest and upright. Second, we will adhere to the proper criteria for selecting and appointing Party and government officials strictly in accordance with the Regulations on the Selection and Appointment of Party and Government Leading Officials. Third, we should hold the principle that the Party supervises officials and place equal emphasis on incentives and constraints while exercising strict supervision and showing kindness. Finally, we will do our utmost to enhance the organizational capacity of community-level Party organizations and build a strong fighting fortress for the new era, publicizing the Party's views and implementing the Party's decisions, leading community-level governance, and rallying the people to promote reform and development.

To promote ethical standards within the Party is to improve the image of the Party, which concerns the support of the people and the survival of the Party. The core of promoting ethical standards is to maintain the flesh-and-blood ties between the Party and the people. Since the 18th CPC National Congress, the Party has launched a series of activities on the mass line. Party officials are required to lead by example in further implementing the CPC Central Committee's Eight-point Decision on Improving Party and Government Conduct. The campaign to fight unhealthy behaviors and tendencies will continue, targeting at, in particular, obsession with formalities instead of substance, too much red tape, indulgence in pleasure, and a penchant for extravagance. The Party has made the "Three Guidelines for Ethical Behavior and Three Basic Rules of Conduct" and "Two Studies and One Action" part of the basic and regular education of Party members. All these measures are aimed at ensuring that officials are able to carry out their duties properly, letting the public have confidence, and uniting the Party and the people with high Party ethical standards. The key lies in solving problems and pursuing practical results. At the same time, we must be prepared to fight a tough and protracted battle, and always remember there will never be an end to ethical standards improvement within the Party.

Discipline enforcement is pivotal to improving governance within the Party. The issue of discipline was included in an overall plan for Party development for a new era at the 19th CPC National Congress, and a series of contents of discipline construction have been enriched and perfected in the Party constitution. This was an innovative, important part of the Party building initiative. General Secretary Xi Jinping has stressed, "the Party must supervise itself and govern itself with strict discipline. It depends on strict discipline." To enforce Party discipline, first of all, we must strictly observe the Party Constitution, the fundamental law of the Party. Second, we should enhance the pertinence and effectiveness of discipline education, let the advanced models play their leading role, and improve the political nature of warning education. Finally, we should deepen the use of the four forms of supervision and discipline enforcement and make disciplinary punishment and organizational adjustment an important means of managing and governing the Party. Party members who seriously violate discipline and the law must be expelled from the Party.

Political awareness initiatives and institution building should go hand in hand. With the institutional construction running through, stronger institutional constraints must be in place at all levels, and so must more institutional oversight over the Party, over any exercise of authority, and over officials. At present, the Party has established a system of intra-Party laws and regulations with the Party Constitution as the foundation, democratic centralism as the core, and other rules and regulations as the main content. To strengthen the Party's institutional construction, another important task is to improve the Party and state supervision system. In this regard, we must strengthen intra-Party supervision, ensure that there are no off-limits areas for intra-Party supervision, deepen political inspection, and link intra-Party supervision with oversight by state departments, CPPCC, and judicial supervision, and oversight by the masses and by public opinion, so as to strengthen the synergy. On the other hand, we should strengthen national supervision and carry out reform of the national supervision system. The 19th CPC National Congress has made important arrangements for advancing the reform of the national supervision system. The Supervision Law of the People's Republic of China was deliberated and adopted at the First Session of the 13th National People's Congress, and the National Supervisory Commission was established. Working together with the Party's discipline inspection commissions, it exercises supervisory and procuratorial powers on behalf of the Party and the state, performs its duty of discipline inspection and supervision, and strengthens supervision over all government officials. In this way, the Party and the state have formed a unified power supervision pattern covering inspection tours, assignment, and supervision and formed an effective mechanism for discovering problems, correcting errors, and fighting against corruption. This has paved the way of supervision with Chinese characteristics to realize the long-term stability of the Party and the state.

Corruption is the most hated by the people and the biggest threat to the Party. The fight against corruption knows no bounds and leaves no ground uncovered. It targets "tigers" (corrupt senior officials), "flies" (corrupt low-ranking bureaucrats), and "foxes" (fugitives abroad suspected of major economic crimes). The cage against corruption is getting stronger, the dam against corruption is being built, and the overwhelming momentum of the fight against corruption has been formed and consolidated. But at the same time, we should be soberly aware that the fight against corruption remains grim and complex. In particular, political and economic issues are intertwined, regional, and sectoral corruption are intertwined, and corruption in the use of personnel and power is intertwined. There are also notable public opinion trends and atmosphere, such as "anti-corruption has nothing to do with the interests of the people," "anti-corruption makes officials idle," "anti-corruption slows down our economy," "anti-corruption is a power struggle," "anti-corruption should be slowly carried out," and so on. Therefore, Xi Jinping said, "we must make it clear that our Party's fight against corruption is not a snobbish affair that discriminates between different people, and it is not a House of Cards power struggle, nor is it a half-finished building."[17] The fight against corruption knows no bounds and leaves no ground uncovered. We will continue to focus on serious coercion and long-term deterrence, and eventually win an overwhelming victory in the fight against corruption.

Five Concepts for Development

Since the 18th Party Congress, General Secretary Xi Jinping has called for "development that is innovative, coordinated, green, open, and inclusive" in accordance with the new requirements of the times and practical development. The new development concept is a fundamental solution to the situation that China's economy has a new normal for economic development and the world's economic recovery is sluggish. As China's economy enters a new normal, the world economy has entered a period of deep adjustment since the international financial crisis in 2008. The original model of extensive development, the simple pursuit of growth rate model no longer works, it is necessary to establish a new concept of development to lead and promote China's economy from the stage of high-speed growth to the stage of high-quality development, optimize the economic structure, and create a new situation of economic development.

The concept is the precursor of practice. Developmental concepts determine the effectiveness and even the success of the development. At the same time, development is also a dynamic process, the development concept changes along with changes in the development concept. The Third Plenary Session of the 11th CPC Central Committee opened up the great course of reform and opened up as well as the road of socialism with Chinese characteristics. In the exploration, based on the actual situation in China, the CPC put forward "a strategic focus on development as the top priority," emphasizing the importance of seizing the opportunity to develop themselves with economic development as the key point. It also put forward that development is the first priority of the CPC to govern and prosper. Moreover, we should adhere to the people-oriented, comprehensive, coordinated, and sustainable development. With the changes in the situation at home and abroad, China is facing new outstanding problems and challenges, mainly in the unbalanced and insufficient development, the quality and efficiency of development are not high, the innovation capacity is not strong enough, the level of the real economy needs to be improved, ecological environmental protection has a long way to go, there are shortcomings in the field of people's livelihood, the task of poverty eradication is difficult, urban and rural regional development and income distribution gap is still large.

The new development concept addresses the outstanding conflicts and problems in China's development and provides scientific guidance to lead profound changes in the overall development of China and achieve development that is of higher quality, more efficient, fairer, and more sustainable. Innovative development focuses on solving the problem of development momentum, coordinated development focuses on solving the problem of unbalanced development, green development focuses on solving the problem of harmonious coexistence between human beings and nature, and open development focuses on solving the problem of internal and external linkage of development, and inclusive development focuses on solving the problem of social equity and justice.

In the five concepts of development, innovation is in the first place, because innovation is the first driving force to lead development. Development momentum determines the speed, efficiency, and sustainability of development. For an economic system of such a large volume in China, it is difficult to achieve high-quality development if the power problem is not solved. General Secretary Xi Jinping pointed out that, seizing innovation, means seizing the key points that affect the whole situation of economic and social development. This requires us to put innovation at the core of the overall national development, to continuously promote theoretical innovation, institutional innovation, scientific and technological innovation, cultural innovation, and other aspects of innovation, so that innovation is everywhere in the works of the CPC and so that innovation becomes a common practice in our society.

The new development concept provides a new answer to the question of "what kind of development we should seek to achieve under the new conditions and how to achieve it." It faces the real problems of China's economic and social development and devotes itself to solving development problems, enhancing development momentum, and cultivating development advantages with a strong sense of problems, writing a new chapter of socialist political economy with Chinese characteristics. According to the new requirements of socialism with Chinese characteristics for a new era and the new expectations of the people, the new concepts for development emphasize more clearly that development is the basis and key to solving all problems in China. Thus, it emphasizes solid development and emphasizes growth model transformation, structural adjustments, and steady growth, and achieves the overall leap in the level of social productivity in China. Moreover, it emphasizes more clearly the constant adjustment of the relations of production to adapt to the productive forces, and emphasizes the decisive role of the market in resource allocation in which the government should play an important role. The removal of institutional barriers to the development of productive forces, the sustainability of the coordination of the social reproduction process, the perfection of the relationship between industries, urban and rural areas, regions, people and nature, home and abroad, people and people, and the handling of the relationship between the current and long-term, local and global, key and general are also emphasized. More distinctly emphasized are adhering to the people-centered development ideology, stressing that the people are the fundamental force to promote development, and adhering to the people's main position. Moreover, we should mobilize the enthusiasm, initiative, and creativity of all parties and promote the sharing of the fruits of development.

The implementation of the new development concept involves, on the one hand, a change in the concept of development as well as the enhancement of knowledge and ability and, on the other hand, the adjustment of interest relations and the innovation of institutional mechanisms. General Secretary Xi Jinping stressed that party members and officials, especially those holding principal leadership positions, should improve their ability to implementation of the new development concept and become professional leaders of economic and social development. They should learn deeply and practically with the use of the dialectic method and innovation. Moreover, they should keep the bottom line and apply the new concept of development throughout the whole process of leadership activities such as decision-making, implementation, and inspection of the work. Moreover, it is important to strive to improve the ability to implement the new concept of development and level and constantly open up new horizons of development. Eloquence is of no value—real action must be taken to realize these concepts. In addition, the implementation of the new concept of development involves not only a change in the way of thinking, behavior, and work but also the adjustment of the relationship between interests and work relationships. We should enhance awareness of the overall situation and strategic awareness, and enhance the ability to be good at thinking in big picture terms and making long-term plan, not just be limited in local, departmental, and immediate view. Moreover, neither can we damage the overall interests for the sake of local interests nor damage our long-term interests for the sake of short-term interests. Only on this basis can we solve the problem and build a mechanism, thus forming a consciousness of thought and action to promote reform. We should ensure that new ideas into new practices, new actions, and the formation of institutional mechanisms conducive to the development that is innovative, coordinated, green, open, and inclusive.

The Five-Sphere Integrated Plan

Since the 18th Party Congress, General Secretary Xi Jinping has repeatedly emphasized the need to adhere to the development of socialism with Chinese characteristics encompassing economic, political, cultural, social, and ecological development in order to lay a solid foundation for the great rejuvenation of the Chinese nation.

The overall layout of socialism with Chinese characteristics has undergone the transformation from "three-sphere" to "four-sphere" and then to "five-sphere." The objective basis of the transformation is the change and the development of social life and practice. Since the founding of New China, in answering the question of how to build a poor and backward agricultural country into a strong socialist modern country, our Party has successively proposed industrialization, the four modernizations, a country with prosperity, democracy, civility, and harmony, and the Chinese Dream of the great rejuvenation of the Chinese nation, which are related and distinct from each other. Accordingly, the general layout of building socialism with Chinese characteristics has been continuously developed and promoted in practice.

As early as the early stage of reform and opening up, Deng Xiaoping clearly proposed to insist on the "two civilizations," and the Twelfth Party Congress in 1982 put forward the requirement of promoting the construction of "two civilizations" and pointed out that the construction of both socialist material and spiritual civilizations depended on the development of socialist democracy. The Sixth Plenary Session of the Twelfth Central Committee of the CPC held in 1986 first clearly put forward the concept of an "integrated plan." *The Resolution of the CPC Central Committee on the Guidelines for the Promotion of Socialist Cultural-Ethical Progress* adopted at this meeting pointed out that the integrated plan of China's socialist modernization is to focus on economic construction, unswervingly carry out reform of the economic and political system, unswervingly strengthen the construction of spiritual civilization, and make these aspects complement each other and promote each other.[18] The 14th Party Congress put the development of a socialist market economy, the building of socialist democracy, and spiritual civilization as the three major goals of building socialism with Chinese characteristics, expanding the overall layout of the "three-sphere." The 15th National Congress of the CPC proposed that "the basic goals and policies of building socialism with Chinese characteristics in economics, politics, and culture are organically unified and inseparable, and constitute the basic principles of the CPC in the primary stage of socialism."[19]

In 2002, the report of the 16th National Congress of the CPC included "fostering social harmony" for the first time in the grand blueprint for building a moderately prosperous society in all respects, proposing to build a more comprehensive moderately prosperous society in the first 20 years of the new century, with the goal of "developing the economy, improve democracy, advancing science and education, promoting cultural prosperity, fostering social harmony, and upgrading the quality of life for the people."[20] In February 2005, Comrade Hu Jintao proposed for the first time in a seminar for leading cadres at the provincial and ministerial levels that building a socialist harmonious society belongs to "social construction" and put it alongside economic, political, and cultural construction, developing the overall layout of socialist construction with Chinese characteristics from "three-sphere" to "four-sphere." He pointed out that

> with the continuous development of China's economy and society, the overall layout of the socialism with Chinese characteristics has been more clearly developed from the three-sphere integrated plan of promoting economic prosperity, political democracy, and advanced culture and ideology to the four-sphere plan that covers economic, political, cultural and social advancement.[21]

In 2007, the 17th National Congress of the CPC further emphasized the need to achieve the goal of becoming a country with "prosperity, democracy, civility, and harmony" in accordance with the five-sphere integrated plan.

The 18th National Congress of the CPC held in 2012 formally incorporated the construction of ecological civilization into the overall layout of the construction of socialism with Chinese characteristics and advanced the "four-sphere" to "five-sphere" integrated plan.

Since the 18th Party Congress, the CPC Central Committee, with Comrade Xi Jinping as the core, has attached great importance to the "five-sphere integrated plan" which promotes the development of socialism with Chinese characteristics encompassing economic, political, cultural, social, and ecological development and put it together with the coordinated promotion of the "the four-pronged comprehensive strategy." It is also emphasized that we should use the five concepts for development to lead the five major construction and constantly create a new situation in China's economic construction, political construction, cultural construction, social construction, ecological civilization construction, and Party construction.

The report of the 19th National Congress of the CPC is based on the new era and puts forward a series of new ideas, new theories, new judgments, and new strategies for the "five-sphere" integrated plan. In terms of economic construction, it emphasizes implementing the new development concept, building a modernized economic system, deepening structural reform on the supply side, accelerating the construction of an innovative country, implementing the rural revitalization strategy, implementing coordinated regional development, and planning and building the Xiong'an New Area at a high starting point and with high standards. In terms of political construction, it was stressed that socialist democracy in China is the most extensive, genuine, and effective democracy that safeguards the most fundamental interests of the people. Moreover, it was stressed that we should adhere to the path of socialist political development with Chinese characteristics rather than rigidly following foreign political models and we should strengthen the centralized and unified leadership of the CPC. Consultative democracy is an important way to realize the leadership of the CPC as well as a unique form and advantage of socialist democratic politics in China. Advancing law-based governance is a profound revolution in national governance. In terms of cultural construction, it emphasizes firm cultural confidence, firmly grasping the leadership of ideological work, promoting the popularization of Marxism, building a system of philosophy and social science with Chinese characteristics, adhering to the correct orientation of public opinion, attaching great importance to the construction and innovation of means of communication, establishing a comprehensive network management system, clearly opposing and resisting all kinds of erroneous views, resisting the erosion of corrupt and backward culture, adhering to the people-centered creative orientation, telling the Chinese story, improving the national cultural soft power, and so on. In social construction, it is stressed that leading the people to create a better life is CPC's unswerving goal. We should grasp the most concerned, most direct, and realistic interests of the people in order to safeguard and improve people's livelihood.

It also attaches great importance to giving priority to the development of education and employment as the greatest livelihood, resolutely winning the battle against poverty, implementing the healthy China initiative, creating a social governance pattern of common construction and sharing, and effectively maintaining national security. In the construction of ecological civilization, it is emphasized that man and nature are a community of life, that a good ecology is the most popular welfare of the people, that green mountains are mountains of gold, that promoting green development, implementing the strictest ecological environmental protection system, and forming a green development and lifestyle.

From the evolution of the "five-sphere" integrated plan, on the one hand, we can see that the CPC has always adhered to the basic direction of economic construction as the center and always responded to the new expectations of the people. On the other hand, we can also see that from concentrating on economic issues to focusing on the development of economy, politics, and spiritual culture, which are the basic aspects of social life, to proposing and emphasizing social construction to improve people's livelihood and social harmony, to proposing and paying attention to the increasingly prominent ecological and environmental issues, to focus on the outstanding issues in the "five-sphere" integrated plan in the new era, our Party has always kept pace with the times and always adjusted its strategy and layout according to the outstanding conflicts and outstanding issues at different stages of China's social development. The adjustments reflect the realism and rationality of the development of the "five-sphere" integrated plan, and reflect the CPC's position and insistence on seeking truth from facts and responding to real problems and people's expectations in a historical and dialectical manner.

Building a Community With a Shared Future for Humanity

According to the report of the 19th CPC National Congress, "the world is undergoing major developments, transformation, and adjustment, but peace and development remain the call of our day." World multi-polarization and economic globalization are gaining momentum, and social informatization and cultural diversity continued to advance, while a new round of scientific and industrial revolution is in the making. The trend of peace and development is irreversible, with the more balanced international power and interconnectedness and interdependence between countries that share a common future. At the same time, our era is one of endless challenges and increasing risks. The world economic growth is sluggish, the cloud of financial crisis persists, and the development gap is widening. Military conflicts occur from time to time, and the ghosts of Cold War mentality and power politics are still lingering. Non-traditional threats to security such as terrorism, cyber security problems, major infectious diseases, and climate change continue to spread. The western-centric view that the international community is dominated by the West and that western values are the main orientation of international relations is no longer sustainable. Western governance concepts, systems, and models are becoming increasingly difficult to adapt to the new international situation and the trend of the times. Various problems are irretrievable, and even major Western powers have their own governance failures. The world is waiting for a new concept of global governance, a new and more just and equitable international system and order, and an even brighter future for mankind. As socialism with Chinese characteristics entered a new era, the path, theory, system, and culture of socialism with Chinese characteristics have further developed. The ways for developing countries to achieve modernization have been expanded, providing new solutions to countries and nations that want to speed up development while maintaining their independence and contributing Chinese wisdom and solutions to the problems facing mankind. As its international influence and voice grow stronger, China is more confident and capable of making greater contributions to the world. Against this background, General Secretary Xi Jinping, standing at the height of the development of human history, has taken on the responsibility of a leader of a major country and deeply thought about issues concerning the destiny of mankind. What kind of world should we build? How to build the world? With great foresight, he put forward the important idea of building a community with a shared future for mankind. This is a Chinese concept and a Chinese plan with a view to human development and the future of the world. It is producing far-reaching global influence, with high praise and active response from the international community, and has been written into UN documents more than once.

Xi Jinping has pointed out that "humanity increasingly finds itself in a global village, with unprecedented levels of interconnectedness, interdependence, cooperation, and synergy between countries. Therefore, a community with a shared future is gradually taking shape, where the interests of all countries are increasingly intertwined."[22] There is only one earth in the universe, and we human beings share one home. In the face of a volatile world and major changes rarely seen in a century, no country can address alone the many challenges facing humanity and no country can afford to retreat into self-isolation. Only through peaceful development and cooperation can we truly achieve win-win outcomes for all.

The idea of building a community with a shared future for mankind is rich and profound. The essence of this vision is, as stated in the report to the 19th CPC National Congress, to "build an open, inclusive, clean, and beautiful world that enjoys lasting peace, universal security, and common prosperity."[23] This reflects the common pursuit of values of human society and is of great and far-reaching significance to China's peaceful development and the prosperity and progress of the world. Efforts are needed in politics, security, economy, culture, and ecology. All countries should respect each other, discuss issues as equals, and take a new approach to developing state-to-state relations with communication, not confrontation, and with partnership, not alliance; commit to settling disputes through dialog and resolving differences through discussion, coordinate responses to traditional and non-traditional threats, and oppose terrorism in all its forms; stick together through thick and thin, promote trade and investment liberalization and facilitation, and make economic globalization more open, inclusive, and balanced so that its benefits are shared by all; respect the diversity of civilizations, replace estrangement with exchange, clashes with mutual learning, and superiority with coexistence in handling relations among civilizations; be good friends to the environment, cooperate to tackle climate change, and protect our planet for the sake of human survival.

To build a community with a shared future for mankind, we need to adhere to the path of peaceful development and build a new type of international relations featuring mutual respect, fairness, justice, and win-win cooperation. China will unswervingly develop friendly cooperation with other countries on the basis of the Five Principles of Peaceful Coexistence, firmly uphold international fairness and justice, and resolutely defend its national interests against hegemonism and power politics. China will never seek hegemony or expansion.

To build a community with a shared future for mankind, we need to improve our diplomacy and build a global network of partnerships. We will develop our friendship and cooperation with other countries in an all-round way, focusing on our neighbors and major countries and on the basis of developing countries. We will promote multilateralism, deepen practical cooperation, strengthen political mutual trust, consolidate social foundation, improve institutional building, and constantly improve China's all-dimensional, multi-tiered and multi-dimensional diplomatic layout. We will promote coordination and cooperation among major countries and build a framework for major-country relations featuring overall stability and balanced development. We will deepen relations with neighboring countries in accordance with the principles for building strong relations with its neighbors based on friendship, good faith, mutual benefit, and inclusiveness, and with the foreign policy of forging friendship and partnership with our neighbors. We will uphold justice while pursuing shared interests and strengthen solidarity and cooperation with other developing countries under the principle of sincerity, real results, affinity, and good faith.

We must also actively and deeply participate in the reform and development of the global governance system. The governance system should be jointly built by all countries for the benefit of all, rather than dominated by any one country. To reform the global governance system is not to tear it down or start all over again but to innovate and improve it. China is committed to upholding the international order and system with the purposes and principles of the UN Charter at its core, promoting democracy in state-to-state relations, and holding that developing countries should increase their representation and raise their voices in international affairs. Global economic governance is an essential part of the global governance system. China will actively support the multilateral trading system as the main channel, promote liberalization and facilitation of international trade and investment, and oppose all forms of protectionism. China participates in and contributes to the existing international order, promotes international cooperation and multilateralism, and actively participates in multilateral initiatives. China will cultivate the positive ways of conduct and philosophy of governance in the Chinese culture to benefit today's global governance. Based on its prevailing national conditions as a developing country, China will seek the right balance between rights and obligations, actively participate in global governance, shoulder international responsibilities, and do our best within our capabilities.

We should unswervingly promote the Belt and Road Initiative so as to further deepen all-round opening up. Carrying forward the spirit of the Silk Road, the Belt and Road Initiative combines China's development with that of countries along the Road and the rest of the world and combines the Chinese dream with the dreams of their people, thus giving the ancient Silk Road a new dimension of the times. The initiative focuses on promoting policy coordination, connectivity of infrastructure and facilities, unimpeded trade, financial integration, and closer people-to-people ties through a consultative process and joint efforts, with the goal of bringing benefits to all. The initiative is committed to building a new landscape of all-round opening up, and is full of vigor and vitality. From 2013 to 2017, China's trade in goods with countries and regions along the Belt and Road exceeded US $5 trillion, and its outward direct investment exceeded US $70 billion. Chinese enterprises built 75 economic and trade cooperation zones in these countries and regions, paying US $2.2 billion in taxes to host countries and creating 210000 jobs. More than 140 countries and regions and more than 80 international organizations have actively supported and participated in the Belt and Road initiative. Unlike the Marshall Plan of the United States, the Belt and Road initiative is open to all countries seeking development, and will never engage in bloc politics or confrontational alliances. The Belt and Road initiative reflects China's clear new international strategy. It aims to promote the development of China's hinterland, countries in the initiative and the world step by step through win-win cooperation, and shoulder its due regional responsibilities and missions as a stable and mature major country in the world.

Commitment to the People-Centered Approach

Adhering to the people-centered approach is the fundamental standpoint and value orientation of Xi Jinping's Thought on Socialism with Chinese Characteristics for a New Era. The report of the 19th National Congress of the CPC lists "people-oriented" as one of the spirits and connotations of socialism with Chinese characteristics in the new era, emphasizing that the people are the creators of history and the fundamental force in determining the future and destiny of the CPC and the country. It is important to uphold the primacy of the people, build ourselves for the public good and exercise power for the people, adhere to the abiding mission, which is to serve the people wholeheartedly. It is also important to implement the party's mass line into all activities of governance, take the people's aspiration for a better life as the goal of struggle, and rely on the people to create a great work of history.

The "People-centered" Approach Adheres to the Basic Principles of Historical Materialism

Historical materialism believes that social history is created by the people. The people are the creators of the material and spiritual wealth of society and are the determining force of social development. This essentially affirms the primacy of the people in the development of social history. General Secretary Xi Jinping pointed out that "the people are the driving force behind the creation of history, the CPC members should not forget the most basic truth of historical materialism at any time."[24] People-centered thought adheres to the basic principle of historical materialism.

People-centered philosophy not only adheres to the basic principles of historical materialism but also combines with the current situation of social transformation, to make further analysis of the main position of the people. First of all, the people are the main body of social development. Xi Jinping has repeatedly stressed: "The people are the true heroes, for it is they who create history." "The Chinese people have, working with diligence, bravery and wisdom, created a beautiful homeland where all ethnic groups live in harmony, and developed a great and dynamic culture."[25] To realize the Chinese dream, we need to rely on the creative work of all the people, and we need generations of Chinese people to work together for it. Second, the people are the main body of social reform. In the process of in-depth reform in all respects, only by fully relying on the power and wisdom of the people can we break through the various obstacles in the process of reform. Whether it is to carry out the top-level design of reform or to break through the fence of solidified interests, it is necessary to understand the people's situation and expectations and to draw wisdom and strength from the people's practice. Finally, the people are the main body of social innovation. "Where do the good measures and solutions of social development come from? The answer comes from the people."[26] Our Party should fully mobilize the enthusiasm and creativity of the people, so that "the people can truly become the subjects of choice and interest."[27]

People-centered philosophy overcomes the limitations of Western humanistic thought and China's age-old tradition of putting people first. Western humanism attaches importance to the concern for human beings themselves and opposes ignoring the existence and value of human beings, but because its core is the abstract individual, it tends to lead to individualism or even "extreme individualism" in the end. China's age-old tradition of putting people first thinking advocates responding to public opinion, protecting the interests of the people, pacifying the people, and implementing moral and benevolent governance, but the "people" are essentially those "common people" who lack subject consciousness. The essence of "people-based" is a technique of "governing" and "managing" the people. The people were still the objects of domination and domination and were even treated as "dumb" and "rogue." This "people-based" ideology also tends to lead to a "mountain-stronghold mentality," and the people become the victims of hilltop divisions. The "people-centered" philosophy recognizes the people as the main force in creating history, emphasizes the concept of "people" as a community, and stresses that the people are the source of social development. It overcomes the individualistic tendency of humanism. It emphasizes "serving the people wholeheartedly" with the basic logic of "people should enjoy what they have created." It overcomes the traditional "people-based" position of imperial power and bureaucracy, and also overcomes the tendency of the "mountain-stronghold mentality" of ganging up, forming parties, and engaging in "cronyism."[28]

The Aspirations of the People to Live a Better Life is Our Goal

The people-centered approach is key to the CPC's political thinking. Since the 18th National Congress of the CPC, the Central Committee with Comrade Xi Jinping at its core has consistently emphasized that

> the original aspiration of the Chinese Communists was to seek happiness for the Chinese people and lead the people to a better life. We must always remain true to this aspiration and always take people's needs for a better life as our goal.[29]

This is a new expression of serving the people wholeheartedly in the new era and is the most vivid expression of the people-centered thinking in the new era.

The answer to whom the Party fights for is the litmus test of a Party and a government. Taking the people's aspiration for a better life as our goal fundamentally answers the question of whom development is for and is a vivid demonstration of the CPC's commitment to serving the public and exercising power for the people.

Since its birth, the Party has always taken serving the people as its fundamental purpose through revolution, construction, reform, and opening up and this new era. With this original aspiration, the Party has led the Chinese nation to achieve a tremendous transformation: it has stood up; grown rich; and is becoming strong. The greatest anti-poverty story in the history of mankind thus has been made. Since the 18th National Congress of the Party, despite the pressure of economic development, people's livelihood indicators have bucked the trend, personal income has continued to increase, and people's sense of gain and happiness has continued to increase.

With the development of the new era and the changes in the principal social conflict, our Party has placed special emphasis on taking the people's aspiration for a better life as its goal. The Party has noticed that the people need not only to be well-off, but also to narrow the gap between them; not just a better living standard, but a better education, a more secure job, and a more secure social security; not only the material and cultural needs but also the needs of a better life that includes the value judgment of different groups, covers a wider range, has higher levels and is more accurately focused. This goal is our Party's initiative to exert self-pressure, and it is also a fulfillment of its commitment to "putting the people first and serving the people" in the historical stage of the new era.

The People Are the Fundamental Strength Upon Which the Party Relies

History and facts have proved that the people are the foundation and strength of the Party and that the people were the main force to rely on in the New Democratic Revolution, as well as in the socialist modernization, reform and opening up, and the great rejuvenation of the Chinese nation. The people are always the true heroes and the fundamental force in determining the future and destiny of the Party and the country.

China is at a crucial stage of securing a decisive victory in building a moderately prosperous society in all respects. Facing new conditions and tasks in the new era, we must respect the people's initiative, maximize their creative enthusiasm, and trust and rely on their strength to turn the blueprint into reality. General Secretary Xi Jinping has pointed out that every breakthrough in terms of practice and knowledge, every new development and creation, and every experience gained in reform and opening up comes from the practice and wisdom of hundreds of millions of Chinese people. Therefore, we must fully respect the will people express, the experience they create, the rights they possess, and the role they play. By implementing the new vision of development, we need to encourage widespread entrepreneurship and innovation, energize the people, and better mobilize talent in all sectors. We will encourage people at the community level to take the lead in experimenting, boldly exploring, and accelerate the development of new technologies, industries, and types of business. In the face of new situations and tasks in the new era, we must regard the practice and creation of the people as the source of vitality, promptly discover and summarize the fresh experience created by the people, and translate it into theories and policies. At the same time, we must mobilize and guide the people to carry out new practices and push forward the cause of the Party and state.

Relying on the people also means insisting on the judgment of the people and taking their satisfaction as the fundamental criterion. Public opinion is the best yardstick to measure the merits and demerits of our work. As Xi Jinping said, the time sets the questions, the Party answers, and the people grade them. The final test of the effectiveness of all our work is whether the people have truly benefited from it, whether their living standards have improved, and whether their rights and interests have been protected. It is "the people's support, approval, happiness, and consent" that should be the starting point and goal of our thinking and handling of problems and work. We must adhere to the standards of the people, address the practice of formalities for formalities' sake, and make the standards strongly binding, so as to earn satisfaction instead of cajole it from the people. Only when the people are satisfied can the Party truly fulfill its solemn promise to the people and truly stand the test of history.

Development Should Be of Direct Benefit to the People

Development should be of direct benefit to the people, which reflects the people-centered approach. General Secretary Xi Jinping has pointed out that national development is a common cause of all the people, and its achievement is also shared by all the people.[30] The Chinese people, living in our great motherland and great era, share the opportunity to contribute, to make their dreams come true, and to grow and develop with the nation and the time.[31] It is our Party's fundamental principle that the fruits of development should be shared by the people, not just a few.

Development should be of direct benefit to the people, which embodies the goal of achieving common prosperity. The concept of inclusive development, one of the five concepts of development, emphasizes shared benefits for all, shared benefits in all respects, shared benefits by all and advancement step by step, which embodies the essential requirements of promoting common prosperity, safeguarding equity and justice, and socialism with Chinese characteristics. The people-centered approach and the approach of development being of direct benefit to the people are highly in accordance with the essence and requirement of the common prosperity. We need to make the "pie" bigger as well as ensure a fair distribution. On the one hand, we will fully mobilize the enthusiasm, initiative, and creativity of the people to promote the cause of building socialism with Chinese characteristics. On the other hand, we must ensure a fair distribution to let the advantages of the socialist system be more fully demonstrated and the people have a greater sense of contentment.

No one should be left behind in building a moderately prosperous society in all respects, and no one should be left behind on the path to common prosperity. General Secretary Xi Jinping has stressed that a moderately prosperous society in all respects covers all fields and represents all-round progress in the Five-sphere Integrated Plan; a moderately prosperous society should cover all the people and benefit all the people; a moderately prosperous society should cover all areas and achieve common prosperity in both urban and rural areas. He says, "the key to a moderately prosperous society depends on the people," and

> when the time comes, we can't say we've failed to achieve it and we have to work for a few more years; nor can we declare that we have completed the building of a moderately prosperous society in all respects while tens of millions of people are still living below the poverty line.[32]

We will focus on targeted poverty alleviation and fulfill the requirements set out in the 13th Five-Year Plan. By 2020, China's GDP and per capita income for urban and rural residents should double that of 2010, and people's living standards and quality should be generally improved. Poverty in rural areas and region-wide poverty should be eliminated by current standards, and all poverty-stricken counties should be lifted, so as to fulfill the Party's promise to the people.

Adhering to the Mass Line

The people-centered philosophy, reflected in the specific practical work of the CPC, is to practice the Party's mass line. The mass line is the lifeline and fundamental working line of the Party, and it is the heirloom of our Party to maintain its youthful vitality and combat power.

General Secretary Xi Jinping attaches great importance to the mass line, which has always been reflected in his path of government and has also been constantly discussed and emphasized the mass line on various occasions. Adhering to the mass line, first of all, lies in public servant consciousness, which requires us to always care about the people. General Secretary Xi Jinping has repeatedly affirmed to members of the CPC that "officials at all levels, regardless of their position, are all public servants and should serve the people wholeheartedly."[33] They should also care about the people's hardships, especially the people with special difficulties to "pay extra attention, extra care, extra concern and do everything possible to help them solve their problems."[34] Second, in the attitude of behavior, we should take the initiative to learn from the masses, the masses as teachers. General Secretary Xi Jinping proposed that we should learn from the masses, and constantly conduct social research. Officials should "consult the people on governance, learn about their needs, seek their advice, understand their opinion, and adhere to democratic decision-making as well as scientific arrangement."[35] Only in this way can we really understand the public opinion and make the right decision. Finally, in the institutional platform, to establish a system of close contact with the masses. We must really put the mass line into practice, we must strengthen the construction of the system, and we must incorporate the mass line into a track that is institutionalized and scientific. For example, mass petitions and official visits are important channels of contact between the party and the masses. The mass petitions are often the negative treatment of problems after the occurrence of problems, while the official visits are a more positive way, which is conducive to the timely detection and solving of problems. General Secretary Xi Jinping attaches special importance to the official visits, requiring leading officials to "conduct a thorough investigation about existing problems, investigate and deal with disciplinary cases in a timely manner and expose them publicly."[36]

The report of the 19th National Congress of the CPC clearly puts forward that the party's mass line should be carried out in all activities of governance. This requires, on the one hand, integrating the mass line into the whole process of economic and social development, implementing the new development concept in all aspects of economic, political, cultural, social, and ecological civilization construction, bringing more benefits to the people through reform and development, ensuring that running of the country by the people is implemented in the political and social life of the country, striving to meet the ever-growing material and cultural needs of the people, safeguarding people's livelihood, and giving them a greater sense of gain, happiness, and security. On the other hand, it is required that the mass line be carried through all the work of the party. Officials should be evaluated based on whether they put the importance of mass work, and whether they are good at dealing with the masses.

Develop Marxism in Contemporary China

Xi Jinping Thought on Socialism with Chinese Characteristics for a New Era focuses on new tasks of the times. It is the latest achievement in localizing Marxism, an important component of the theoretical system of socialism with Chinese characteristics, representing Marxism for contemporary China in the 21st century.

The Ideological Banner and Fundamental Guideline of the Party and Country in the New Era

Chairman Mao Zedong once said, "doctrine is like a banner; only when the banner is unfurled can we have goals and know where we are headed."[37] During the period of revolution, construction, and reform, our Party has always vigorously promoted the localization of Marxism, making major theoretical innovative achievements such as Mao Zedong Thought, Deng Xiaoping Theory, the Important Thought of Three Represents, and the Scientific Outlook on Development, which have guided the Party and the country on their way forward. As socialism with Chinese characteristics has entered a new era, the CPC Central Committee with Comrade Xi Jinping at its core has shouldered the political responsibility of continuing to write a major article on socialism with Chinese characteristics. By combining theory with practice, Xi Jinping Thought on Socialism with Chinese Characteristics for a New Era has systematically answered the question of what kind of socialism with Chinese characteristics we should uphold and develop in the new era and how we should uphold and develop it.

Xi Jinping Thought on Socialism with Chinese Characteristics for a New Era takes upholding and developing socialism with Chinese characteristics as its core, and constantly deepens our understanding and thinking on it. Since the 18th CPC National Congress, General Secretary Xi Jinping has put forward a series of major propositions and thoughts. He stressed the need to correctly understand the relationship between the "two 30 years" before and after the start of reform and opening up and clarified that the construction and development of socialism in China is continuous and coordinated from a historical and political perspective; he pointed out the historical origin, ethnic gene, and practical basis of socialism with Chinese characteristics and stressed that the socialism with Chinese characteristics is the achievement of the great practice of more than 40 years of reform and opening up, the outcome of the 70 years of ongoing exploration of the People's Republic of China, the result of over 90 years of the practice of great social revolution carried out by the people under the leadership of the Party, the choice made after a history of more than 170 years from decline to prosperity of the Chinese nation since modern times, the inheritance and development of the 5,000 years of Chinese civilization; he emphasized that the defining feature and advantage of socialism with Chinese characteristics is the leadership of the Communist Party of China, which is the most important achievement of the Party and the people's understanding of upholding and developing socialism with Chinese characteristics and the most fundamental summary of the law; he added "confidence in its culture" to the existing "three matters of confidence" (confidence in the socialist path, theory and system), which enriched and expanded the connotation of socialism with Chinese characteristics, and provided profound ideological support for us to deepen our understanding and to follow our own path.

Its core content is summed up in "eight areas" and "fourteen points," providing fundamental guidelines for the political and social life of the Party and the country. "Eight areas" lays stress on the theoretical level of high generalization, while "fourteen points" lays stress on the practical and strategic level. Together they define the overarching objectives, tasks, plans, strategies, directions, external conditions, and political guarantees for the new era, as well as the model and drivers of development, which has charted the course for the Party to lead the Chinese people in securing a decisive victory in building a moderately prosperous society in all respects and realizing the great rejuvenation of the Chinese nation.

Make Original Contributions to the Development of Marxism in China

The most fundamental reason why Marxism has shown strong vitality in China lies in our party's commitment to the organic unity of adherence to Marxism and the development of Marxism. On the one hand, Xi Jinping Thought on Socialism with Chinese Characteristics for a New Era, being the most realistic and vivid Marxism of the present era, always runs through the basic standpoints, views, and methods of Marxism, demonstrating the theoretical character and spirit of Marxism. On the other hand, based on the practice and problems of the new era, it puts forward a series of original new ideas and new views, and new judgments, developing Marxism in a new era. Xi Jinping Thought on Socialism with Chinese Characteristics for a New Era has made original contributions to Marxism, which is reflected in the following aspects:

It is based on Chinese practice, facing Chinese problems directly. Xi Jinping Thought on Socialism with Chinese Characteristics for a New Era, which has brought vitality to China, is the product of combining the basic tenets of Marxism with the contemporary characteristics and the national conditions of China. This thought views the essence and characteristics of the new era from the height of the 500-year history of socialism in the world and emphasizes that the entry of socialism with Chinese characteristics into the new era means that scientific socialism in China in the 21st century has emerged with great vitality. This is an important basis for us to maintain firm confidence in Marxism and conviction in scientific socialism. This idea focuses on Chinese problems, summarizes Chinese experience, takes Marxism as the guide, recognizes and develops the law of ruling of the CPC, the law of socialist construction, and the law of development of human society, and on this basis proposes the goals, tasks, layout, and strategies for building socialism with Chinese characteristics in the new era. It proves with the actual development of socialism with Chinese characteristics that the Western development model is not the "only" model of modernization, but just "a" model.

It draws on Chinese culture and focuses on the cultural dimension. Emphasizing the importance of culture and highlighting the cultural dimension of socialism with Chinese characteristics is an important feature of Xi Jinping Thought on Socialism with Chinese Characteristics for a New Era. General Secretary Xi Jinping has repeatedly stressed that culture is a country and a nation's soul. Our country will thrive only if our culture thrives, and our country will be strong only if our culture is strong. Xi Jinping has spoken about culture and civilization on many occasions at home and abroad, emphasizing that the profound Chinese excellent traditional culture is our spiritual gene and spiritual lifeline and that we should promote innovative transformation and development of traditional Chinese culture. In a series of important speeches and articles and writings of General Secretary Xi Jinping, we can often see references to traditional cultural classics, such as quoting "every concern of the people weighs in our heart" to express love for the people and for the people's heart, using "successful governance relies on solid action" to illustrate the truth that empty talk is harmful to the nation while doing practical work will make it thrive. The meaning of reform and innovation is highlighted by the saying that "a wise man changes as time and event change."

It also stands at the forefront of the times and expands its international vision. In this era, the trend of multi-polarization and economic globalization is developing, the international environment is complex and ever-changing, the competition for comprehensive national power is becoming increasingly fierce, the number of unstable and uncertain factors affecting peace and development has increased, and we will still face the pressure of the developed countries' dominance in the economy, science and technology and the ideological competition for a long time, and face many foreseeable and unforeseeable risks and challenges. For China, we have gone from "standing up" to "getting rich" and are now experiencing "getting strong." Now there are major changes in social conflicts and we are entering a new stage of development. Based on the problems and challenges of the times, Xi Jinping's Thought on Socialism with Chinese Characteristics in the New Era puts forward strategic new ideas and perspectives on how China can solve its own problems, face the new opportunities and challenges of economic globalization, draw on the achievements of human civilization, and make its own contributions to the world.

To Provide Spiritual Strength for the Realization of the Great Rejuvenation of the Chinese Nation

Achieving great rejuvenation is the greatest dream of the Chinese nation since modern times. Xi Jinping Thought on Socialism with Chinese Characteristics for a New Era has distinctly put forward and systematically discussed the major proposition of the Chinese Dream, profoundly elaborated the basic connotation of national rejuvenation, profoundly revealed our position in the historical process of national rejuvenation, scientifically planned the path and strategic steps for national rejuvenation, and injected a new connotation for adhering to and developing socialism with Chinese characteristics in the new era. Under the guidance of this ideology, we are more confident and capable than ever to accomplish the historical mission of the CPC in the new era and realize the Chinese dream of national prosperity, national revitalization, and people's happiness.

An important reason why Xi Jinping thought on socialism with Chinese characteristics for a new era can provide great spiritual power is the thoroughness of its theory. Marx once said: "Theory is capable of gripping the masses as soon as it demonstrates ad hominem, and it demonstrates ad hominem as soon as it becomes radical. To be radical is to grasp the root of the matter."[38] The thoroughness of Xi Jinping thought on socialism with Chinese characteristics for a new era is reflected in the fact that, on the one hand, it grasps the fundamental interests and demands of the people and is always rooted in the people. It adheres to the people-centered philosophy, grasps the changes in the needs of the people, recognizes the historical changes of the main social conflicts, deeply grasps that the changes in the needs of the people are not only quantitative changes and expansion of the field, but more crucial is the improvement of quality, the issue of "goodness," and pays more attention to the people's aspirations for a better life and real feelings.

On the other hand, it is unambiguous with the key issues related to the future destiny of the party and the country. For example, in emphasizing the overall leadership of the CPC, the report of the 19th National Congress of the CPC emphasizes that "the Party exercises overall leadership over all areas of endeavor in every part of the country."[39] Xi Jinping Thought on Socialism with Chinese Characteristics for a New Era makes many things clear. Among them, the eighth is to make clear that the defining feature of socialism with Chinese characteristics is the leadership of the Communist Party of China; the greatest strength of the system of socialism with Chinese characteristics is the leadership of the Communist Party of China; the Party is the highest force for political leadership. It sets forth the general requirements for Party building in the new era and underlines the importance of political work in Party building. General Secretary Xi Jinping profoundly stressed, "we must recognize that China's greatest national condition is the leadership of the Communist Party of China. What are Chinese characteristics? This is the Chinese characteristics." History proves that the Communist Party of China has led the Chinese people from standing up, and getting rich to becoming strong. Maintaining the spirit of self-revolution, the CPC has led the Chinese people to overcome one seemingly insurmountable hurdle after another. The CPC has constantly achieved an orderly change of state leadership, always ensuring a smooth and orderly transition of state power, providing a strong political guarantee for the country's long-term peace and security and the people's well-being. The CPC also has promoted the modernization of the national governance system, providing a strong political guarantee for the sustainable and healthy development of the country and the happiness of the people. In addition, in emphasizing the issue of adhering to and improving the socialist system with Chinese characteristics, General Secretary Xi Jinping repeatedly stressed that the socialist system with Chinese characteristics is distinctive in features and efficiency. The reason why a socialist political system with Chinese characteristics works and has vitality is that it grows up from the soil of Chinese society and has its own superiority, such as centralized power to do great things, self-improvement and self-development, unity of stability and vitality, etc.

Contributing Chinese Wisdom and Chinese Solutions to the World

We are witnessing major changes unfolding in our world, something unseen in a century. Starting from the subjectivity of Chinese civilization, Xi Jinping Thought on Socialism with Chinese Characteristics for a New Era and insists on exploring the path of socialism with Chinese characteristics and summing up the experience of the practice of socialist modernization, building an ideological system, value system, institutional system, and strategic system that adhere to the basic tenets of Marxism, reflect the characteristics of Chinese civilization and are independent of the Western model and Western discourse, and providing the world with a Chinese solution for the better development of human society. This program illustrates and announces to the world the end of the "end of history" with China's practice and tells the world that there is not only one way to promote the modernization of a country. We have declared with facts the bankruptcy of the "end of history" and the bankruptcy of the view of history that all countries will ultimately end up with the Western system model. Besides that, we have also declared the bankruptcy of the so-called Western universal values that Westerners believe. China's development has broadened the way for developing countries to modernize, offering a new choice to those countries and nations in the world that want to accelerate their development while maintaining their independence.

The Chinese wisdom and solutions that contemporary China has contributed to the world are also reflected in the community with a shared future for humanity and the "Belt and Road" initiative proposed by Xi Jinping Thought on Socialism with Chinese Characteristics for a New Era. Since the international financial crisis, the world economy has undergone deep adjustments, the division between the rich and the poor has intensified, anti-globalization and populism are on the rise, and the development of new technologies, especially artificial intelligence, may aggravate inequality and instability, making the problem of unbalanced development in the world more prominent. In such a context, should we choose to develop in a predatory manner by eating the weak, or to develop by seeking common ground while reserving differences and seeking co-prosperity? Today, China has proposed the "community with a shared future for humanity" and is working to promote the "Belt and Road" construction, grasping development as the greatest common denominator, focusing on the common dream of people around the world to pursue peace and development, and sharing China's development with other countries around the world. This reflects China's global vision, global mind, and responsibility in unifying its own development with that of the world.

Xi Jinping Thought on Socialism with Chinese Characteristics for a New Era has written a new chapter of the localization of Marxism and has demonstrated its powerful power of truth, unique ideological charm, and great practical power in the historical process of the Party leading the people to carry out great struggles, build great projects, advance great undertakings and realize great dreams in the new era. Under the guidance of Xi Jinping Thought on Socialism with Chinese Characteristics for a New Era, the road of socialism with Chinese characteristics will become broader and we will become more confident, and the Communist Party of China will lead the Chinese people to seize the great victory of socialism with Chinese characteristics in the new era, realize the Chinese dream of the great rejuvenation of the Chinese nation, and realize the people's aspiration for a better life.

Notes

1 Central Literature Research Office of the Communist Party of China. *Selected Documents of the Central Committee of CPC*, vol. 24. Beijing: People's Publishing House, 2013, p. 248.

2 Compiling Group of *Guide Book of the Report of the 19th National Congress of the Communist Party of China*. *Guide Book of the Report of the 19th National Congress of the Communist Party of China*. Beijing: People's Publishing House, 2017, p. 12.

3 Jin Yinan. A Great Transformation from Standing Up, Getting Rich to Becoming Strong. *Xinhua Daily*, July 17, 2018.

4 Compiling Group of *Guide Book of the Report of the 19th National Congress of the Communist Party of China*. *Guide Book of the Report of the 19th National Congress of the Communist Party of China*. Beijing: People's Publishing House, 2017, p. 10.

5 Literature Research Office of the CPC Central Committee. *Collected Works of Mao Zedong: Volume 5*. Beijing: People's Publishing House, 1996, p. 343.

6 Xi Jinping. *Speech at the Celebration of the 95th Anniversary of the Founding of the Communist Party of China (July 1, 2016)*. Beijing: People's Publishing House, 2016, p. 12.

7 Mao Zedong. *Selected Works of Mao Zedong*. vol.1, 2nd ed. Beijing: People's Publishing House, 1991, p. 111.

8 Xi Jinping. Speech at the Symposium on Philosophy and Social Sciences. *People's Daily*, May 19, 2016.

9 Compiling Group of *Guide Book of the Report of the 19th National Congress of the Communist Party of China*. *Guide Book of the Report of the 19th National Congress of the Communist Party of China*. Beijing: People's Publishing House, 2017, p. 40.

10 Xi Jinping. *The Governance of China*, vol. 2. Beijing: Foreign Language Press, 2017, p. 72.

11 Xi Jinping. Explanatory Notes for the 'Decision of the CCCPC on Some Major Issues Concerning Comprehensively Deepening the Reform. *People's Daily*, November 16, 2013.

12 Xi Jinping. *The Governance of China*. Beijing: Foreign Language Press, 2014, p. 71.

13 Party Documents Research Office of the CPC Central Committee. *Excerpted Expositions of Xi Jinping on Comprehensively Deepening Reform*. Beijing: Central Party Literature Press, 2014, p. 18.

14 *Study Guide for Reports of the 19th CPC National Congress* Compiling Group. *Study Guide for Reports of the 19th CPC National Congress*. Beijing: People's Publishing House, 2017, p. 21.

15 Literature Research Office of the CPC Central Committee. Selected documents since the 18th CPC National Congress: ii. Beijing: Central Literature Publishing House, 2018, p. 589.

16 Compiling Group of *Guide Book of the Report of the 19th National Congress of the Communist Party of China*. *Guide Book of the Report of the 19th National Congress of the Communist Party of China*. Beijing: People's Publishing House, 2017, p. 61.

17 Xi Jinping. *Speech at the Sixth Plenary Session of the 18th Central Commission for Discipline Inspection*. Beijing: People's Publishing House, 2016, p. 30.

18 Party Literature Research Center, CPC Central Committee. *Selected Important Documents Since the 12th CPC National Congress*, vol. 3. Beijing: People's Publishing House, 1988, p. 1173–1174.

19 *Compilation of Documents of the 15th National Congress of the Communist Party of China.* Beijing: People's Publishing House, 1997, p. 20.

20 Party Literature Research Center, CPC Central Committee. *Selected Important Documents Since the 16th CPC National Congress,* vol. 1. Beijing: People's Publishing House, 2005, p. 14.

21 Party Literature Research Center, CPC Central Committee. *Selected Important Documents Since the 16th CPC National Congress,* vol. 2. Beijing: People's Publishing House, 2006, p. 696.

22 Xi Jinping. Adapting to the Trend of The Times and Promoting World Peace and Development: Speech at the Moscow Institute of International Relations. *People's Daily (Overseas Edition),* March 25, 2013.

23 Compiling Group of *Guide Book of the Report of the 19th National Congress of the Communist Party of China. Guide Book of the Report of the 19th National Congress of the Communist Party of China.* Beijing: People's Publishing House, 2017, p. 58.

24 Publicity Department of the Communist Party of China. *A Reader of Xi Jinping's Important Speeches.* Beijing: People's Publishing House, 2016, p. 128.

25 Xi Jinping. *The Governance of China.* Beijing: Foreign Language Press, 2014, pp. 4–5.

26 Xi Jinping. *Essays of Chinese Chairman Xi Jinping.* Zhejiang: Zhejiang People's Publishing House, 2007, p. 61.

27 Xi Jinping. *Essays of Chinese Chairman Xi Jinping.* Zhejiang: Zhejiang People's Publishing House, 2007, p. 246.

28 Li Yi and Xiao Shaobin. Theoretical innovation and practical implications of the "people-centered approach" for development. *Studies of Marxism,* 2017;7.

29 Xi Jinping's Speech at the First Plenary Session of the 19th CPC Central Committee on October 25, 2017. *Qiu Shi,* 2018;1.

30 Literature Research Office of the CPC Central Committee. *Excerpts from Xi Jinping's Remarks on Building a Moderately Prosperous Society in all Respects.* Beijing: Central Literature Publishing House, 2016, p. 149.

31 Literature Research Office of the CPC Central Committee. *Selected literature since the 18th National Congress of the Communist Party of China (PART I).* Beijing: Central Literature Publishing House, 2014, p. 235.

32 Literature Research Office of the CPC Central Committee. *Excerpts from Xi Jinping's Remarks on Building a Moderately Prosperous Society in all Respects.* Beijing: Central Literature Publishing House, 2016, p. 154.

33 Xi Jinping. Speech at the Concluding Meeting of the Party's Mass Line Education and Practice Activities. *People's Daily,* October 9, 2014.

34 Party Literature Research Center, CPC Central Committee. *Selected Important Documents about the Mass Line.* Beijing: Central Party Literature Press, Party Building Books Publishing House, 2013, p. 128.

35 Xi Jinping. *Essays of Chinese Chairman Xi Jinping.* Zhejiang: Zhejiang People's Publishing House, 2007, p. 245.

36 Xi Jinping. Speech at the Concluding Meeting of the Party's Mass Line Education and Practice Activities. *People's Daily,* October 9, 2014.

37 Literature Research Office of the CPC Central Committee. *MAO Zedong's Chronicle (1893–1949),* vol. 1. Beijing: People's Publishing House, Central Literature Publishing House, 1993, p. 71.

38 Central Compilation and Translation Bureau for the Works of Marx, Engels, Lenin and Stalin. *The Complete Works of Marx and Engels,* vol. 1. Beijing: People's Publishing House, 2009, p. 11.

39 *Guide book for Reports of the 19th CPC National Congress* Compiling Group. *Study Guide for Reports of the 19th CPC National Congress.* Beijing: People's Publishing House, 2017, p. 20.

References

Ai Siqi. *The Complete Works of Ai Siqi*. Beijing: People's Publishing House, 2006.

Ai Siqi. *Twenty-two years of Chinese Philosophical Thought*. Shanghai: Fudan University Press, 1989.

Central Compilation and Translation Bureau for the Works of Marx, Engels, Lenin and Stalin. *The Complete Works of Lenin*, vol. 60, 2nd ed. Beijing: People's Publishing House, 1990.

Central Compilation and Translation Bureau for the Works of Marx, Engels, Lenin and Stalin. *Selected Works of Stalin*, part 2. Beijing: People's Publishing House, 1979.

Central Compilation and Translation Bureau for the Works of Marx, Engels, Lenin and Stalin. *The Complete Works of Marx and Engels*, vol. 1. Beijing: People's Publishing House, 2009.

Central Compilation and Translation Bureau for Works of Marx, Engels, Lenin and Stalin. *Marx/Engels Collected Works*, vol. 10. Beijing: People's Publishing House, 2009.

Central Compilation and Translation Bureau of the Works of Marx, Engels, Lenin and Stalin. *Collected Works of Lenin*, vol. 2, 2nd ed. Beijing: People's Publishing House, 1995.

Central Literature Research Office of the Communist Party of China, National Archives Administration of China. *Selected Important Documents Since the Founding of the Party (1921–1949)*, vol. 15. Beijing: Central Literature Publishing House, 2011.

Central Literature Research Office of the Communist Party of China. *Writings of Mao Zedong*, vol. 1. Beijing: People's Publishing House, 1993.

Central Literature Research Office of the Communist Party of China. *Writings of Mao Zedong*, vol. 6. Beijing: People's Publishing House, 1993.

Central Literature Research Office of the Communist Party of China. *Biography of Mao Zedong*, vol. 4, 2nd ed. Beijing: Central Documents Publishing House, 2011.

Central Literature Research Office of the Communist Party of China. *Writings of Mao Zedong*, vol. 7. Beijing: People's Publishing House, 1999.

Central Literature Research Office of the Communist Party of China. *Chronology of Mao Zedong (1949–1976)*, vol. 4. Beijing: Central Documents Publishing House, 2013.

Central Literature Research Office of the Communist Party of China. *Biography of Mao Zedong*, vol. 5, 2nd ed. Beijing: Central Documents Publishing House, 2011.

Central Literature Research Office of the Communist Party of China. *Writings of Mao Zedong*, vol. 7. Beijing: People's Publishing House, 1999.

Central Literature Research Office of the Communist Party of China. *Writings of Mao Zedong*, vol. 8. Beijing: People's Publishing House, 1999.

Central Literature Research Office of the Communist Party of China. *Selected Important Documents Since the Founding of the People's Republic of China*, vol. 11. Beijing: Central Literature Publishing House, 1995.

Central Literature Research Office of the Communist Party of China. *Biography of Liu Shaoqi*, vol. 2, 2nd ed. Beijing: Central Literature Publishing House, 2008.

Central Literature Research Office of the Communist Party of China. *Biography of Chen Yun*, vol. 2. Beijing: Central Literature Publishing House, 2005.

Central Literature Research Office of the Communist Party of China. *Selected Important Documents Since the 18th National Congress of CPC*, vol. 2. Beijing: Central Literature Publishing House, 2016.

Central Literature Research Office of the Communist Party of China. *Jiang Zemin's Remarks on Socialism with Chinese Characteristics (Excerpts by Topics)*. Beijing: Central Literature Publishing House, 2002.

Central Literature Research Office of the Communist Party of China. *Selected Important Documents Since the 16th National Congress of CPC*, vol. 2. Beijing: Central Literature Publishing House, 2005.

Central Literature Research Office of the Communist Party of China. *Selected Important Documents Since the Reform and Opening Up*, vol. 1. Beijing: Central Literature Publishing House, 2008.

Central Literature Research Office of the Communist Party of China. *Selected Important Documents Since the Reform and Opening Up*, vol. 2. Beijing: Central Literature Publishing House, 2008.

Central Literature Research Office of the Communist Party of China. *Selected Important Documents Since the 15th Party Congress*, vol. 2. Beijing: Central Literature Publishing House, 2001.

Central Literature Research Office of the Communist Party of China. *Selected Documents of the Central Committee of CPC*, vol. 24. Beijing: People's Publishing House, 2013.

Chen Jin. The Communist Party of China and the Theoretical Innovation. *Studies on Mao Zedong and Deng Xiaoping Theories*, 2013;5, pp. 1–6.

Chen Yun. *Selected Works of Chen Yun*, vol. 3, 2nd ed. Beijing: People's Publishing House, 1995.

China Li Dazhao Research Association. *The Collected Works of Li Dazhao*, vol. 3. Beijing: People's Publishing House, 1984.

Compilation of Documents of the 15th National Congress of the Communist Party of China. Beijing: People's Publishing House, 1997.

Compiling Group of Guide Book of the Report of the 19th National Congress of the Communist Party of China. *Guide Book of the Report of the 19th National Congress of the Communist Party of China*. Beijing: People's Publishing House, 2017.

Deng Xiaoping. *Selected Works of Deng Xiaoping*, vol. 2, 2nd ed. Beijing: People's Publishing House, 1994.

Deng Xiaoping. *Selected Works of Deng Xiaoping*, vol. 3. Beijing: People's Publishing House, 1993.

Deng Xiaoping. *Selected Writings of Deng Xiaoping*, vol. 1, 2nd ed. Beijing: People's Publishing House, 1994.

Deng Zihui. *Writings of Deng Zihui*. Beijing: People's Publishing House, 1996.

Fang Songhua, Chen Xaingqin, Jiang Youfu. *Outline of Academic history of Marxism in China*. Shanghai: Academia Press, 2011.

Reports of the 19th CPC National Congress Compiling Group. *Study Guide for Reports of the 19th CPC National Congress*. Beijing: People's Publishing House, 2017.

Guo Jianning. "Harmony" Does Not Equal to No Conflict or Struggle. *People's Tribune*, 2013;16, pp. 42–43.

Guo Jianning. *A Contemporary Perspective on the Adaptation of Marxist Philosophy to Chinese Conditions*. Beijing: People's Publishing House, 2009.

Guo Jianning. Adapting Marxism to Chinese Conditions and Constructing a Shared Spiritual Homeland. *Journal of Peking University (Philosophy & Social Sciences)*, 2010;4, pp. 13–16.

Hou Huiqin. *Thirty Years of the Theoretical Innovation of the Adaptation of Marxism in Chinese Conditions (1978–2008)*. Beijing: China Social Sciences Press, 2008.

Hu Weixiong. One hundred years of Translation and dissemination of Marxist works in China. *Journal of China Executive Leadership Academy Yan'an*, 2013;2, pp. 75–82.

Jiang Zemin. *On Socialist Market Economy*. Beijing: Central Literature Publishing House, 2006.

Jiang Zemin. *Selected Works of Jiang Zemin*, vol. 1. Beijing: People's Publishing House, 2006.

Jiang Zemin. *Selected Works of Jiang Zemin*, vol. 3. Beijing: People's Publishing House, 2006.

Jin Yinan. *A Great Transformation from Standing Up, Getting Rich to Becoming Strong*. Xinhua Daily, 2018-07-17.

Li Nan and Zhou Jianhua. On the Subject of Theoretical Innovation of Contemporary Adaptation of Marxism to Chinese Conditions. *Jianghan Tribune*, 2010;5, pp. 15–21.

Li Rui. *Mao Zedong: A Life of Reading*. Shenyang: Volumes Publishing Company, 2005.

Li Yi and Xiao Shaobin. Theoretical Innovation and Practical Implications of the "People-centered approach" for Development. *Studies of Marxism*, 2017;7, pp. 26–33.

Li Zonggui. A Brief Discussion on the Characteristics of Traditional Chinese Philosophy. *Academic Forum*, 1988;5, pp. 27–29.

Literature Research Office of the CPC Central Committee. *Collected Works of Mao Zedong: Volume 5*. Beijing: People's Publishing House, 1996.

Literature Research Office of the CPC Central Committee. *Excerpts from Xi Jinping's Remarks on Building a Moderately Prosperous Society in all Respects*. Beijing: Central Literature Publishing House, 2016.

Literature Research Office of the CPC Central Committee. *MAO Zedong's Chronicle (1893–1949)*, vol. 1. Beijing: People's Publishing House, Central Literature Publishing House, 1993.

Literature Research Office of the CPC Central Committee. *Selected Documents Since the 18th CPC National Congress: ii*. Beijing: Central Literature Publishing House, 2018.

Literature Research Office of the CPC Central Committee. *Selected Literature Since the 18th National Congress of the Communist Party of China (PART I)*. Beijing: Central Literature Publishing House, 2014.

Liu Shaoqi. *Selected Works of Liu Shaoqi*, vol. 1. Beijing: People's Publishing House, 1981.

Mao Zedong. *Selected Works of Mao Zedong*, vol. 3, 2nd ed. Beijing: People's Publishing House, 1991.

Mao Zedong. *Selected Works of Mao Zedong*, vol. 1, 2nd ed. Beijing: People's Publishing House, 1991.

Mao Zedong. *Selected Works of Mao Zedong*, vol. 2, 2nd ed. Beijing: People's Publishing House, 1991.

Mao Zedong. *Selected Writings of Mao Zedong*, vol. 4, 2nd ed. Beijing: People's Publishing House, 1991.

National Archives Administration of China, Central Literature Research Office of the Communist Party of China. *Selected Documents of the Central Committee of CPC*, vol. 24. Beijing: People's Publishing House, 2013.

National Archives Administration of China, Central Literature Research Office of the Communist Party of China. *Selected Documents of the Central Committee of CPC*, vol. 36. Beijing: People's Publishing House, 2013.

Party Documents Research Office of the CPC Central Committee. *Excerpted Expositions of Xi Jinping on Comprehensively Deepening Reform*. Beijing: Central Party Literature Press, 2014.

Party History Research Office of the Central Committee of the Communist Party of China. *History of the Communist Party of China*, vol. 1, part 2, 2nd ed. Beijing: History of the Communist Party of China Publishing House, 2011.

Party History Research Office of the Central Committee of the Communist Party of China. *History of the Communist Party of China*, vol. 2, part 1, 2nd ed. Beijing: History of the Communist Party of China Publishing House, 2011.

Party History Research Office of the Central Committee of the Communist Party of China. *History of the Communist Party of China*, vol. 2, part 2, 2nd ed. Beijing: History of the Communist Party of China Publishing House, 2011.

Party Literature Research Center, CPC Central Committee. *Selected Important Documents Since the 15th National Congress*, vol. 3. Beijing: People's Publishing House, 2003.

Party Literature Research Center, CPC Central Committee. *Selected Important Documents Since the 12th CPC National Congress*, vol. 3. Beijing: People's Publishing House, 1988.

Party Literature Research Center, CPC Central Committee. *Selected Important Documents Since the 16th CPC National Congress*, vol. 1. Beijing: People's Publishing House, 2005.

Party Literature Research Center, CPC Central Committee. *Selected Important Documents Since the 16th CPC National Congress*, vol. 2. Beijing: People's Publishing House, 2006.

Party Literature Research Center, CPC Central Committee. *Selected Important Documents About the Mass Line*. Beijing: Central Party Literature Press, Party Building Books Publishing House, 2013.

Publicity Department of the Communist Party of China. *A Reader of Xi Jinping's Important Speeches*. Beijing: People's Publishing House, 2016.

Study Guide for Reports of the 19th CPC National Congress Compiling Group. *Study Guide for Reports of the 19th CPC National Congress*. Beijing: People's Publishing House, 2017.

Sun Daiyao. Understanding the Three Dimensions of the "Three Confidence": Study Note No. 20 of Learning General Secretary Xi Jinping's Series of Important Remarks. *Frontline*, 2013;12, pp. 86–89.

Sun Mingzhang. On the Development and Features of Ancient Chinese Dialectics. *Journal of Xiamen University (Arts & Social Sciences)*, 1985;6, pp. 75–82.

Theoretical Bureau of the Publicity Department of the CPC Central Committee. *Ten Lectures on Marxist Philosophy.* Beijing: Learning Press, 2013.

Wei Jianlin. The Tradition of Dialectics in Chinese Culture Has Great Significance in Reality. *Chinese Social Sciences Today.* November 22, 2011.

Xi Jinping Stressed During the 18th Collective Study of The Political Bureau of the CPC Central Committee that We Should Remember Historical Experience, Lessons, and Warnings, which Supply Useful References for the Modernization of National Governance Capacity (October 14, 2014). http://politics.people.com.cn/n/2014/1014/c1001-25826596.html.

Xi Jinping. Adapting to the Trend of The Times and Promoting World Peace and Development: Speech at the Moscow Institute of International Relations. *People's Daily (Overseas Edition)*, March 25, 2013.

Xi Jinping. *Essays of Chinese Chairman Xi Jinping.* Zhejiang: Zhejiang People's Publishing House, 2007.

Xi Jinping. Explanatory 'Notes for the 'Decision of the CCCPC on Some Major Issues Concerning Comprehensively Deepening the Reform'. *People's Daily*, November 16, 2013.

Xi Jinping. Explanatory Notes for the Decision of the CCCPC on Some Major Issues Concerning Comprehensively Deepening the Reform. *People's Daily*, November 16, 2013.

Xi Jinping. Note on the Decision of the CPC Central Committee on Some Major Issues concerning Comprehensively Deepening Reform. *People's Daily*, November 16, 2013.

Xi Jinping. Speech at the 18th Meeting of Politburo Standing Committee with Chinese and Foreign Journalists. *People's Daily*, November 16, 2012.

Xi Jinping. *Speech at the Celebration of the 95th Anniversary of the Founding of the Communist Party of China (July 1, 2016).* Beijing: People's Publishing House, 2016.

Xi Jinping. Speech at the Concluding Meeting of the Party's Mass Line Education and Practice Activities. *People's Daily*, October 9, 2014.

Xi Jinping. *Speech at the First Session of the 12th National People's Congress.* Beijing: People's Publishing House, 2013.

Xi Jinping. *Speech at the Gathering Celebrating the 40th Anniversary of Reform and Opening up* (December 18, 2018). http://www.xinhuanet.com/2018-12/18/c_1123872025.htm.

Xi Jinping. *Speech at the Sixth Plenary Session of the 18th Central Commission for Discipline Inspection.* Beijing: People's Publishing House, 2016.

Xi Jinping. *Speech at the Symposium on Philosophy and Social Sciences (May 17th, 2016).* Beijing: People's Publishing House, 2016.

Xi Jinping. The Communist Party of China's 90 Years of Guiding Ideology and Basic Theory of The Times and Historical Enlightenment. *Study Times*, June 27, 2011.

Xi Jinping. *The Governance of China.* Beijing: Foreign Languages Press, 2014.

Xi Jinping. *The Governance of China,* vol. 2. Beijing: Foreign Language Press, 2017.

Xi Jinping's Remarks on Cultural Confidence Since the 18th Party Congress (October 13, 2017). http://www.xinhuanet.com/politics/2017-10/13/c_1121796384.htm.

Xi Jinping's Speech at the First Plenary Session of the 19th CPC Central Committee on October 25, 2017. *Qiu Shi,* 2018;1, pp. 3–8.

Xu Qingpu and Shi Jialiang. On the Research Trend of Sinicized Marxism in Modern Times. *Studies on Marxism,* 2007;3, pp. 64–69.

Yun Daiying. *Collected Works of Yun Daiying,* vol. 1. Beijing: People's Publishing House, 1984.

Zhang Dainian and Wang Dong. The Modern Rejuvenation and Comprehensive Innovation of the Chinese Civilization. *Teaching and Research,* 1997;5, pp. 9–14.

Zhang Dainian, Cheng Yishan. *Chinese Culture and Debates on Culture.* Beijing: China Renmin University Press, 1990.

Zhou Enlai. *Selected Writings of Zhou Enlai,* vol. 2. Beijing: People's Publishing House, 1984.

Zhu Qiaosen, Li Lingyu and Liu Jianhui (eds.). *A Study of the Historical Experience of the Communist Party of China.* Beijing: CPC Central Party School Press, 1997.

Index

Note: *Italic* page numbers refer to figures.

Printed in Great Britain
by Amazon